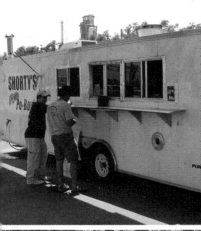

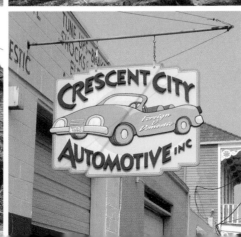

Delirious New Orleans

Roger Fullington Series in Architecture

UNIVERSITY OF TEXAS PRESS ❖ AUSTIN

Delirious New Orleans

Manifesto for an Extraordinary American City

Stephen Verderber   FOREWORD BY Kevin Alter

Publication of this book was made possible in part by support from Roger Fullington and a challenge grant from the National Endowment for the Humanities as well as a generous subsidy from Clemson University.

Requests for permission to reproduce material from this work should be sent to:
   Permissions
   University of Texas Press
   P.O. Box 7819
   Austin, TX 78713-7819
   www.utexas.edu/utpress/about/bpermission.html

♾ The paper used in this book meets the minimum requirements of ANSI/NISO Z39.48-1992 (R1997) (Permanence of Paper).

LIBRARY OF CONGRESS CATALOGING-IN-PUBLICATION DATA

Verderber, Stephen.
   Delirious New Orleans : manifesto for an extraordinary American city / Stephen Verderber ; foreword by Kevin Alter.
      p.   cm. — (Roger Fullington series in architecture)
   Includes index.
   ISBN 978-0-292-71753-4 (cloth : alk. paper)
   1. Vernacular architecture—Louisiana—New Orleans.   2. Outsider art—Louisiana—New Orleans.   3. Urban renewal—Louisiana—New Orleans.   4. City planning—Louisiana—New Orleans.   5. Hurricane Katrina, 2005.   6. New Orleans (La.)—Buildings, structures, etc.
   I. Title.
   NA735.N4V47   2009
   720.9763'35—dc22
                                           2008031036

Photo and Illustration Credits—2.1–2.3, 2.13, 4.1–4.3, 4.11, 4.14, 4.16–4.18, 4.24: Courtesy, United States Library of Congress; 2.12, 2.24, 4.4, 4.5: Courtesy, The Historic New Orleans Collection; 2.19: Alphonse Goldsmith, Photographer. Courtesy, The Historic New Orleans Collection; 3.32, 3.33, 4.30: Courtesy, Worldwide Photos; 4.6–4.10, 4.12: Courtesy, Leonard V. Huber, and Pelican Publishing Company, Gretna; 4.13: Courtesy, Allen Freeman, Photographer; 4.15: Alfred Ward, Illustrator. Courtesy, New Orleans Public Library; 4.19: Frank Leslie's Illustrated Newspaper. Courtesy, New Orleans Public Library; 4.20, 4.21: Courtesy, New York Historical Society, and Pelican Publishing Company, Gretna; 4.22, 4.23: Courtesy, New Orleans Public Library; 4.31: Courtesy, United States Geological Survey; 5.3: Courtesy, The Times-Picayune; 6.3: The Estate of Nathaniel Curtis. Courtesy, Southeastern Architectural Archives, Tulane University; 6.4, 6.6, 6.13, 6.15–6.17: Frank Lotz Miller, Photographer. Courtesy, Lois Frederick Schneider; 6.5, 6.7, 6.11, 6.14, 6.18: Alexander G. Verderber, Photographer; 6.8, 6.9: Courtesy, Frances Curtis; 6.10: Courtesy, Arthur Q. Davis, Curtis & Davis, and the Southeastern Architectural Archives, Tulane University; 6.12: Courtesy, Southeastern Architectural Archives, Tulane University

All other photos by Stephen Verderber. © Stephen Verderber, 2008.

Contents

Foreword

Kevin Alter

ERUSING THE PAGES OF CONTEMPORARY journals and books on architecture, the architectural observer is struck by the innovation and dynamism of an array of individual buildings. Typically portrayed as stand-alone edifices, architecture is generally communicated in terms of an easily consumable object and valued by the degree of formal dexterity and innovation that it might display. Much harder to grasp are the vicissitudes of place and culture in which a building finds its place, and more generally, its meaning. In contrast to the implications put forth through these publications, the keen observer finds that a building's ultimate meaning and power lie not in understanding it in isolation, but rather in the context of the various conditions of its circumstance—physical, climactic, cultural, and social. Moreover, many of the most powerful examples in the field are firmly rooted in their situation, and a deep understanding of that situation is paramount in posing a poignant and meaningful piece of architecture. Indeed, there are celebrated architects such as Glenn Murcutt, whose work is published internationally, but who also categorically refuses to build outside of the realm in which he is intimately familiar. Rather than accepting the implied meaning of his work, which might be transmitted through the glossy pages of a journal or monograph, the value of his buildings is rooted to a deep understanding of, and intervention into, the context of which the buildings are a part.

Beyond a visceral knowledge of a given place, borne of many years of living and working within it, architects oftentimes search for ways to achieve deep insight into the places in which they might propose working. Interrogations of place abound, and regularly form the basis of meaningful architectural interventions. Particularly noteworthy in this regard are studies such as Rem Koolhaas's seminal 1978 book, *Delirious New York: A Retroactive Manifesto for Manhattan*, to which *Delirious New Orleans* owes its title and desires a conscious comparison. Koolhaas's book reveals New York City in a brilliant new light, and in the process identifies and underlines those aspects of the city that he finds valuable. In addition to the insight it has provided into the field, the book is a roadmap to those aspects of the contemporary city to which his much-celebrated work relates. The notion of *cross-programming* that he identifies as particularly poignant in Manhattan, for example, resounds everywhere within his own work.

Turn now to another great and beguiling American city, New Orleans. While teaching at Tulane University's School of Architecture, Stephen Verderber set himself on a project of photographing poignant examples of local vernacular architecture as a means of identifying those aspects of the physical culture of New Orleans that do not often make it into academic discussions about the city. After Hurricane Katrina changed the face of that city forever, Verderber, one of the many refugees of the storm, found himself with an awesome opportunity: to bring into focus the invaluable collection of vernacular architecture that graced the city, and was, along with its attendant culture and values, in very probable danger of disappearing altogether. Armed with the photographs taken just prior to Katrina, Verderber returned to these same places to document their post-hurricane state. The comparison speaks for itself, and the potential loss is compelling. From this basis, Verderber proceeds to write his own manifesto for the city of New Orleans, and offer his insights into the dangers, dilemmas, and culture of the city.

Delirious New Orleans begins as a poignant photo-essay and personal reflection on a particularly outspoken collection of vernacular architecture in New Orleans. In a variety of ways, the book points to the importance of these representations of culture, particularly in distinction to their high architecture counterparts. The photographs especially capture a vibrant culture, and in pairing images taken both before and after the hurricane, leave open the question about the role (or lack thereof) of such artifacts in the rebuilding of the city. The images taken before the hurricane document the rich life of New Orleans in ways not present in the arguments currently being made for rebuilding strategies, and the images taken after make vividly clear another devastating chapter of loss for the city. *Delirious New Orleans* makes the argument that this collection of vernacular architecture serves as a cultural touchstone, and that its presence is a necessary component to the great American city of New Orleans.

Delirious New Orleans promises to be a contribution to the field: it documents an important collection of cultural artifacts and it enters into the debate about the rebuilding efforts of the Gulf Coast—something that heretofore had gone without much attention. Because of J. B. Jackson's seminal works, attention to vernacular architecture is hardly new to the field. However, focusing our attention on these artifacts over a time period that spans the disaster of Hurricane Katrina is profound. *Delirious New Orleans* records the hurricane in an unexpected and intimate fashion, marks the importance of vernacular building stock vis-à-vis the culture of which it is a part, and makes the argument that this kind of authentic cultural artifact must be present in any effort to rebuild. Speculating on the various ways in which this rebuilding might be made manifest is the pleasure that follows the book's conclusion.

I hope that *Delirious New Orleans* will be useful to design professionals in general, and urban designers and planners in particular, as they plan and project the future of our cities and coastal regions.

05.02.08
Kevin Alter
Sid W. Richardson Centennial Professor in Architecture
Director of Architecture Programs
The University of Texas at Austin, School of Architecture

Preface and Acknowledgments

I WAS RAISED IN A CHICAGO SUBURB A MILE FROM the world's second McDonald's. As the years passed, and my life and culinary tastes evolved, I witnessed the destruction of its initial spirit—its sense of place. That location was used as a testing site for new architectural concepts, and it was constantly being renovated and expanded in an unending cycle of change. Much later, the work of nonarchitects, particularly Herbert Gans's seminal writings on the dialectic between high and popular culture, influenced me greatly. I had been taught in architecture school up to that point to reject the everyday vernacular because it was contaminated and therefore unworthy of serious study by an aspiring architect. These so-called contaminated building types—gas stations, drive-ins, motels, neon signs, free-form rural churches, and amusement parks—fascinated me. These places reminded me of the sense of liberation I had felt while sitting many an afternoon on that shiny red and white tile bench at McDonald's when I was a kid.

My perspective of "acceptable" versus "unacceptable" in architecture was permanently altered. Everyday vernacular architecture remained outside the margins of theoretical discourse to most purists in Chicago, my place of birth and the domain-stronghold of modernist Miesian discourse. These buildings and places were viewed as no more than idiosyncratic "outsider" buildings, as unself-conscious artifacts. To me, however, these outsider buildings and places were the analogues of my experience with the then-exploding language of pop music—rock in particular—and the evolving language of pop(ular) architecture. Their packaging and marketing were analogous as well: communicating with a mass audience through the use of memorable visual, spatial, and sonic "hooks" not unlike a melody or chorus you can't shake from your head. Both were centered on mass consumption, immediacy, and associated products consumed in multiple places simultaneously. It was about being fully immersed in popular culture as a way of taking part in a civic dialogue. Here, everyone was invited—invited to experience "the latest," "the new and improved," be it the Beatles' latest number one hit or a new hamburger variation, such as the Big Mac—only all at once.

Over time I built up a sizeable collection of images of these places, and the growing number of books on this unorthodox subject came as little surprise. I came to realize that many others shared this same passion for the vernacular of the ordinary, everyday realm. Soon, the National Trust for Historic Preservation was carrying the banner in grassroots campaigns to save vintage movie theaters, gas stations, neon signs, early McDonald's restaurants, and so on. Remnants of the vanishing inventory of the architecture of the road—including the earliest McDonald's restaurants—were now taken in some quarters as serious "works." Interest had grown in Japan and Europe in this quintessentially American phenomenon.

By 2005, I had lived in New Orleans for twenty years, and because of other professional pursuits and priorities, I had not devoted much serious attention to the city's wealth of unique twentieth-century commercial buildings, signage, and artifacts. New Orleans is undoubtedly among the greatest American cities for the study of architecture and urbanism. I continued to be fascinated by the city's relative compactness, enforced by the geographic limits of its location and its being surrounded by water on all sides. By compactness, I am referring to the core city and its interwoven inventory of colonial, Greek revival, Victorian, modernist, and unself-conscious, everyday building types and artifacts.

Throughout the nearly twenty-two years I lived in New Orleans, I became embroiled in certain preservationist battles in the city and its suburbs. These occurred, pre-Katrina, when particularly insensitive developers or politicians tried to ramrod particularly miserable proposals through the review processes, and I wrote (published) letters to the editor at the *Times-Picayune*. Perhaps the most flagrant example I witnessed during the two decades I lived in New Orleans before Hurricane Katrina was the senseless destruction of the Rivergate Convention Center, designed with bravado by the very talented New Orleans firm Curtis & Davis. Designed in the early 1960s in the International Style, the Rivergate had been highly regarded by historians and architects far beyond New Orleans. Its destruction in 1996 was tragic. Unfortunately, in retrospect, I felt I did not help enough in the cause. I promised myself to not stand on the sidelines the next time a similarly important modernist civic landmark was threatened with destruction.

In my own neighborhood, in the Uptown section, I fought to save a vintage mom-and-pop grocery located a short walk down the street from where I lived. It had changed hands three times in recent years, and yet the newest owners persevered. They continued to sell sno-balls and po-boys to the kids of the neighborhood, delectables for which the place had been known for six decades.

Katrina changed just about everything in New Orleans. A few days before the storm, I had casually convinced the owner of a nearby 1950s drive-in (Frostop) to dig through the cache of personal photos he had collected of the place from its inception. In the back of my mind, I had hoped to convince the owner to fully restore the place. They were stored in old boxes in his attic, and he told me he hadn't gone through them in years. The Friday before Katrina he brought a handful of the old photos and offered them to me. The drive-in would take on five feet of Katrina's floodwaters, and the materials he had brought to show me that day were completely destroyed.

New Orleans's role was central in the history and development of American outsider, or folk, vernacular building types, including the gas station, the fast-food franchise, the movie palace, the roadside motel, the sno-ball stand, and the post–World War II commercial strip. But it was just as important as a place where important American modernist works by firms like Curtis & Davis were built. My appreciation of the dialectic between elite and everyday, popular architecture in New Orleans would ultimately be driven by my close involvement in trying to spare yet another modernist masterpiece by Curtis & Davis from senseless destruction. This dialectic would inadvertently come to function as the operative bookends of this project, post-Katrina. It would also for me provide insight into the mysteriously intersecting functions of race, class inequalities, aesthetic tastes, the art of politics, and the peculiar, below-sea-level geography of the place.

New Orleans's indigenous culture remains complex and contradictory. Two of its most celebrated annual events are the world-renowned Mardi Gras spectacle and the somewhat lesser-known but equally important New Orleans Jazz and Heritage Festival. Locals refer to the latter as simply Jazzfest. Locals and visitors alike become enrapt in the spirit of these two events. Each expresses a collaged visual and sonic landscape. Both are temporal, fleeting, here then gone. Each lasts two weeks. Mardi Gras, tied to the Lenten calendar, usually falls about eight weeks before Jazzfest.

Jazzfest is very much ingrained in the neighborhood where it is staged, and it touches the Esplanade Ridge, Gentilly, and Mid City neighborhoods. On the final Sunday of Jazzfest in 2005, as I walked from the New Orleans Fairgrounds (where Jazzfest is staged each year), people were playing chess on tables on the street corner, and impromptu pickup jam bands were wailing away on sidewalks in front of the rows of shotgun houses. We (David Quinn and I, plus our two teenage

sons) came upon iconic Liuzza's Restaurant, in operation since the 1920s. There, a street party and crawfish boil was happening on this near-perfect afternoon. To me, this scene epitomized the good side of life in New Orleans. It was a positively delirious, upbeat scene. That next week I began to document via photos the offbeat places, buildings, and artifacts I had grown to love over the years, all over the city, with a passion I could neither explain nor fully understand myself.

From east to west, suburb to swamp, sampling this visual landscape itself was, for me, a genuinely delirious (in the most positive sense of the word) experience. The traditions of escapism persisted. I hold many fond memories of riding the roller coasters with my two young children and their friends at the Jazzland (later Six Flags New Orleans) amusement park in the years just before Katrina. It is now in ruins. Delirious behavior—and by extension, delirious places—after all, had always been elevated to the status of civic virtue in New Orleans. For this reason, *Delirious New Orleans* became the obvious choice for the title of the project. It was chosen four months before Katrina, and was influenced by Rem Koolhaas's inspiring book *Delirious New York* (1978). Twentieth-century architecture amid New Orleans's inimitable cultural gumbo would be the central focus. By the weekend Katrina struck, over one hundred buildings, places, and artifacts (such as signs) had been documented. In many cases, the same subject matter was reshot at different times of day in an effort to capture its expressively delirious qualities.

My wife, Kindy, or my son, Alex, sometimes joined me on these sojourns, pre-Katrina. Friends and colleagues offered suggestions once they heard what I was up to. Why was I compelled to do this now, after having lived for twenty years in the city? I still was not really sure, but one thing was certain in retrospect, post-Katrina: Katrina rudely interrupted and yet further rekindled my on-again, off-again love affair with the city. As it was for everyone, my sense of sudden dislocation was real and profound. After a fourteen-hour evacuation car ride–exile march, and three very surreal nights in a Houston hotel with what seemed like multitudes of evacuees (and their pets), my wife and our two teenagers journeyed onward to Austin, Texas. Our dear friends, Charles and Christy Heimsath, provided us with shelter and, a few days later, helped us find a small house to rent until the end of the year, when we could return to repair our flooded home. That first week in Austin, Fritz Steiner, the dean of the School of Architecture at the University of Texas at Austin, offered academic refuge there. In my delirium (in the most negative sense) brought on by the cataclysmic events of that first week, I had described to him the pre-Katrina *Delirious New Orleans* project and its possible ramifications post-Katrina.

I am greatly indebted to him and to the faculty, students, and staff of the UT School of Architecture for their support, kindness, and shelter during the fall semester of 2005, while Tulane University remained shuttered. Parts 1 through 4 of this book were largely assembled in Austin.

Professors Kevin S. Alter and Michael Benedikt, codirectors of the Center for American Architecture and Design at the School of Architecture, were important supporters of this project. Their insights, encouragement, and pivotal role in critically and graphically making this into a book are greatly appreciated. Jim Burr, the humanities editor at the University of Texas Press, also was a great source of encouragement at an unstable moment in my life and career. Thanks are also due to Victoria Davis, at the University of Texas Press, and freelance copy editor Kip Keller for their diligent editing and checking of the manuscript. Many thanks to Raquel Elizondo, assistant dean (now retired) of the University of Texas School of Architecture, to Professor Steven Moore and the students in his graduate design studio, and to Eric Hepburn, Tisha Alvarado, Tara Carlisle, Tracey E. McMillan, Christine Wong, and Kerry Coyne. Special thanks to Jason Heinze, my research assistant while in residency at Texas (and later at Tulane), and to Jessica Gramcko, Breeze Glazer, and Dori Hernandez, my research assistants at Tulane. Jason Heinze himself was affected by the tragedy, since his parents lost their home in the Lakeview section of New Orleans. For reading a draft of most of the manuscript, special thanks to Dr. Eugene Cizek. Gene is a close colleague, architect, and preservationist of the highest caliber. Also, thanks to Dean Reed Kroloff of the Tulane University School of Architecture, who understood my decision to remain domiciled in Austin in Katrina's aftermath. Thanks to St. Stephen's Episcopal School in Austin and its head, the Reverend Roger Bowen, for taking in my two "Katrina kids," Alexander and Elyssa Leigh. The St. Stephen's faculty, staff, students, and parents were a source of kindness and inspiration. Without question, this project is dedicated to my wife, Kindy, for her unwavering support and understanding for so many years.

Thanks also to Sony for inventing the 2 GB memory stick. Following the catastrophe, it was a challenge indeed to photograph a city whose power grid was rendered nearly completely dysfunctional. In between house repairs during the fall of 2005 and 2006, I was in the field, so to speak, on post-Katrina reshoots. I made many day trips to New Orleans from Baton Rouge and the home of the late Reverend Miller Armstrong and his wife, Maryann. To their hospitality and support, I am indebted. Thanks to dear friends Mary Martha Quinn and David Quinn. Post-Katrina, *Delirious New Orleans* took on new meaning. It was now as much about the dark side of deliriousness, delirium, as about its joyous aspects. Conceived at first as celebratory and upbeat, the project became shadowed by the question whether it would be possible to portray pre-Katrina conditions in the face of Katrina's devastation—the massive dislocation, destruction, and upheaval of the storm's aftermath. Readers should bear in mind that the book's title is more meaningful and resonant to me now than before the hurricane. In no way is the title meant to be insulting in any way to anyone or to any place.

The city was technically "closed" and evacuated when I first returned to survey the jaw-dropping damage ten days after the disaster. The ruined neighborhoods and the scope of the destruction were shocking. Being there then felt eerily like being thrust into a war zone, and a remnant of that initial feeling stayed with me thereafter, day in and day out. That first visit, however, remained the most haunting. The mold-infested stench of the toxic waters that engulfed everything in and around my home remains vivid to this day. The flood-waters had receded from my neighborhood only a few days earlier. The situation in Mississippi seemed different: the Mississippi coast was wiped clean by an act of nature, while New Orleans sat poisoned by the multiple failures of its poorly constructed government-built levees.

In the weeks and months following the catastrophe, pundits around the globe speculated wildly on the city's future, including its architecture. There is insufficient space here to refute the various misperceptions widely reported. Suffice it to say, not all the rich people lived on high ground before Katrina, and not all the poor people lived on low ground. In a period of nearly three hundred years, the historical condition that had evolved across time and space was far more complex. It is true that high concentrations of African Americans lived in the lowest-lying neighborhoods, which were the most severely flooded, though middle-class and upper-class whites in other neighborhoods, such as Lakeview, also lost everything. Overall, could more lives have been saved through better predisaster planning? Of course. But it makes little sense here to excoriate those responsible for the total breakdown in leadership at all levels of government that the world witnessed in the immediate aftermath of Katrina. That subject will be left to others to explore in the years ahead.

This book has six parts. In Part 1, pre- and post-Katrina images are presented. The latter images are presented to convey the post-Katrina delirium that so forcibly transformed the city, literally overnight. It is a set of complex conditions, including starkness, desolation, sadness, loss of place and collective memory, and the rising public anger as it became clear that the disaster was largely man-made. Part 2 examines the language of commercial vernacular architecture in New Orleans. Part 3 extends this language to embrace vibrant, expressive folk architecture—the soul, funk, and hip-hop expressions—in the African American neighborhoods of the city. Pre-Katrina, a compelling, culturally resonant, and provocative "on our own" architectural dialect had begun to flourish and inform placemaking in these neighborhoods. Part 4 attempts to examine the causes of the complex and contradictory conditions that resulted in the bifurcation of New Orleans's contemporary architectural traditions. These conditions are viewed largely in relation to institutionalized racism and racial intolerance, class inequalities, clandestine political maneuverings, and how these determinants are expressed in the Mardi Gras subculture. Part 5 looks at the aftermath of Katrina, especially the armada of FEMA trailers that descended upon the city and its suburbs and invaded the commercial vernacular landscape. Part 6 describes the intense battle I became very closely engaged in to save a National Register–caliber landmark modernist church from 1963 by Curtis & Davis: St. Frances Xavier Cabrini Church, in Gentilly. This was an intense, pitched battle between an invading force bent on total destruction and those who saw the loss of the church as a critical setback for the rebuilding of the city. Sadly, the church was destroyed in early June 2007 after the failure of an eleventh-hour effort to save it for future generations of New Orleanians.

I am indebted to the Friends of St. Frances Xavier Cabrini Church (the ad hoc organization I helped form) for its intense devotion to saving this masterpiece. This group includes David Villarrubia, Robin Brou-Hatheway, Patricia Schreiber, Arthur Scully, Jim Logan, Frank Silvetti, Maurice Malochee, Frances Curtis, Arthur Q. Davis, Nell Curtis Tilton, Walter Gallas, Karen Gadbois, Mark Folse, David Gregor, Elliott Perkins, Stephen Braquet, Breeze Glazer, Steve Dumez, Fritz Suchke, Georgi Anne Brochstein, Lois Frederick Schneider, Kendall Frederick Pron, Barry Bergdoll, John Hildreth, Pete Rizzo, Michel Ragon, John Klingman, Steve Dumez, Ellen Weiss, Grover Mouton, the hundreds of loyal Cabrini parishioners who did not want to lose their beloved church and parish, and a handful of brave students at the Tulane School of Architecture. Thanks to my son, Alexander, who fearlessly navigated the rubble of the church to document its demise.

I am also grateful for generous support from Clemson University, my new academic home after more than two decades of teaching at Tulane. My leaving Tulane for Clemson had absolutely *nothing* to do with the church controversy, contrary to rumors spread by uninformed antichurch blogger-agitators. A grant from Clemson helped pull the project through the home stretch to completion. I joined the faculty in the School of Architecture at Clemson in 2007. Thanks to the Clemson Advancement Foundation and its director, LeRoy S. Adams; to Ted Cavanaugh, chair of the architecture program; to Esther Kaufman and Brandon Walter for their support; and to Jan Schach, former dean of the College of Architecture, Art and Humanities at Clemson.

Delirious New Orleans has been a fascinating and daunting project, and no one should make the mistake of underestimating the challenges that lie ahead in reconstructing New Orleans. These include global warming and its effects on rising sea levels and the increasing ferocity of hurricanes; determining how to protect a city that lies below sea level and is subsiding significantly in many areas; the severe loss of coastal wetlands because of shortsighted human interventions over the course of many decades of environmentally irresponsible development; and the urgent need to repair long-entrenched and fragile racial, social, class-based differences within the city and its metro area.

New Orleans is a city living on a knife's edge. Sadly, two years out, the rebuilding process remains stymied by a severe leadership vacuum. New Orleans suffered as nearly a fatal blow as any American city has ever experienced. A tremendous percentage of the city's housing stock was decimated. Countless homeowners and renters have been locked out of returning to their homes. The city's population has dropped by half. Insurance problems are worsening. Without a place to live, who can come back? The reconstruction of buildings alone will not bring New Orleans or New Orleanians back home, although this is of critical importance in the recovery process. A city is about its spirit, grit, and soul as much as its physicality. This book is therefore as much a cautionary tale as it is a call to arms to protect, rebuild, and preserve the architecture and cultural heritage of a truly extraordinary American city.

AUGUST 2007
Stephen Verderber
New Orleans

Delirious **New Orleans**

A Delirious Landscape

What does not destroy me, makes me stronger.
—FRIEDRICH NIETZSCHE

Baumer Foods (Crystal Preserves), Tulane Avenue Overpass
Baumer Foods was founded in New Orleans in 1923. The plant was located on Tulane Avenue in Mid City. This colorful, intricately detailed billboard was a fixture in New Orleans from 1954 to 2006. Motorists on their way to and from downtown viewed a worker stirring a large vat of spicy red sauce. The production plant over which the sign rests was heavily damaged by Katrina's floodwaters. Before Katrina, three million gallons of Baumer's Crystal Hot Sauce was shipped around the world every year. The sign sat atop the shuttered plant beside the Tulane–I-10 interchange. In 2006 the plant was destroyed to make way for a housing development.

Coliseum Theatre, Camp and Thalia

Built in 1938, the Coliseum Theatre was considered the city's premier art-deco-era movie palace. Its beautiful architectural motifs included an illuminated spire of rings that ascended upward directly above a circular street-level ticket booth. Its exterior was sleek and streamlined. The circular glass-encased ticket booth and the neon tracing along the main canopy at the entrance were among its most memorable architectural features. A few years ago, an unsightly freeway-access ramp that had blocked views of the theater and cut it off from its neighborhood context was demolished. Fully restored in the 1990s, the theater then served as a media production studio. Katrina tore off its roof; later, the entire theater burned to the ground because of a careless construction worker. An ad hoc community shrine, placed by admirers amid the ruins of this "cathedral" to cinema, conveyed the neighborhood's sadness and grief.

05.18.06
2:20 PM

05.18.06
2:35 PM

South Claiborne Hardware, South Claiborne and Napoleon

This sign, on a small independently owned neighborhood hardware store in the Broadmoor section, features a larger-than-life girl straddling an immense adjustable wrench. It has been a source of some distraction to motorists for decades. Her 1950s-era Vargas-like *Playboy* pose and coy smile are pure vintage cheesecake and, together with her perfect white gloves, ballet slippers, and perfectly primped hat, serve to accentuate her more alluring attributes. Feminists in most large American cities would most likely have long ago demanded the removal of a sign like this; its longevity in New Orleans might best be explained by the storeowners' being Harley-Davidson motorcycle aficionados. Katrina filled the store with six feet of grimy floodwater; it reopened nine months later. It is now closed.

Jackson Food Store, Jackson and Willow

The Jackson Food Store mural was a tribute to the members of 4 Kings Entertainment, an on-the-rise rap-music promoter in pre-Katrina New Orleans. Curiously, only two of the three people depicted were identified by name on the mural (Ronald and Chev). The background depicted a street scene from the nearby, partially demolished (2004) C. J. Peete housing project. Pre-Katrina, this mural was noteworthy for its large scale and graffiti-like artistry. In the post-Katrina photo, the tears shed by Ronald appear in retrospect to be for Katrina's victims. Soon thereafter, unfortunately, this mural was completely eradicated.

05.18.06
11:45 AM

06.12.05
9:35 PM

Lenny's Piccadilly Lounge, University Place near Canal
Lenny's Piccadilly Lounge, a popular watering hole in the central business district for six decades, is located across the street from the grand entrance to the Roosevelt Hotel (the Fairmont Hotel before Katrina). It was located midway between New Orleans's two most opulent vintage live theaters, the Orpheum and the Saenger, and the now-shuttered large movie palaces on Canal Street (the Saenger Theater and the State Palace). Lenny's exuded a Cotton Club–like, New York-in-the-1940s ambiance. It was the place to be seen among the late-night after-theater crowd. The place somehow preserved and maintained its Sinatra-esque after-hours smoke-filled feel in the age of MTV and the Internet. Lenny's personified New Orleans cosmopolitanism at its best. One can only hope it will reopen.

LJ's Body Shop, Oak Street
The day of the first shot (pre-Katrina), the owner told me the bright red car on the sign was a replica of his own fully restored vintage 1949 Lincoln coupe. This stretch of Oak Street, in the historic Carrollton neighborhood, was built in the mid-nineteenth century, and many of the original frame commercial establishments (with apartments above) still remain, as is the case here. This section of Carrollton did not flood, because it was so near the Mississippi River levee. In the unflooded neighborhoods, property values escalated dramatically in the first months after the storm along what is now routinely referred to as the "sliver by the river."

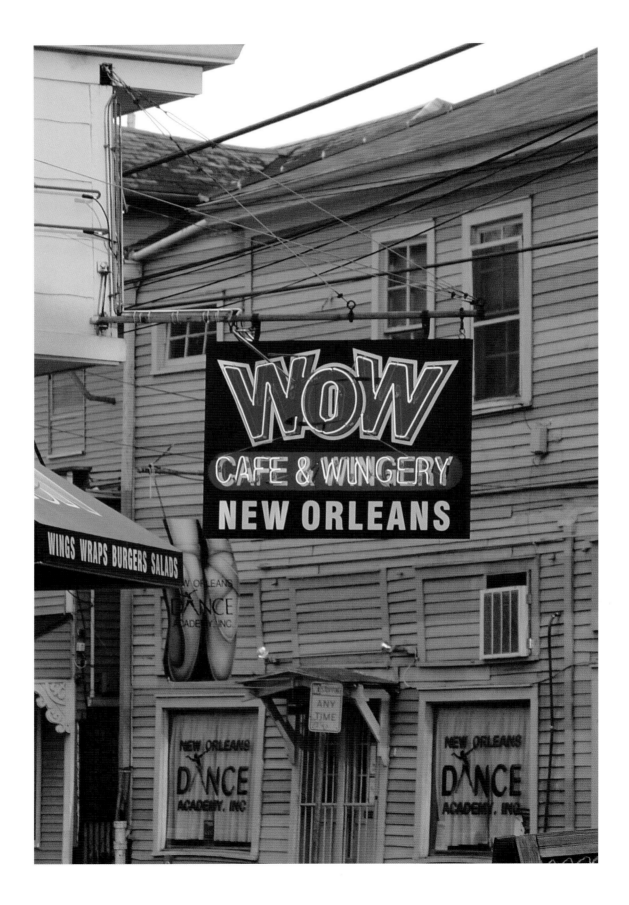

**WOW Café and Wingery,
Magazine and State**
The WOW Café is one of a small
chain of eateries. The juxtaposition
of its neon sign and the pointed
ballet slippers of the New Orleans
Dance Academy sign across the
street was haunting. The lean-to
frame façade bordering Magazine
Street conveyed the impression
that the building itself was sway-
ing to the movement of the dancers
within. Post-Katrina, the boarded-
up entrance to Reginelli's Pizzeria
conveyed the owner's desperation
to locate his dispersed staff so
he could reopen as soon as possible. This was the first restaurant
I dined in in the city post-Katrina,
and it was an emotional experience
to witness so many friends and
strangers alike swap war stories.

Burger Orleans, South Claiborne and Harmony
Burger Orleans was a chain founded in New Orleans in the late 1990s. Like Rally's, another locally based chain, Burger Orleans featured walk-up and drive-through windows, but no indoor seating. A pair of colorful jazz murals adorned the façades. One depicted a jazz band with brass and rhythm sections. The mural on the other side of the building depicted tourist-postcard-like images of the St. Charles Avenue streetcar line and a sax player whose melody wafted through the air along with the aromas from a plate of crawfish étouffée. The murals, signed "Angela 250 Draw," disappeared in Katrina's aftermath.

06.14.05
11:14 AM

06.14.05
6:35 PM

10.05.05
3:35 PM

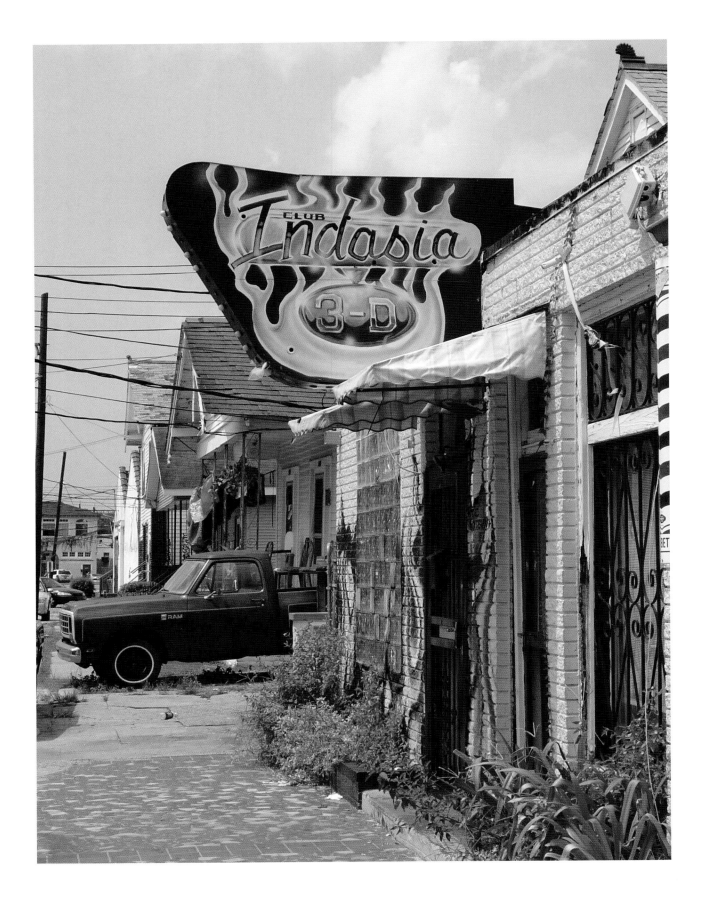

Club Indasia 3-D, Fourth near Dorgenois

Club Indasia was an after-hours bar in a low-lying section of a declining, working-class neighborhood in Mid City. It was a few blocks from one of the city's most notorious public housing projects, and also near the infamous Pumping Station Number 1, one of many pumping stations that utterly failed during Katrina. The flames painted on the façade and the sign contrast starkly with the comparatively benign imagery of the barbershop next door. It was unusual in New Orleans for these two functions to share the same building. Post-Katrina, the adjacent shotgun houses were tagged with orange kiss-of-death "Condemned" stickers because they were judged to pose a public health threat.

Hip Hop Clothing, North Broad near Esplanade
The Hip Hop gear store on North Broad Street was covered with a wraparound graffiti-like mural painted on a monolithic, modest wood-frame structure. Here, mural and building were one and the same—the quintessential decorated shed. A large *2* was emblazoned on the side, positioned at the end of a street scene depicting the 'hood at night. The rendering of a street lamp bathing a desolate streetscape was simultaneously poetic and menacing. On the front elevation, the perspective in the mural was from curb level; a storm drain was rendered larger than life at lower left. A sidewalk led to a set of stairs and the front porch of someone's shotgun house.

Keystone Motel, Airline Highway
Before Interstate I-10 was built in the 1970s, Airline Drive (renamed Airline Highway about a decade ago in an attempt by Jefferson Parish to spruce up its tawdry image) was the main commercial thoroughfare linking New Orleans and Baton Rouge. Among its vintage, pre–World War II roadside-strip attractions were a number of ingratiating yet decisively low-budget courtyard, or motor court, motels along the Jefferson Parish segment of the strip leading from Moissant Airport (since renamed Louis Armstrong International in a similar rebranding effort in the 1990s) into downtown New Orleans. The Keystone Motel is high-style vintage roadside Americana, invoking a bygone era when families mainly took automobile vacations. Sadly, these places are vanishing daily.

Monte Carlo Motel, Chef Menteur Highway

The Motel Monte Carlo was built along "The Chef" strip—the other pre–World War II era roadside strip leading into the city. The Chef extended into the city from the east, and was lined with long-since-destroyed destinations: a Frostop drive-in, walk-up-only McDonald's restaurants, assorted diners, and seedy by-the-hour motels. This motel was built in the mid-1950s. The Chef was the eastern counterpart to Airline Highway, linking the city to Pass Christian, Biloxi, Mobile, and points beyond along the Gulf Coast. Note the painted-over "Air Conditioned" on the handsome masonry wall that doubled as a sign armature pre-Katrina, and the "Color TV" appendage signage. The Monte Carlo had fallen on hard times before Katrina, as evidenced by its fractured sign. Regardless, the turquoise arrow with its flashing neon and the fractured letters "M-O-T-E-L" were no match for Katrina.

Haydel's Flowers, South Claiborne
Though diminutive in scale, this neon sign was a landmark on South Claiborne Avenue for more than sixty years. The delicate neon tracing of roses above "Flowers" was sublime, and "Haydel's" was discreetly stated within the composition. At the same time, the ubiquitous lean-to utility poles and power lines are a reminder of the problems which hinder burying them in the spongy soil of a city that sits below sea level. This sign was a work of art although its fate remained unknown following its disappearance six months after Katrina. In the background, the immortal Louis Armstrong sadly presides over this loss of urban authenticity, post-Katrina.

09.17.05
3:40 PM

05.18.06
3:45 PM

Causey's Country Kitchen, Chef Menteur Highway

This was a Frostop drive-in until it was purchased by the Causey family in the 1980s and converted to Causey's Country Kitchen. The large sign along Chef Menteur Highway, topped by a mug, stood little chance against Katrina. The adjacent Causey's restaurant was renovated to create a partially enclosed eating area after it was purchased from the previous owner. The thin diagonal structural support struts remain visible from the exterior. The huge rotating Frostop root beer mug, at one time mounted atop the flat roof at its center, had long since been removed. In a "circle the wagons" plan of defense, and with the family's bus business suspended in Katrina's aftermath, the buses were redeployed as a sort of protective shield of armor.

08.26.05
10:56 AM

10.07.05
12:05 PM

Frostop Drive-In, South Claiborne and Miro

At Ted's Frostop, across the street from Tulane University, the iconic root beer mug sat for decades high above the sidewalk. This drive-in had been renovated and expanded over the years, nearly obliterating its 1950s minimalist, structurally expressive attributes. As at all Frostops, the root beer mug, in the beginning, rotated atop the roof and was brightly illuminated at night. Also remaining were not fully concealed vestiges of the Jim Crow era, i.e., a "for colored only" walk-up window to the rear. Regardless, this much-altered building retained its original charm. Six feet of floodwater from Katrina swamped the place. The mug had not rotated for over twenty years yet remained a neighborhood landmark. In the storm's aftermath, the owner decided to leave the mug upside down on the ground and disaster memorialization T-shirts are now sold inside.

Frostop Drive-In, Jefferson Highway near Cleary

The Frostop on Jefferson Highway in Jefferson Parish was also a local landmark. Unlike the Frostop on South Claiborne, it had retained its mug on the roof, although this mug also no longer rotated. The prominent diagonal struts of the original design remained. The open-air dining area had been enclosed at some point, and tacky, backyard, suburban-style masonry benches and tables, and a small wooden picket fence were added. However, the interior remained largely intact. Two days after Katrina, the gas station next door exploded due to a gas leak. Miraculously, the flames did not engulf its adjacent neighbor. Through the owner's sheer will, lunch was being served only a matter of days after Katrina. In 2008, this Frostop was threatened with demolition for a high-rise condominium project designed by Daniel Liebskind.

Marshall Art Digital Imaging (Soulja Slim mural), North Claiborne and Pauger
The Soulja Slim mural was painted in memory of an on-the-rise local rapper who was gunned down in 2003 in front of his mother's house one afternoon in the Gentilly section of New Orleans. The slogan "Stop the Killing" was often encountered around the city during the past few years—at bus stops, on large billboards atop buildings, and as small signs placed on utility poles; a murder epidemic had been ravaging inner-city neighborhoods before Katrina took her turn. In this example, commemoration commingled with commerce, since the message was presented as part of an advertisement for a local T-shirt shop. Post-Katrina, Soulja appears disgusted at the sight of his devastated hometown as he gazes upon the ruined furnishings piled on the curb across the street.

**Stereo Lounge,
Causeway Boulevard**
The Stereo Lounge sign was pure 1940s-vintage neon. "Morris Motel, ½ Block, Turn Right" were the instructions given passing motorists. It stood out amid a nondescript stretch of Causeway Boulevard in Jefferson Parish near Jefferson Highway. This area did not flood. The sign's deep blue color was intense, urbane, yet welcoming, and its white neon letters and half-tipped martini glass provided animation. The sign had been protected by a Plexiglas shield before Katrina. This sign deserved to be fully restored and granted landmark status, but unfortunately it disappeared six months later (as did the structure in 2008).

10.06.05
3:30 PM

05.18.06
1:45 PM

Bayou Specialties, River Road, Jefferson

This boat looks as if it were ripping through the outer wall of the building in an attempt to catapult itself up over the top of the Mississippi River levee across the street and into the river. This establishment, which sold fishing and boating supplies, was located just across the parish line in Jefferson Parish on River Road. The area did not flood, since it was located on high ground, but elevation alone could not protect buildings from winds that peaked at 130 mph. The sign was iconic in the unself-conscious tradition of the greatest roadside signs of the 1930s and 1940s, e.g., a donut shop shaped like a donut, a camera shop with a camera on the front façade, or a music store shaped like a piano.

**Sugar Bowl Courts,
Airline Highway**
New Orleans has been the home of the Sugar Bowl holiday football classic since the first game was played on New Year's Day in 1935. This vintage motor court, built in the 1940s, attained local infamy years ago because of its association with the world's oldest profession. It was architecturally noteworthy for the singular, iconic Sugar Bowl Courts neon sign that adorned its roof before Katrina. This stretch of Airline Drive (formerly Airline Highway), having dissipated into a down-on-its-luck strip of bars and rent-by-the-hour motels, lost a key component of its remaining mid-twentieth-century authenticity when Katrina knocked out this exquisite sign.

Broad Street Overpass, Broad Street and I-10
This is a scene representative of New Orleans's version of the inner-urban postindustrial belt found in most large American cities. Along the Tulane Avenue corridor, the landscape of neglect consisted of derelict manufacturing plants, bars, and vacant graffiti-covered warehouses. This Budweiser sign had been a longtime landmark along the section of I-10 leading from the suburbs to downtown. The abandoned Falstaff brewery (now converted to apartments) is shown to the immediate right. This overpass, like other nonflooded, high-elevation roadways in the city, was transformed into an ad hoc refuge for thousands of homeless survivors after Katrina. Discarded pillows and blankets reveal the true misery.

Doerr Furniture Co., Elysian Fields near St. Claude
This sign simply disappeared post-Katrina. It was a local favorite because of its art deco composition and thin white neon lettering set against a chocolate brown background. It was located in the Faubourg Marigny section on the rear side of the venerable furniture company, which occupied a full city block. Doerr has been located in this neighborhood for more than eighty years, and its print and televised ads are well known to generations of New Orleanians.

Aeren Supermarket, Washington and South Dorgenois

This establishment has been in the Broadmoor neighborhood for more than fifty years. Its 1950s-era streamlined modern sign and the adjacent supermarket, set in a sea of asphalt, contrasted with the zero-lot-line urban context: a walkable neighborhood filled with early-to-mid-twentieth-century raised bungalows. Many houses were demolished in the name of progress in the 1950s to make way for customers who opted to drive to this store, one of the new one-stop "super" markets where they could "make groceries." Post-WWII white flight to the suburbs caused this neighborhood to decline.

08.18.05
7:50 PM

Piazza d'Italia, Poydras and Camp

This plaza, celebrated as the "poster child" building of the postmodern movement in architecture in the 1970s, graced the covers of both Charles Jencks's landmark book *The Language of Postmodern Architecture* and a national architecture magazine. The team of Charles Moore with Perez Architects received much praise for their design. It was commissioned by leaders of the city's Italian American community to recognize the long-neglected contribution of Sicilian immigrants to the city's history. It received many awards, and then languished as the world's first postmodern ruin before it was rescued and restored by the Loews hotel chain in 2003. Post-Katrina, this remarkable place was reduced to a staging area for out-of-town disaster mitigation specialists and their army of RVs.

Big Daddy's Bottomless Topless Club, Bourbon Street

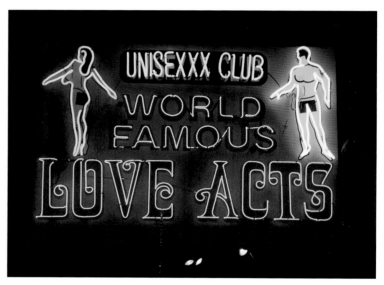

Unisexxx Club, Bourbon Street

On Bourbon Street, sex has long been a major commodity, celebrated for generations. However, post-Katrina, something about the signs that hawked sex seemed quaint in retrospect: these signs and façades in the Vieux Carré had typically exhibited only facsimiles, not the real thing itself. On cleverly composed neon signs, the figures' genitals were even blacked out in one case. Post-Katrina, a nearly all-male army of post-disaster workers overran New Orleans, transforming it into a schizoid twenty-first-century version of the American Wild West—part war zone, part stage set. Storefronts suddenly functioned as display cases for live models—Amsterdam on the Bayou.

Unisexxx Club

**Sandpiper Lounge,
Louisiana near Barone**
Vintage neon from the mid-
twentieth century had, sadly, been
disappearing from New Orleans
in recent years. Lacking landmark
protection, their fate was left to the
whims of their owners. The decline
of the surrounding neighborhoods
where many of the best examples
were located had also contributed to
their demise over the years. Worse,
these properties tended to change
hands frequently. In spite of all this,
the Sandpiper Lounge managed to
endure. It was featured in the 2004
film *Ray*. Katrina nearly dislodged
the neon letters "M-U-S-I-C," but
the delicately rendered cocktail
glass held its own. This area flooded,
and recreational boats used in ad
hoc rescue missions were scattered
everywhere.

10.06.05
1:42 PM

10.07.05
1:54 PM

London Lodge Motel, Airline Highway

This motel on Airline Highway was the preeminent motor court of its era in New Orleans, even though it had fallen on hard times before Katrina. While its name, an apparent reference to England, never made much sense, passersby in their autos were taken with the neon sign's eye-catching sunburst tracing at the pinnacle as well as the "Old World" lettering within the sunburst, set against a 1950s-era brick veneer wall and poplar trees. It is the best remaining example of a Las Vegas–strip-style post–World War II motor court in New Orleans, and for this reason alone it is worthy of landmark status. It was renovated in 2007 after having endured seven feet of floodwater.

Crescent Schools, South Broad near Orleans

The long tradition of sign making in New Orleans was evident at the Crescent Gaming and Bartending Schools. Set midblock, this storefront operation was located on an aging commercial strip that runs through the heart of the city. A restaurant, Henry's Soul Food & Pie Shop, was downstairs. The city's nickname is referenced in the hand-painted crescent figure, shown confidently balancing a tray of beverages in one hand and a fist full of aces in the other. There, one could learn to become a big-time black-jack dealer at the Harrah's casino palace down on Canal Street. In the '40s or '50s, this sign would probably have been grandly executed in neon.

32 Inches Po-Boy, Barataria and Belle Terre
This establishment, in Marrero on the west bank of the Mississippi River, is known simply as "32 Inches Po-Boy." A beautifully rendered sign above the roof eave depicted its namesake—an enormous shrimp and crawfish po-boy fully "dressed" on a loaf of French bread. In the background, a white halo of sorts surrounded the po-boy, setting it apart from a background field of mustard yellow. A single spotlight illuminated the sign, perhaps as a substitute for the high cost of a neon sign. This po-boy deli was the site of a former Super Saver food store.

Frozen Pops Snowballs, Fourth and South Derbigny

This sno-ball stand is located in the area between Uptown and Central City, and it looked rundown and forlorn long before Katrina. Located across the street from a New Orleans Recreation Department (NORD) playground and basketball pavilion, it is a prime example of a *nomadic* sno-ball stand, since it could be transported anywhere. It could easily be shuttled, for instance, to an athletic event, picnic, and church event in the same weekend. The stand's color, materials, siting, and roof pitch mimic those of the shotgun house in the background. The neighborhood took a beating from Katrina.

David Crockett Fire Station, Lafayette Street, Gretna
This fire station on Lafayette Avenue in Gretna was in full glory on the day this photo was taken, pre-Katrina. The equipment was on display, gleaming from a fresh wash that morning, as were the large storefront windows. Pride and self-confidence were unmistakably in the air. This moderne station, built in the 1960s, was, for fire stations in New Orleans, unique in its design, with a gently sloped roofline (metal gabled roof added later), expansive windows, and elaborate brickwork. The scene, sadly, changed significantly after the hurricane. The fire trucks retreated, not unlike the heads of turtles in the face of uncertainty.

Gretna Gun Works, Inc., Lafayette and Third

The entire world saw televised images of looting in the downtown area during that harrowing first week after the hurricane flooded 80 percent of the city. In the first three days alone, looters cleaned out virtually all the firearms and ammunition from every gun store. New Orleanians watched horrified along with the rest of the world as a city fell into anarchy. "What could be next?" observers and evacuees alike asked aloud as a wave of disturbing events unfolded. Was this handgun on the façade really the last available weapon left to steal in the city?

Commercial Vernacular Architecture in New Orleans

There are only two kinds of levees—those that have failed and those that will.
— NATIONAL ASSOCIATION OF STATE FLOODPLAIN MANAGERS, 2005

THE PATCHWORK QUILT OF NEIGHBORHOODS that is New Orleans remains a source of fascination to residents and visitors alike. The courtyards, gardens, parks, housing, churches, civic buildings, and cemeteries of the city have been the subject of scholarly interest for many generations. This inventory has been documented in particular with respect to the legacy of New Orleans "high architecture."[1] Federalist, Greek revival, late Victorian, Richardsonian Romanesque, and the other styles are prevalent throughout the city's urban core. The language, or vocabulary, associated with these architectural styles and building typologies, some indigenous to New Orleans and others imported and adapted, is extensive and well known in American architectural history and within the canon of the history of American urbanism.[2] Moreover, this inventory is appreciated internationally for the unique heritage it represents.[3] The story of New Orleans's architectural and urban landscape is difficult to convey with any accuracy without also describing the multiple cultural dialects it expresses. It is a narrative interwoven with the lives of builders, patrons of civic life, philanthropists, and political power-brokers as well as a cast of exotic and quixotic characters who have inhabited New Orleans throughout the city's history.[4]

Any architectural, urban design, or landscape design language of New Orleans, however, remains incomplete—fragmented—if centered only on the city's high architecture—only those buildings and places that represent the values and accomplishments of the elite classes through the past three hundred years. These were the buildings and places built by and for the wealthy and influential. The literature on New Orleans's high-style built environment has largely neglected the everyday vernacular of the folk architecture of the ordinary environment. Some aspects of the everyday vernacular, including shotgun houses, double shotguns, camelback shotguns, Creole cottages, former slave quarters, and various offshoots, have received scholarly attention, and these typologies have been well documented. This attention has most often focused on housing types built by and for working-class immigrants in the Irish Channel, Ninth Ward, Faubourg Marigny, and Bywater.[5]

Similarly, typologies associated with the high architecture of banks, schools, churches, and so on have been well documented by historians and preservationists.[6] It is not the intent to reinvent those wheels here, and it goes without saying that that research remains extremely valuable and will be an extremely important resource in the rebuilding of the post-Katrina New Orleans. But what about the flip side of the coin? What about all of the poor-cousin, offbeat, funky, quirky, on-our-own buildings, artifacts, and places that over the years have been dismissed as incidental and therefore inconsequential by historians and preservationists?

This discussion is therefore a reaction to that dismissive attitude, but it is not necessarily revisionist, either. It is not an attempt to revise our view of this substantial body of past work. It is centered instead on the intersection of popular culture and architecture. It is about irony, fragmentation, and schism. It is about the everyday places that are celebrated within a community. It is about how that which is celebrated by one neighborhood can be completely ignored by a nearby neighborhood. It is about architecturally modest yet insightful shrines to the human struggle for self-empowerment. It is about appreciating that which is authentic within an inclusive language of the everyday vernacular.

One definition of *shrine* is, in part, "any structure or place consecrated . . . a place or object hallowed by its history or associations . . . a receptacle for sacred relics."[7] There has been little research on New Orleans's everyday commercial vernacular folk architecture. From the inception of New Orleans as a French trading outpost and strategic military installation on the Mississippi River up to 1945, any mention of this inventory of outsider buildings and places has usually been off-the-cuff. Pictures of, say, the White City amusement park are rare finds today. Few if any scholarly analyses or popular texts have singularly focused on New Orleans's twentieth-century commercial vernacular folk architecture. Perhaps this is because New Orleans has always preferred to think of itself as a pre-automobile city, not unlike an aging film star remaining locked in her past.

The Role of New Orleans in American Commercial Vernacular Architecture

Despite the general inattention to this subject in New Orleans, a sizable literature exists on the architecture of the American roadside. New Orleans possessed outstanding examples of both pre-auto and auto-age sensibilities. The national literature on the subject might best be characterized as three streams of inquiry; the first centers on nostalgia for the road and the bygone era of two-lane highways, before the start of the construction of the interstate highway system in 1956. These books tend to glamorize the road and traveling by automobile. "See the USA in a Chevrolet" was a slogan that immediately symbolized the umbilical link between the automobile and the American psyche. As prosperous Americans became obsessed with their cars, they became less and less interested in the old, walkable, inner-urban neighborhoods where they grew up.

Chester Liebs's *Main Street to Miracle Mile: American Roadside Architecture* (1985) remains one of the best treatments of the subject.[8] Related scholarship on commercial vernacular architecture includes histories of the neon signs of fast-food roadside restaurants, the architecture of motels, gas stations, travel lodges and resorts, funky and bizarre signs, 1920s and 1930s stainless-steel diners, and the rise and fall of the American movie palace and drive-in theater.[9] Dozens of Web sites have been established by devotees of these subjects, and their creators are people who share a passion for the American roadside and its colorful history. Among the most extensive of these Internet sites is Debra Jane's *Roadside America*, where she presents many of her more than five hundred photographs categorized by state and building type.[10]

A second stream of inquiry centers on saving vintage signs, particularly along America's highways. These include both neon signs and unusual, iconic sculptures that are either freestanding or affixed to structures. These one-of-a-kind roadside attractions are among the dwindling examples of the fixtures of the commercial establishments that dotted the American roadside landscape from 1920 to the present, particularly from 1920 to 1940, and from 1945 to 1975. Scholars have also examined the aesthetics and functions of derelict, in-ruins vernacular and populist artifacts, such as rusted-out "dead" neon signs and related artifacts.[11] Among the most studied signs and roadside commercial places are those in Los Angeles along the city's vintage commercial strips, such as Sunset Boulevard and Wilshire Boulevard.[12]

A third stream of inquiry, perhaps the most architectural of the three, focuses on specific commercial vernacular building types. This area is centered on the prefranchise and early franchise eras of American mass-consumer culture: fast-food restaurants, diners, movie palaces, motels, gas stations, department stores, resorts, spas, and related commercial building types. Book-length treatments of various building types have appeared, including Paul Hirshhorn and Steven Izenour's *White Towers*.[13] The rise of suburbia and the effects of suburban sprawl across the postindustrial American landscape are within the scope of this area of inquiry as well. National organizations, most notably the Society for Commercial Archeology (SCA), have assumed a leadership role in heightening public awareness of the significance of this facet of the American built environment.[14] More recently, the National Trust for Historic Preservation has become active in increasing awareness of the need to save these rapidly disappearing examples of American roadside consumer culture.[15]

New Orleans had all types of commercial vernacular architecture in abundance, and remains today a remarkable place to study the pre-auto-age American city as well as the American metropolis in the age of the automobile and the road.

The Pre-Auto Age

In New Orleans, an ancient city by American standards, all of the American city's many periods of development can be studied firsthand. Therein lies the second reason why a book on this subject was needed: in the pre-auto age of the city's growth and development, the land situated nearest to the Mississippi River was settled first because it was the highest ground. The streetcar line running along St. Charles Avenue connected the Vieux Carré (literally, "Old Square," known in English as the French Quarter) and the downriver French-speaking *faubourgs* (suburbs) with the burgeoning English-speaking American Sector along the upriver (Uptown) side of Canal Street. The streetcar line also fostered much new development. Streetcar lines soon ran along dozens of other neighborhood arteries. Seventy-two streetcar lines were in operation by 1945.

As the back sections of Uptown and Mid City were dredged from the "back of town" swamps and became available for development, new streetcar lines were created, and existing lines were extended to reach out to these new neighborhoods. These included the City Park area, Gentilly, Ninth Ward, Esplanade Ridge, and Broadmoor. On the west bank of the Mississippi, the early commuter communities of Algiers and Gretna were built in the mid- to late nineteenth century. Streetcars also served them and fostered access to downtown across the river by ferry. The purchase of autos by more and more families expedited the growth of these neighborhoods. Commuters could still choose public transit as a way to get downtown, but it was almost always the slower option, since streetcars stopped at every major intersection; people seemed to prefer the newfound personal autonomy of commuting to work in their own cars.

Later, although the freeways and strips eventually became clogged with multitudes of drivers in New Orleans and in other large American cities, the allure of auto commuting did not diminish. New Orleans, unlike nearly every other major

2.1: *Canal and Carondelet Streets, New Orleans, 1906.*

American city, however, maintained a modicum of streetcar service (the St. Charles line) during this period. The Canal Street line disappeared in 1963. In time, the St. Charles line took on historic significance. The car barn on Willow Street which served this line also took on historic status.[16]

Still, it remains curious that specialists in the field of commercial vernacular architecture overlooked the seminal importance of New Orleans. In bustling late-nineteenth-century New Orleans, visionary advertisers knew that they could reach many potential new customers through the use of architecturally scaled advertisements. Large billboards were erected on the façades of commercial buildings on main streets across America. The New Jackson Square Cigars sign on the front façade of the building at the corner of Canal and Carondelet was visible to anyone moving between the Vieux Carré and the American Sector on the other side of Canal (Fig. 2.1). Passersby were in horse-drawn carriages along with pedestrians and streetcar passengers.

This advertisement was among dozens that had appeared on façades and rooftops along Canal Street by 1900, although

2.2: *Camel cigarettes advertisement, Royal Street near Canal Street, 1907. Note the autos parked in front of the Hotel Monteleone.*

there is evidence of this practice having occurred as early as the 1840s.[17] During the early twentieth century, it was generally considered crass to advertise directly on buildings. Exterior advertising had been limited to pedestrian-scaled signs suspended from second-story galleries on building fronts in the Vieux Carré and in the central business district. This tradition continues today. Some signs were suspended far above the street in order to be viewed from afar. Such was the case with the Camel cigarettes figure suspended above Royal Street, looking toward Canal Street, in a 1907 photograph

(Fig. 2.2). The use of a suspended figure was a clever way to sidestep the garish effect of such advertising on the ornate hotels and commercial establishments along Royal, which continues to serve today as one of the city's premier commercial streets. When electricity was introduced, these signs exploded with color and special effects.

In walkable areas within New Orleans's historic core, and particularly in areas along the river, advertising within the streetscape was scaled to the individual and to the rate at which someone could effectively process information while

2.3: *"Smallest Newsstand in New Orleans," 103 Royal Street, 1903.*

on foot or on a bicycle. Not only the signs but also the smells emanating from these places contributed to the essence of the city. In New Orleans, small mom-and-pop commercial places flourished. The caption of a 1903 photo of the smallest newsstand in New Orleans, a news and magazine vendor located across the street from the Hotel Monteleone on Royal Street, is telling in this regard (Fig. 2.3). This stand closed in 1995, having fallen victim to a combination of the novel allure and immediacy of the Internet as much as to rising real estate values in the Vieux Carré.

New Orleans is an excellent example of a pre-auto-age American city that was transformed into an auto-age metropolis without ever completely turning its back on its past, i.e., its historic core. As New Orleans's early auto-age fringes grew in population, new roads were built, and the city extended and widened existing roads wherever feasible, in the process sometimes destroying the beautiful live oak trees lining the miles of neutral grounds (this is discussed further in Part 3). Along the streetcar routes, a number of neighborhood family-run restaurants soon appeared, and other establishments were adapted from former residential structures. Two notable freestanding examples of the former type were Compagno's (now Vincent's), operated by the Compagno family for four generations, and the Bungalow in Gretna, across the river. Compagno's was composed as a series of three progressively smaller, almost telescoping architectural elements—scalar serialization—with all three frame "houses" contiguous to one another (Fig. 2.4). The front element housed the main dining room and a bar, the midsection housed the kitchen, and the third component served as back storage. This white frame structure, with its striking side profile and roofline, has been a landmark in the Carrollton section along St. Charles Avenue since the 1920s.

Another architecturally noteworthy neighborhood eatery-bar was the Bungalow, built in the 1930s in Gretna. It was also located on a streetcar line. This structure, designed in the art deco style popular at the time, was a variation on the camelback shotgun style, and was appropriated (as was Compagno's) from nearby private dwellings built in the 1870–1920 period (Fig. 2.5). The curved glass windows gave the place, from within, a fishbowl look. An attached two-level camelback residence to the rear was somewhat reminiscent of a steamboat pilothouse. This structure remains intact and extremely close in appearance to this photograph from 1938. Both the former Compagno's and the Bungalow were built on high ground near the Mississippi.

In a pedestrian- and streetcar-scaled city, the introduction of neon signs in the 1930s caused a minor sensation. This new type of sign could be seen from farther away than

2.4: *Vincent's Italian Restaurant, St. Charles Avenue, 2005 (pre-Katrina).*

2.5: *Bourres's Bungalow, Gretna, 1938.*

2.6: *Half Moon Bar & Restaurant, Camp Street near Magazine, 2005 (pre-Katrina).*

its predecessors. Neon allowed for new possibilities in color, form, scale, and imagery. The Half Moon, on Camp near Magazine Street (Uptown), depicted a smiling neon-lit moon-face (Fig. 2.6). Similarly, The Pearl oyster bar on St. Charles, near Canal Street, was a particularly strong example of the kinetic potential of neon, its flickering arrow at the bottom beckoning patrons to come inside to dine or drink (Fig. 2.7). The restaurant's namesake was very cleverly placed within an oyster pearl.

New Orleans's indigenous culinary traditions are known the world over, and the representation of these traditions has always been an integral visual element in the signs displayed outside its eating establishments. In particular, the representation of nautical life has endured as a central, often whimsical theme since the city's founding. Myriad signs depict crawfish, oysters, shrimp, and, to a lesser extent, alligators and catfish. Shrimp in particular continue to be depicted in the signs on many family-run corner restaurant establishments and in those on roadside-strip eating establishments in the suburbs. Alligators tend to be depicted when a whimsical theme is sought. For example, the neon sign at the Cajun Cabin beckons patrons with a depiction of an alligator frolicking in a tub of beer. It remains hard to tell if the alligator is simply enjoying the "Live Cajun Music" within or is just unaware or even unconcerned—New Orleans is often

referred to as the City That Care Forgot—of his ultimate fate (Fig. 2.8). Such evocative signs, while designed primarily for pedestrians, are also effective for those in autos whizzing by at 30 to 40 miles per hour or faster. They were conceived in the spirit of the pedestrian age but were used later in the age of the suburban roadside strip. Many pre-auto-age neon signs in the oldest neighborhoods in the city were therefore later adapted to suburban settings. This dualism was most often expressed in Metairie, where the signs for Café Du Monde, the Morning Call Café, and Gambino's Bakery were nearly identical to their earlier counterparts in the old neighborhood. The wedding-cake sign of Gambino's Bakery on Veteran's Memorial Boulevard, in particular, is highly iconic, like the oyster at the center of The Pearl neon sign in the central business district; only here the cake *is* the sign in its totality: cake as sign, sign as cake in this clever composition. It is beautifully designed as well. The attention to detail is stunning, including the realism of the candles (especially when lit at night), the white frosting, and the realistic cake lettering in the center. The candles are illuminated at night in bright neon colors (Fig. 2.9). The intriguing aspect of this and similar neon signs remains their effectiveness in pedestrian as well as roadside-strip contexts. One could just as easily take in their detailed artistry during an encounter along a sidewalk.

2.7: *The Pearl Oyster Bar & Restaurant, St. Charles near Canal, 2005 (pre-Katrina).*

2.8: *Cajun Cabin, Bourbon Street, 2005 (pre-Katrina).*

2.9: *Joe Gambino's Bakery, Veteran's Memorial Boulevard, Metairie, 2005 (pre-Katrina).*

Similarly, the Oak Street shopping district was built in the pre-auto age. However, with the introduction of the automobile, people opted to drive to places they had previously walked to. So in the 1940s the owner of Meisel's Fabrics, on Oak Street, opted for a neon sign to signal its presence to this new type of customer—the driver (Fig. 2.10). In the case of the Lamplighter Lounge, located on the older section of the Veteran's Memorial Boulevard commercial strip, the sign works at both a pedestrian scale and from a passing auto. This sign and the Gambino's sign are located five miles apart on "Vets" Boulevard (Fig. 2.11). Luckily, all of the abovementioned vintage signs survived Katrina intact.

The Age of the Automobile

The automobile profoundly influenced the American urban and suburban landscape in the post–World War II period.[18] This impact has given rise to a strong backlash. A chorus of critics has charged for years that the car, the superhighway, and the interstate highway system were the three most important determinants—or culprits—in the rise of sprawl. These factors were strongly associated with having spurred the decline of historic urban centers across the United States, New Orleans included.[19] Ample statistical evidence supports this thesis, since downtowns suffered from benign neglect due to steady depopulation.[20] Many neighborhoods that were forsaken and left behind soon bore telltale scars, becoming crime-ridden war zones. In New Orleans, the persistent out-migration from pedestrian-scaled—and, later, streetcar-scaled—pre-automobile neighborhoods was the main reason why these neighborhoods fell into a precipitous decline.[21]

By the 1940s, the automobile had aggressively pushed its way into dominance, clogging street traffic on Canal Street, the city's main commercial thoroughfare. The car had replaced horses and then streetcars as the status seeker's preferred mode of transportation. Despite the congestive, intrusive impact of the auto on Canal Street, the changing times fostered yet another new generation of neon signs along Canal, all competing now for both the pedestrian's and the motorist's attention. Signs for Regal Beer, Mother's Home Made Pies, the Hotel New Orleans, Loew's Theatre, and myriad others stretched the limits of neon-sign technology (Fig. 2.12). The bombastic display put up each holiday season at the Holmes department store included a five-story Santa Claus standing atop the main entrance canopy over the sidewalk.

The auto age gave rise to a new building type, the gas station. At first, the density of New Orleans left few sites available on which to build freestanding gas stations. Oil companies, however, jockeyed for prime, high-visibility locations. It became a sort of arms race for prominence and status among

2.10: *Meisel's Fabrics, Oak Street, 2005 (pre-Katrina).*

2.11: *Lamplighter Lounge, Veterans Memorial Boulevard, Metairie, 2005 (pre-Katrina).*

2.12: *Canal Street, 1948.*

2.13: *Texaco station and garage, Lee Circle, 1928.*

the most powerful oil companies—Standard, Gulf, Texaco, Shell—and others that built impressive facilities in a number of large American cities. Texaco built a mixed-use facility on Lee Circle in New Orleans. Barthelemy Lafon designed this circular area in 1807, at the spot where St. Charles Avenue intersected with Howard Avenue. This spot, originally called Place du Tivoli, initially served as a pleasure garden, with outdoor lights, tables, a dance floor, and brass bands on the weekends. In the 1840s, Italianate mansions just coming into fashion were built around the circle. Later, many of these beautiful mansions gave way to impressive new civic buildings, including Temple Sinai (1872), the Howard Memorial Library (1899), and the New Orleans Public Library (1908).[22] When it was constructed in 1926, this ornate gas station and service garage was designed to conform in style to the former prestige of the neighborhood and to St. Charles's status as the city's premier residential address (Fig. 2.13). It was demolished in the 1960s in favor of a generic "rubber stamp" gas station.

The compactness of New Orleans meant that the interstate highway system would have a less intrusive effect on the historic fabric of the city than it did in most other large American cities. However, its mitigation was also the result of an intense and suspenseful battle that played out in the 1960s to halt a riverfront elevated expressway, a project that would have decimated the historic riverfront for the entire length of the Vieux Carré. This grassroots battle pitted state and federal highway planners against a small but passionate coalition of civic activists. This fight has been documented in detail.[23] The locals won. As a result, Interstate 10 was built instead along Claiborne Avenue behind the Vieux Carré, and a bypass loop was constructed east to west through the 6,000-plus-acre City Park, the largest urban park in the United States, with a spur built along Howard Avenue to connect I-10 with the Greater New Orleans Bridge, later to be rechristened the Crescent City Connection. A local renaming contest was sponsored by the local paper, the *Times-Picayune*, in 1990. The range of proposed names, many of them politically satirical, was deliriously funny.

When the *Times-Picayune* built its new main offices and printing plant on Howard Avenue near the interstate in the 1970s, it adopted the motif of a "newspaper column" as its signature identifying element so that the building could be

2.14: *Times-Picayune main office and plant, Howard Avenue, 2005 (pre-Katrina).*

2.15: *Clarinet (mural), Holiday Inn Downtown, Loyola Avenue, 2005 (post-Katrina).*

clearly seen by passing motorists on I-10. The large white column was meant to be read from the adjacent expressway and the nearby Broad Street overpass. The column was topped with an entablature bearing the paper's name depicted in illuminated letters (Fig. 2.14). This landmark was designed to have maximum impact on commuters to and from downtown and those crossing the Greater New Orleans Bridge.

Orienting motorists passing along I-10 to the downtown area was the inspiration behind Richard Haas's immense fourteen-story clarinet mural he painted on the blank wall of the Downtown Holiday Inn. This mural immediately became

a landmark when it was completed in 1990. It pays homage to Pete Fountain, the legendary New Orleans clarinetist, and to the city's incomparable jazz legacy. Fountain performed on Johnny Carson's *Tonight Show* a record thirty-two times. The post-Katrina scene at the hotel featured huge decontamination trucks trying to combat the mold problem inside the flooded first floor of the hotel (Fig. 2.15). The rooftop of this hotel was also the base for a deadly sniper's attack on innocent citizens across the street in Duncan Plaza in the 1960s.

New Orleans contains many strong examples of what Robert Venturi described in 1972 as a "decorated shed."[24] Often appearing as bland "shoeboxes," these structures, including many industrial buildings, were enlivened with color and arresting graphics on their front façades. Wild Wayne's Seafood Shack on Airline Drive in Metairie was painted in a bright hue of yellow. Flanking the doorway were two playful graphics, one of a crawfish wearing a hat, with "Po Boys" emblazoned beneath, and a second depicting a crab on the verge of succumbing to a boiling kettle, with the words "Boiled Seafood—Live" below (Fig. 2.16). The Point restaurant was housed in a classic decorated shed in an industrial area along the River Road in Gretna. It was impossible to miss its main attractions—beer and burgers (Fig. 2.17).

Often a business will employ architecture to establish a close affinity between its sales objectives and its customers' predilections, even to the point of concealing or masking its true function. The designer of the main building for Lumber Products, Inc., located on Airline Highway (now Drive) in Metairie, purposefully made it look identical to a suburban

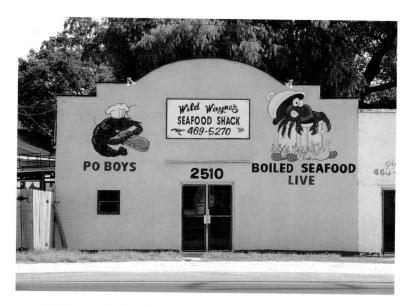

2.16: *Wild Wayne's Seafood Shack, Airline Drive, Metairie, 2005 (pre-Katrina).*

2.17: *The Point, Gretna, 2005 (pre-Katrina).*

house, just like the ones being built in the surrounding community. This building was built in 1940 (Fig. 2.18). Jefferson Parish experienced explosive population growth in the post–World War II period, and this lumber company's modest blue building (repainted green post-Katrina), complete with roof dormers, wood siding, small-paned "picture windows," and a covered front "porch," emulated nearby residential architecture.

McKenzie's bakery was the most well-known name in New Orleans baking throughout the twentieth century. The chain was founded over seventy years ago, and its history was thoroughly interwoven with that of the Mardi Gras king cakes that are sold by the tens of thousands each year during Carnival season. Folklore has it that in the seventeenth century Louis XIV took part in a Twelfth Night festival at which a bean or ceramic figure was hidden in a cake, which became known as the *gâteau des rois* (kings' cake). The cakes, baked throughout the city, were originally round in order to portray the circular route taken by the magi to confuse King Herod, who was trying to follow the wise men so he could kill the Christ child. Hidden away somewhere in a few of

the cakes was either a small bisque or china doll, a trinket, or a bean, usually a red bean that was sometimes covered in silver or gold leaf. The finder became king, or queen, for the day. Today, a plastic baby is baked inside the king cake, and according to local tradition, whoever receives the baby in their piece of cake must buy the next king cake.

The first king cakes Donald Entringer made were commissioned for a Carnival group called the Twelfth Night Revelers. In 1935, his father, a baker in Biloxi, Mississippi, had bought a bakery on Prytania Street in New Orleans, keeping its original owner, Henry McKenzie, on as manager. The Revelers supplied porcelain trinkets to McKenzie's every year. The shop baked five or six cakes each year for the group's annual Carnival ball. An additional half dozen or so cakes would be sold, and that was all. The porcelain doll was switched out with a plastic baby in the early 1950s. The phrase "I got the baby!" is exclaimed by the person who received the baby, and this phrase remains as much a Mardi Gras ritual as the phrase "Throw me something, mister!"

By the early 1950s, a McKenzie's bakery outlet could be found in nearly every New Orleans neighborhood. The store

2.18: *Lumber Products, Airline Drive, Metairie, 2005 (pre-Katrina).*

in the Gentilly section (1957) possessed all the trademark architectural features of in-vogue 1950s strip-center architecture. It was sheathed in green 2' × 2' porcelain Bakelite panels. These panels were applied to a brick surface in a grid pattern. The name of the bakery was outlined in white neon letters, set against the shimmering green panels. The appearance, combined with the extruded-aluminum full-height storefront windows, was that of streamlined moderne. The grid wrapped around the corner of the box, in this case a corner site within the shopping district. The progressive design of this McKenzie's Gentilly Woods store embodied the spirit of the city during the post–World War II period of major civic growth and prosperity.

The growth in popularity of king cakes helped fuel the growth of McKenzie's so much that by 2000 there were forty-two outlets in the metro area, and the main kitchen employed a staff of more than two hundred who baked pastries and bread continually.[25] That same year, the world's longest king cake was baked, measuring one thousand feet in length and weighing more than a ton.[26] The operations were sold that year, and the chain began to experience financial problems. Many stores were closed in the five years preceding Katrina, and the chain's future remained uncertain in Katrina's aftermath.

In recent years, the increasing cost of neon signs has forced inventive storeowners to turn to other media of expression. The Crescent City Automotive, Inc., sign was among the new wave of non-neon commercial signs. These relied on sculpted, raised lettering and images set against a wood or metal background and aperture. In this case, a vintage convertible, rendered in turquoise, is depicted as it rumbles down a street, and "Automotive" appears in cursive immediately below.

Vines, Cows, Alligators, and Crawfish

The city's many fine restaurants have been a source of plenty of unusual sights, but perhaps none so bizarre as the huge wisteria vine that wound its way through the interior of Maylie's Restaurant on Poydras Street for decades. In 1876, Bernard Maylie and Hypolite Esparbe opened an eatery that catered to the butchers of the nearby Poydras Street market. Maylie's served only men until 1925. A unique feature of the restaurant was the immense, almost threatening vine whose trunk, more than a foot in diameter, thrust upward through the dining room and out onto the balcony above Poydras Street. Maylie's closed in 1986 and is the present site of a Smith and Wolinsky's steakhouse (closed since Katrina). In 1941, an advertisement was produced that featured this strange sight and the flowers in full bloom on the balcony (Fig. 2.19).[27]

2.19: *Maylie's Restaurant, Poydras Street, 1941.*

In the tradition of the immense papier-mâché sculptures that have adorned Mardi Gras floats for one hundred fifty years, large sculpted figures of animals and food continue to intrigue New Orleanians. The Brown's Dairy cows have been a landmark for decades. In 2000, the ninety-five-year-old Brown's Velvet Dairy changed its name to Brown's Dairy, but the slogan "Smooth as Velvet" remained on its cartons. Brown's Dairy also remains the owner of a pair of twelve-foot-high fiberglass cows. These cows towered over Interstate 10 in Metairie for twenty-seven years, and they were brightly decorated every Christmas and Mardi Gras season. The dairy now takes the cows out on promotional tours to local schools and grocery stores. Here they are shown at rest outside the main dairy processing plant, located in the Central City neighborhood (Fig. 2.20).

Much of the area surrounding New Orleans remains a swamp. The imagery of the swamp is expressed in myriad signs, from the quirky to the idiosyncratic, and on building adornments, from the aforementioned neon of the Cajun Cabin on Bourbon Street, to the folk architecture expressions found at swamp-tour sites in the marshes remote from the city, to brass rappers on ornate Garden District mansions. The nearby wetlands, home to nutria, alligators, and the seafood for which New Orleans became famous internationally, remain a prime source of inspiration to entrepreneurs. Crawfish, alligators, crabs, oysters, and catfish are but five main attractor-themes on commercial signs. At Airboat Tours, in Des Allemands on the west bank, a taxidermied alligator beckons customers, its jaws hanging over the side of a white

2.20: *Brown's Dairy cows, Central City, 2005 (post-Katrina).*

2.21: *Cajun Swamp Tours, Des Allemands, 2005 (pre-Katrina).*

2.22: *Semolina's, Metairie, 2005 (pre-Katrina).*

picket fence as if the alligator were alive, just having crawled up out of the water. Nearby, the Cajun Swamp Tour's main entrance off Highway 90 in Des Allemands is flanked by a pair of heroically New Orleans–themed, although thoroughly Disney-ish, fiberglass gators depicted as fishermen, each holding fishing gear, one wearing a scarf, boots, and a plantation hat (Fig. 2.21). These examples function as sign-sculptures and blur the line between one-of-a-kind Mardi Gras sculptures, which adorn floats, and mass-culture amusement-park attractions.

Similarly, the crawfish perched on the roof of Semolina's restaurant in Metairie was for a number of years a familiar sight to motorists on Interstate 10. This large red fiberglass sculpture appeared to be climbing out of a gigantic holding tank to escape being served as someone's dinner in the restaurant below (Fig. 2.22). Semolina's was founded in New Orleans in the 1980s and operates a number of locations in

the metro area. It is a sit-down-only restaurant, and the food is traditionally prepared and served. This location remains shuttered in Katrina's aftermath, and the whereabouts of the crawfish remains unknown.

The Lucky Dog

To people around the world who visit the Big Easy, the Lucky Dog is a well known larger-than-life sculpted figure. Perhaps the best-known Lucky Dog vendor is Ignatius J. Reilly, protagonist of the novel *A Confederacy of Dunces*. The Lucky Dog is a highly iconic hot-dog pushcart, and these carts, combined with their inimitable vendor-operators, have been a presence in the Vieux Carré for decades (Fig. 2.23). In the late 1940s, brothers Stephen and Erasmus Loyacano first wheeled their unique vending carts out onto the streets of the city. By 1949, the brothers decided to market their popular invention nationally. At a national convention, when hundreds of del-

2.23: *Lucky Dog vendor, Bourbon Street, 2005 (pre-Katrina).*

egates asked them for more information, the brothers decided to forgo sales and branch into franchising instead. Their advertisement read, "Cruise the midway. Get around town. You and Lucky Dog follow the crowd. A red-hot steam job that will roll up profits everywhere you go. Steam cooks 100 dogs, buns, and chili. Stores everything for 300 more. A fleet of eight carts now successfully operating in New Orleans." But by 1952 they had given up on the franchising concept, and after twenty-three years they sold the business. The new owners, Doug Talbot and Peter Briant, purchased Lucky Dogs Novelty Cart, Inc., in 1970. Its original location was 1304 St. Charles Avenue. Imagine how hard it must have been to push a fully loaded seven-foot-long hot-dog cart from there to the Vieux Carré, almost a mile.[28] Pre-Katrina, the carts were rolled only a few blocks from a kitchen located on Gravier Street in the central business district. Post-Katrina, the Lucky Dog carts have been far fewer in number.

Bowling Alleys

Within the canon of populist roadside architecture, the bowling alley has yet to receive the credit it is due. At this writing, some scholarly work has appeared, although no full-length books have been devoted solely to this unique American building type.[29] Bowling was a major American pastime from the 1940s through the 1970s, and bowling places—alleys— could be found in most cities and towns from coast to coast. These places were associated with the proliferation of the auto and rise of suburbia. One could drive to the nearest bowling alley, park out in front amid a sea of asphalt, and spend an evening with friends in a relaxing social atmosphere while pretending to get a bit of exercise playing an indoor sport. Most bowling alleys saw their best days pass long ago, although three remaining vintage bowling alleys in New Orleans aptly represent the best of this building type from the 1940–1975 period.

The first is Mid City Bowling Lanes, since 1988 known locally simply as the Rock 'n Bowl. The Rock 'n Bowl is an eighteen-lane facility located at Tulane and Carrollton, across the street from the site of the former White City amusement park and later Pelican Stadium, a minor-league baseball venue (see Part 4). Mid City enjoyed many glory years within a busy sports neighborhood until the stadium was razed in 1958. Larger, more modern-moderne bowling centers opened in the surrounding suburban areas. By 1988, the local chapter of the Knights of Columbus, the then owner, found itself saddled with an aging relic. This bowling establishment is unusual in that it was built on the second floor, above a row of street-level stores. The building, constructed in 1941, is the city's oldest bowling alley, and was set back from the street to allow for a parking lot in front. The look and feel of the bar and the lanes remain original. On a stage off to the side, live bands perform many nights during the week. It is known for Cajun, zydeco, blues, and straight-ahead rock and roll. Large murals on the walls near the stage depict New Orleans street scenes from the 1940s and 1950s. Rock 'n Bowl is not typical of most bowling alleys, since it is in a dense urban context and was built at a time when bowlers could have gotten there by streetcar as easily as by automobile.[30] The strip mall of which this establishment was a part was renovated in 2008. Fortunately, the vintage neon "bowling" sign was retained.

A second example, this from the age of the roadside strip, is Orbit Lanes, built in 1963 on the Chef Menteur Highway strip in New Orleans East. The Orbit lanes were meant to be reached by car. The name was inspired by the space race occurring at the time between the United States and the USSR. A large globe with spikes revolved atop a large pole next to the main entrance. The building began at the front sidewalk property line, with parking to the side and rear.

A third example is Gretna Lanes, on the west bank. Also built in the 1960s but set back far from the street to allow for a large parking lot in front, Gretna Lanes was noteworthy for the mural on its front façade: a bowling ball crashing into a set of pins against a sky blue backdrop.

Drive-ins in the Big Easy

The drive-in restaurant was a popular building type in mid-twentieth-century New Orleans, and its popularity was paralleled in other large U.S. cities. Few sites were available for their construction, because of rising land costs and because only three major commercial strips led into the city from the American mainland. In the Vieux Carré, the old Morning Call coffee stand in the French Market had long been a purveyor of French-drip coffee. Established in 1870, it was patronized by locals and tourists alike before being relocated to Metairie in the 1960s. Where horses once were hitched, now autos were parked, as depicted in a postcard scene from the 1940s (Fig. 2.24). As the city expanded outward into the drained swamps that surrounded the city during the interwar period, the three main roadside commercial strips remained Airline Highway

2.24: *Morning Call coffee stand, French Market, 1949.*

(from the west), Chef Menteur Highway (from the east), and Highway 12 (from Slidell). These arteries soon were packed with an array of drive-in restaurants, drive-in theatres, and assorted other commercial building types. Later, in the post–World War II decades, the Veterans Memorial strip would be built in Jefferson Parish, along with numerous others throughout the metropolitan area.

By 1957, the Frostop regional drive-in fast-food chain had established a particularly strong presence in New Orleans. Frostop is a name that at its zenith was familiar to millions of Americans. In 1926, L. S. Harvey opened the first Frostop root-beer stand in Springfield, Ohio. It was an immediate success because of the creamy root beer served in frosted mugs. Frostop drive-ins were built in many parts of the United States until 1941. During World War II, expansion was greatly curtailed because of shortages of materials, labor, and the ingredients needed for root beer. By 1960 there were seven Frostop outlets in the New Orleans area. The chain flourished during the early days of rock and roll, when the pioneering AM station WILD boomed the Top 40 hits of Fats Domino, Elvis Presley, Chuck Berry, and others from dashboards as teenage carhops served teenage customers in their cars. The main attractions included root beer, malts, sodas, and "Castle Burgers," modeled on the White Castle chain's small hamburgers in the Northeast.

Distinctive, appointed with fixed exterior seats and tables so that you could eat outside as well as in your car, they were noteworthy architecturally for their flat roofs and thin diagonal "strut" roof supports. By night, the roof elements appeared to form a shimmering wafer-thin plane hovering above the carhops, and by day they looked like legs holding up a stainless-steel-bordered pearl-like Formica kitchen table. The brown, beige, and yellow trademark color palette was artfully highlighted in neon. The most notable feature, architecturally, was the revolving frosted mug of root beer that gently rested atop the roof (see Figs. 1.15 and 1.16 in Part 1).[31] The New Orleans flagship opened at 3321 St. Charles Avenue in 1952. It possessed most of the classic attributes of Googie architecture (also known as populuxe or doo-wop architecture)—an open-air, carhop format; ultramodern larger-than-life iconic elements (the illuminated rotating mug); an in-vogue 1950s color palette of brown and beige; stainless-steel and glazed-tile interiors; and neon tracing around the perimeter of the roof.[32] Eventually, the Frostops in New Orleans would be eclipsed by newer and more aggressive fast-food chains, such as Rally's, McDonald's, Wendy's, and others.

One of the competitors that grabbed market share from Frostop was the Rally's drive-in chain, a unit of Checker's

Drive-in Restaurants, Inc. Rally's copied many of Frostop's attributes, but does not provide indoor sit-down dining. It has become one of the nation's largest chains adhering to the traditional concept of the drive-in. Rally's was founded and incorporated in Tennessee in 1984, opened its first restaurant in 1985, and adopted a double drive-through configuration for its restaurants; most also provide outdoor patio seating. The imagery clearly is reminiscent of the 1950s. This set it apart from its larger competitors such as McDonald's, Burger King, and Wendy's, and for this reason Rally's was a particularly appropriate fit with vintage neighborhoods and commercial strips in New Orleans and with the city's "the past is safer than the future" mentality. Before Katrina there were over a dozen outlets in the area. The theme colors are black, white, and red. An outlet on South Claiborne opened in 2005 on the site of a former A1 Appliances store (Fig. 2.25).[33]

Similarly, the Airline Drive strip is home to a strong example of a Dot's Diner. Dot's is a national chain, but the New Orleans location on Airline embodies the charm of a classic streamlined deco diner from the 1930s. It has a stainless-steel overhang; corrugated metal sides in horizontal bands of red, white, and blue; and a stainless-steel interior with a sit-down counter.

New Orleans is well known as the home of the first Popeyes Chicken restaurant in America. This chain grew from a single location in Chalmette in 1975. In time, outlets were established across the United States. In 1972, Popeyes founder and New Orleans native Al Copeland opened a fast-food restaurant called Chicken on the Run, serving a traditional mild chicken recipe. After several months of lackluster sales, he rechristened his fledging restaurant Popeyes, after the Popeye Doyle character in the movie *The French Connection*. With this new concept, Copeland would make his mark on the world. He tinkered with his chicken recipe by adding Cajun spices to the batter. In 1976, the first Popeyes franchise restaurant opened, on Airline Highway in Baton Rouge. The marketing tagline "Love That Chicken from Popeyes" quickly caught on with the public, and the five hundredth franchise outlet opened in 1985. This placed the brand on an equal footing with earlier competitors such as Kentucky Fried Chicken (KFC).

Popeyes opened its first "double drive thru" in Ponchatoula, Louisiana, in 1987. By 1988 there were 700 restaurants operating in the United States. Popeyes bought the Church's Chicken restaurant chain in 1989. By 1991, the first international location opened, in Kuala Lumpur, Malaysia. Outlets also opened in Germany and elsewhere throughout Europe, and in 1993, AFC Enterprises bought out both Popeyes and Church's and moved the headquarters from New Orleans to Atlanta. At that time, sixty Pioneer Chicken restaurants in

2.25: *Rally's drive-in, South Claiborne, 2005 (pre-Katrina).*

2.26: *Popeyes, Carrollton and Earhart, 2005 (pre-Katrina).*

Los Angeles were purchased, increasing Popeyes's presence on the West Coast. An agreement with the Kroger grocery-store chain resulted in the opening of a number of outlets in Kroger stores. The hundredth Popeyes in South Korea opened in 1997, and by 1996 the thousandth location opened worldwide. In 1998, sixty-six former Hardee's restaurants were purchased. By 2000, worldwide sales had reached $1.2 billion. The chain continued to expand globally in subsequent years.[34]

By 2005 it was decided that an architectural facelift was called for. Most franchise locations underwent a major renovation. Gone were the gaudy red-tile mansard roofs, the faux black stonework on the building's sides, and the original signage. Instead, the chain attempted to attract a more upscale clientele, as did many of its competitors (Fig. 2.26). Faux stucco (Dryvit) was applied to the exteriors, a modest red-trimmed parapet was wrapped around the building, a "New Orleans–style" wrought-iron railing and a faux balcony were added, and large murals were painted on the building's sides in an attempt to depict and celebrate the local culture

of Louisiana (Fig. 2.27). At night, these modifications were rather successful, since the murals and the balcony were dramatically bathed by floodlights carefully positioned along the perimeter of the parking lot.

Other fast-food chains founded in New Orleans include The Ground Pat'i. Founded in 1971, this chain struggled over the years to gain a regional foothold. By 2006 it was operating only a handful of outlets in the metro area, including a strong example on Causeway Boulevard in Metairie.[35]

Another growing national chain, Smoothie King, was founded in New Orleans in 1973. Steve Kuhnau and his soon-to-be wife, Cindy, were its founders. Kuhnau suffered as a teen with severe allergies and hypoglycemia. He was a soda jerk during high school at Hoppers Drive In, and began experimenting with a high-protein drink in his off hours. He discovered that his concoctions elevated his blood-sugar level while simultaneously suppressing his appetite.

By the time he met his future wife, he was working at Dixie Health Foods, a local health-food store. He was surprised at how successful his drinks were, and in 1989 he and his wife

2.27: *Exterior mural, Popeyes.*

opened their first Smoothie King, on Baronne Street in the central business district. Three other locations opened soon thereafter. Unfortunately, no attempt was made to develop an architectural identity for the chain, at least at its fixed-site stores. However, the nomadic Smoothie King outlets are very colorful, with a larger-than-life Smoothie King Styrofoam cup surrounded by graphics of succulent fruit depicted on the front panel (see Part 5). The tradition of enjoying fine yet very fattening food in New Orleans made it very difficult for this health-food chain to flourish on its home turf. Therefore, the decision was made to expand the chain practically everywhere except New Orleans. By 2006, as a result of this strategy there were more than 350 Smoothie King locations across the United States.[36]

Masker Buildings: Make Your House Anything It Wants to Be
New Orleans, as the above discussion makes clear, has played a significant role in the franchising of America, in the form of the locally founded Popeye's, Smoothie King, and, to a lesser extent, The Ground Pat'i restaurant chains. On the other

hand, some unique, even peculiar, homegrown building types have for the most part remained indigenous to the city. The masked, or masker, building, is perhaps the best example of these indigenous types. A partial definition of *mask* is "a covering for a part of the face, worn to conceal one's identity . . . anything that disguises or conceals . . . a covering, as of wire or gauze, a protective shield . . . a cosmetic preparation applied to mask one's intentions."[37] In the case of a building, a shield or mask functions much like a person's mask. The act of masking denotes a deliberate change, although in people this change is usually temporary, as when taking on an entirely different persona at a Carnival ball. Masking requires a desire or need to alter how one is perceived, and the before-after condition establishes the visual and behavioral limits of this experience.

Buildings also may masquerade briefly, and in New Orleans this most often occurs during the Mardi Gras season, when houses and commercial establishments are festooned with brightly colored banners. Such draperies cover façades and balconies, often in the form of flags, and are not

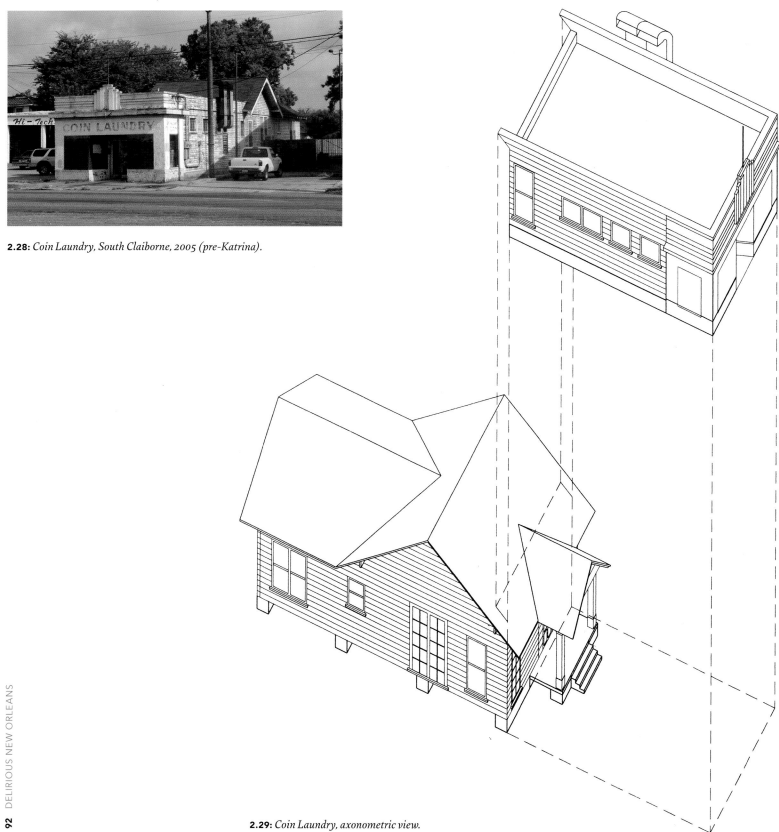

2.28: *Coin Laundry, South Claiborne, 2005 (pre-Katrina).*

2.29: *Coin Laundry, axonometric view.*

intended to completely or permanently obscure a building's underlying identity.

In most cases this ritual is not unlike decorating a house with Christmas ornamentation. Architecturally, decorating a building for a short-term masquerade is related to permanently masking a building's function, although these are not fully interchangeable rituals in New Orleans. The former tends to occur only in holiday seasons, while the latter denotes an act of permanent alteration. What differs is the means by which a building is permanently masked to conceal some or all of its prior identity. In New Orleans, a long tradition exists of masking everyday small-scale buildings to achieve functional transformation. Building masking occurs, for instance, when a private residence is transformed into a corner grocery store or a Laundromat without necessarily relinquishing its initial function.

Masking therefore occurs when residences are adapted to a second function, usually a commercial function, or to a mixed-use commercial-residential hybrid. The Coin Laundry on South Claiborne was originally a single-family frame dwelling built in the Craftsman style about 1920. The original residence was built with a setback to provide a front yard. The yard was soon seen as prime real estate, and the family realized that they could continue to live on the premises while operating a business if an addition were built out toward the sidewalk. Note the horizontal frame siding extended to the stucco frontispiece parapet, designed in the late 1920s or early 1930s in the then-popular art deco style and painted in white (Figs. 2.28 and 2.29). The frame for the sign that at one time was likely suspended above the sidewalk, perpendicular to the building, may have doubled as a flagpole. Zoning laws were modified in many neighborhoods to allow for new property uses such as this to be reclassified for light commercial use, their original residential classification having been grandfathered. Hence, these buildings were almost always mixed use, or *transprogrammatic*.

Similarly, Neeb's Hardware, at Lafayette Street and Fourth, in Gretna, was a prime example of masking a private residence, in this case a camelback shotgun residence, into a commercial headpiece-frontispiece. The private residence in this case was of somewhat earlier vintage (circa 1900), and like the Coin Laundry on Claiborne, was sited with its front facing the street. The hardware store has much else in common with the laundry. In the formerly open front yard, a box-shaped extension was constructed with an internal connection to the rear zone. An art deco vocabulary, rendered in white, was incorporated into the front and side street façades, and serves to make its new identity known without completely obscuring its prior identity (Figs. 2.30 and 2.31).

Neeb's has been operated continuously as a hardware store, even in the face of recent stiff competition from the nearby big-box retailers such as The Home Depot and Lowe's. Both Neeb's and the Coin Laundry are delicately proportioned and elaborately detailed, with modest side entrances that contribute to their enduring domestic scale, along with modest yet effective signage (for the period), and neither disrupts the scale of its streetscape context.

The Kid's World Day Care Center, at St. Claude and Alvar, circa 1920, was also originally a single-family dwelling on a corner lot. Since the setbacks from St. Claude were only eight feet from the sidewalk, there was less room to project a commercial mask element outward. Regardless, a stucco-sheathed mask element was built, then topped with a stepped gable parapet, not unlike a miniature version of the Alamo. This mask extension was first used for a corner drugstore, which was later adapted into its current use. In this post-Katrina photo, note the camelback rear (later) addition to this once double-shotgun house (Fig. 2.32). It was located across the street from a large public high school, and this was likely why the adaptation from drugstore to day care took place. When it was a drugstore, students would walk over from school and sit at the soda fountain. These days, in the age of mega-franchisers such as Walgreens, the city's soda fountains are long gone, and an acute need exists for affordable childcare.

The Bluebird Café on Prytania Street across from the Touro Infirmary was also constructed as a single-family shotgun dwelling in the 1920s. In the 1950s a mask-addition was built, extending the building out to the sidewalk's edge. Great care was taken to conceal this building's former identity, as was done with all genuine masker buildings in New Orleans. When someone wears a Carnival mask, it usually conceals only the face, seldom extending behind the ears. Similarly, the sides of masker buildings are also usually visible, yet only somewhat. Beyond this, few clues are provided about the true identity of the building lurking behind the mask. In the case of the Bluebird, the mask itself is compositionally stark; only its bright yellow exterior and a blue awning to protect the patrons, who wait in line outside, sometimes for more than an hour, enliven it. Note the caricature of the Bluebird logo painted on the side façade, high above the sidewalk. Its placement ensures its visibility to passersby in autos, and also keeps it out of reach of graffitists (Fig. 3.31). The Bluebird did not continue to house a private residence after its transformation, unlike the prior three examples of maskers. In the case of all four of these masked buildings, however, symmetry ruled: the front door is generally situated in the center and flanked by storefront windows

2.30: *Neeb's Hardware, Gretna, 2005 (pre-Katrina).*

2.31: *Neeb's Hardware, axonometric view.*

2.32: *Kid's World, St. Claude Avenue, 2005 (post-Katrina).*

to either side. In addition, in each case the entire building, mask and all, is painted the same color or similar colors.

Tee-Eva's, a restaurant on Magazine Street near Napoleon Avenue, was built as a hamburger and sno-ball stand. Its mask, with its walk-up window, is a holdover from its earlier incarnation. Tee-Eva's continues to sell sno-balls, and this mask device conceals a private dwelling in the rear. The brightly rendered, animated murals on the face of this mask were painted by Miami artist David LeBatard, who signs his work as LEBO (Figs. 2.33 and 2.34). The menu is ambitious, including Creole soul food in addition to sno-balls, pies, and pralines. Tee Eva is the cousin of Antoinette K-Doe (see Part 3). Tee-Eva's mask, unlike the previous four maskers, contrasts with the building it conceals. This is due to the façade's bright color palette and playful graphic imagery. This strategy is necessary since Tee-Eva's is situated midblock in a pedes-

trian-oriented commercial strip where many densely sited buildings compete for the attention of auto traffic.

Another masker, the Meauxbar (pronounced meow-bar) Bistro, on the corner of Rampart and St. Philip, on the edge of the Vieux Carré, was even more architecturally daring. The mask applied to the building was a total concealment, semi-autonomous from the dwelling it concealed, almost as if rejecting what was being masked. Nevertheless, the Meauxbar achieved its individuality through an aesthetic vocabulary of composition, surface pattern, and materiality that was generally similar to that used in the preceding examples. If Tee-Eva's succeeds in conveying a loose funkiness for locals, Meauxbar seeks to project a "proper" or more formally upscale image for tourists. The Meauxbar Bistro's formidable masonry walls conceal a mid-nineteenth-century Creole cottage that was initially classically proportioned and

2.33: *Tee-Eva's Creole Soul Food, Magazine Street, 2005 (post-Katrina).*

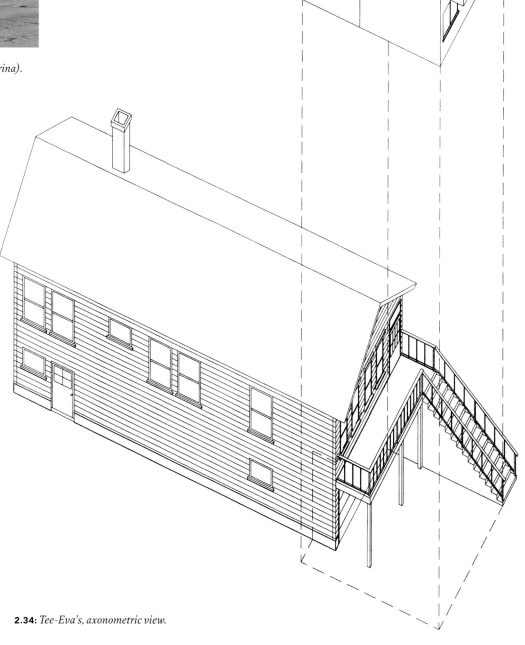

2.34: *Tee-Eva's, axonometric view.*

2.35: *Meauxbar Bistro, Rampart Street, 2005 (post-Katrina).*

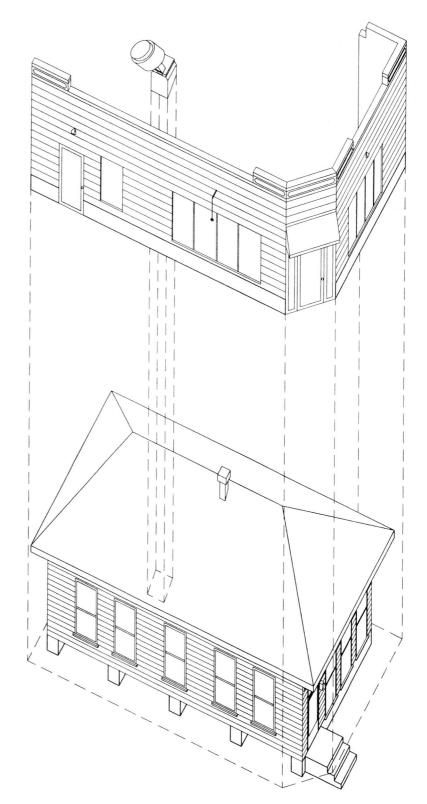

2.36: *Meauxbar, axonometric view.*

2.37: *Steiner Electronic Service, North Galvez, 2005 (post-Katrina).*

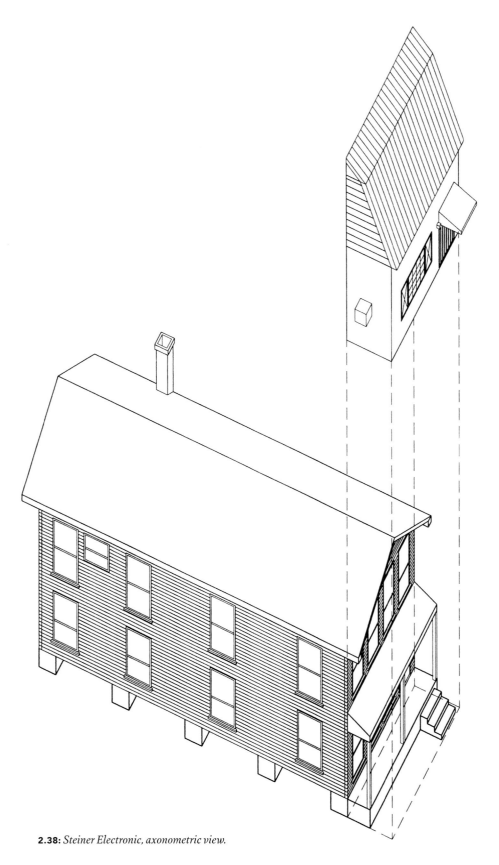

2.38: *Steiner Electronic, axonometric view.*

that abutted the sidewalk on two sides in a zero-lot condition (Figs. 2.35 and 2.36). The masking of this cottage was constructed autonomously from the frame house it conceals. The cottage did not serve either as a structural aperture for the mask or as a surface upon which the mask was directly applied. The repositioning of the main entrance to a corner diagonal position from the initial entry on the Rampart Street side completed the transformation. In the end, the walls appear formidable, even institutional. Here, the Creole cottage seems to be held captive within the strict confines of its mask.

In the case of Steiner Electronic Service, on North Galvez near Iberville, a Bavarian-village storefront, a streetscape in Old Amsterdam, or a rural village in Switzerland seems to have inspired its mask. It stands in sharp contrast with its neighbors, all of which were typical New Orleans Victorian or Creole cottages, some one level in height and others two levels. Most were raised on pier foundations with open undersides, but only slightly above the base elevation level. The building concealed was a two-level frame residence with a front porch. The mask, constructed in the late 1940s, contained small-paned windows, wood shutters, a rusticated wood door, and a stucco exterior (Figs. 2.37 and 2.38). In the accompanying illustration, the tin-roof cladding appears to have originally been a mansard roof of tile or patterned shingles. In this post-Katrina photo, the high floodwater line is visible, and is indicative of the severity of the damage sustained within. Steiner's is threatened with demolition as it sits at the center of the seventy-four acres targeted for the new LSH and VA replacement hospitals. The National Trust placed this neighborhood on its most endangered list in 2008.

A final example of a masker, Jolie's/Gretna Gun, on the corner of Lafayette and Third Streets in Gretna, was a highly ironic expression—a fusion—of two building types: an unusual, even bizarre, synthesis of a decorated shed with a sidesaddle mask. Their combined expression in this long-established residential neighborhood, a block from the river levee, was ironic both aesthetically and functionally (Fig. 2.39). A private shotgun residence was demolished on the site of the gun shop that was subsequently built on the corner. A side yard once separated the two residences with a white picket fence. This was demolished as well. The remaining structure (nearest the levee) was retained, and the gun store now abutted its side elevation. A portion of the site of the demolished residence became a parking lot. Finally, this hybrid composition, with its juxtaposition of an exquisite wall mural in collision with the stark functionality of a gun store, straddled a fine line between playful illusion and surreptitiousness. The plastic handguns on the exterior were

2.39: *Jolie's/Gretna Gun Shop, Gretna, 2005 (pre-Katrina).*

stolen (together with all the guns inside) in the widespread looting that ensued in Katrina's aftermath (see Part 1).

Most architectural masking in New Orleans occurred in the older, more established residential neighborhoods. By 1940, many of the private residences along North and South Claiborne Avenue, as well as other commercial streets, including Canal Boulevard in Mid City, Carrollton Avenue, St. Claude, Elysian Fields, Broad Street, Magazine Street, and Tulane Avenue, had acquired commercial masker buildings, not unlike the examples discussed above. Many dozens of these transformations from single use to mixed use, or to a completely commercial zoning classification, occurred, e.g., barbershops (Big Al's), drugstores (Carrollton Rexall), hardware stores (Neeb's Hardware), restaurants (Liuzza's, Mandina's), bars (Igor's, Madigan's), sno-ball stands (Plum Street Sno Balls, Hanson's), and bakeries (Gambino's, McKenzie's). This trend was fueled by several motivations: expand an existing business that may have been operated entirely out of the original house, capitalize on a prime location that was previously a private residence, "modernize," or simply keep up with the Joneses. Much innovation occurred despite the tight lot sizes in a pedestrian-scaled city, zero side-lot lines, and minimal setbacks from the street or one's neighbors—seldom more than three to five feet—in dramatic contrast to the excessive setbacks mandated by most current suburban building codes in the United States.

Of the eight masker buildings discussed above, four were situated midblock (the Coin Laundry, Bluebird Café, Tee-Eva's, and Steiner Electronic Service) and four were on corner lots (Neeb's Hardware, Kid's World, Meauxbar Bistro, and Jolie's/Gretna Gun). In general, the four main architectural attributes of maskers are, first, their small scale, since most were built originally as private residences; second, most such interventions were designed to fit tightly into their immediate site and streetscape contexts; third, the majority were owner-occupied, their mom-and-pop owners living in the none-too-opulent quarters in the rear of the masked structure; and fourth, nearly every such act of architectural masking in New Orleans occurred before the late 1950s—not coincidentally, when white flight spawned the explosive growth of the suburbs around the city and resulted in the abandonment, as mentioned earlier, of these older neighborhoods. Masked buildings have endured in New Orleans for many reasons, including the city's compact, pedestrian scale, the large number of people who continue to walk or ride public transit to these places rather than drive to the suburbs, and the high percentage of city dwellers who cannot afford to own an auto.

Soul, Funk, and Hip-Hop

In New Orleans, music is in the air we breathe.
—ALLEN TOUSSAINT, 2001

THE DEBATE OVER THE VALIDITY OF EVERYDAY vernacular folk architecture parallels the debate over the term *vernacular* in the field of American folk art. The term *vernacular* has been in use by architectural historians since the 1850s, and was borrowed from linguists. One definition that folklorist Henry Glassie has proposed for studying folk traditions in architecture is rooted in linguistic structural principles used to diagram the lexicon of possible expressions within an architectural "grammar."[1] First, the language of vernacular folk architecture—architecture without architects—evolves around a shared understanding of proven architectural conventions between a builder and a client. This relationship dates from the earliest American settlements, where frame farmhouses were designed and built according to shared assumptions regarding occupancy, functionality, construction standards, and symbolic objectives. Similarly, folk art expresses the concerns of everyday, ordinary human activity and endeavor.[2] Second, predilections evolve out of a growing self-confidence, self-awareness, and place awareness. In time, there emerges an indigenous set of building types and aesthetic standards that are made by and for the people of a given place. In New Orleans, for purposes of this discussion, it is argued that soul, funk, and hip-hop are the three main visual-musical media through which urban folk-architecture sensibilities are expressed, and that the collective influence of these media is in keeping with Glassie's definition.

Folk art and folk architecture are rooted in pride, principles of self-expression, and individuals' search for self-empowerment. The buildings and places that host this expression of community pride and spirit include schools, housing, commercial establishments, places of worship, resorts, places devoted to recreation, and, in particular, food and drinking establishments. The overriding emotion conveyed by the wealth of American folk art and architecture illustrating these themes is a pride barely contained within the physical boundaries of a given artwork, sign, or building.[3]

This pride has ripple effects, as can be seen with urban folk architecture in New Orleans as it has evolved to express indigenous cultural traditions.

In the American South, and in New Orleans in particular, the average home was generally more modest than its northern counterpart. New Orleans's origins were in shipping, as the United States' southernmost link with Latin and Central America and the Caribbean. Shipping ties with West Africa during the main decades of the slave trade, specifically Senegal and the Ivory Coast, played a significant role in the origin of Afro-American folk arts and crafts.[4] Jazz was born from these diverse influences, and this fact is accepted around the world. In the case of architecture, the norm was small houses with kitchens built separately and to the rear of the main structure because of the warm, humid climate and the need for ventilation. This division gave rise to the shotgun house: a narrow one-story building with gabled roof, one room wide and one or more rooms deep, with circulation bisecting the rooms from front to back. This housing type first appeared in New Orleans in the early nineteenth century, and is rooted in Haitian and West African origins. This early appearance meant that New Orleans urban folk architecture had a seminal role in American roots architecture, just as New Orleans indigenous, or roots, musical traditions—namely, jazz, rhythm and blues, and, most recently, hip-hop—have had a seminal role in American roots music.

Later, with the spread of railroads across the North American frontier, architectural styles, like music, could be broadly disseminated.[5] The rise of international shipping lanes and American railroads coincided with the Victorian era in architecture and design (1840–1900).[6] Not surprisingly, Victorian house designs and architectural details were widely disseminated. Industrialization, combined with new modes of transportation, meant that decorative architectural trim, paints, and tools could be sent inland via ship or rail freight from New Orleans to remote points across the continent. To this day, the bright hues, including yellow, red, tangerine, magenta, blue, maroon, violet, and mauve, that were extolled in New Orleans Victorian-era shotgun-house exteriors are traceable to the city's Caribbean and West African roots. New Orleans was therefore both a receiving point and a distribution point for roots-influenced cultural invention.

New Orleans's eclectic culinary traditions similarly date from its inception as a port and trading center. These traditions remain alive today in the city's kitchens, and this is why food remains at the heart of the city's culture and its importance to the rest of America. The culinary tradition of borrowing from Latin and Caribbean immigrants extends to a desire for the interiors and exteriors of restaurants to express their influence. The exterior of Jacques-Imo's Café on Oak Street, with its animated color palette, is a folk-inspired reinterpretation of a Victorian shotgun. In this case, the basic residential type is elevated, allowing a commercial storefront on the ground level. An artist named Rain Webb painted the pair of vehicles that are eternally parked in front of the restaurant, colored in festive hues to match those of the restaurant.

The residence and studio of folk artist Dr. Bob, in the Bywater neighborhood on Chartres Street, is an interesting blend of a subset of these influences. Dr. Bob (Shaffer) resides in a vintage Airstream trailer on the site. He has decorated his trailer home with a mural of a street scene of Chartres, looking from his studio toward his Faubourg Marigny neighborhood (Fig. 3.1). Dr. Bob included himself in the mural (at far right). An array of popular-culture artifacts, at first appearing randomly placed, creates the visual effect of being in a garden of plastic icons. The gate to his studio and workshop is made of an array of highly colorful hand-painted surfboards (Fig. 3.2). The main themes in his paintings and sculptures include colorful shotguns, his friends in the neighborhood, and scenes of nature, all rendered in his folk-inspired visual vocabulary.[7] Dr. Bob's spread and Jacques-Imo's are two examples of the eclectic passions of a chef and an artist, both white, seeking to create (and perpetuate) a multicultural visual eclecticism through an assimilation of African and Caribbean influences.

On the north shore of Lake Pontchartrain, in the bedroom community of Abita Springs, the UCM Museum of folk art and architecture was begun in 1992. The UCM Museum seeks to express the diversity and multicultural history of New Orleans. The buildings and grounds express the idiosyncratic vision of its founder, builder, curator, artist, and administrator, John Preble. The collections are housed in three buildings. The main structure was an abandoned filling station. It now houses the gift shop and the main reception area (Fig. 3.3). This is connected to a gallery containing a highly eclectic collection of artifacts on roadside Americana, Louisiana folk culture, and popular culture. A series of miniature dioramas are housed in glass cases. These include "Lil Dub's BBQ," a New Orleans rhythm-and-blues juke joint circa 1940, a Mardi Gras parade, a jazz funeral, and a hotel in New Orleans's infamous Storyville red-light district circa 1900. Thousands of glass and mirror fragments cover the House of Shards, which sits next to the workshop gallery and across from the Bottle House, whose walls are made entirely of soda and beer bottles set in mortar (Fig. 3.4). Near this is the "Wreck of the UFO," which in fact is a "crashed" vintage Airstream trailer with a family of (mannequin) aliens onboard.

The Web site contains many vintage postcards of roadside diners in New Orleans.[8]

The work of a young black artist, Terrance Osborne, is rooted in his native New Orleans's love of color and the poetic urban language of decay in the architecture of its oldest neighborhoods. His most well known works are of shotgun houses stacked on top of one another in random assemblages. In a large mural he was commissioned to paint on the exterior of New Orleans Riverside Hilton (2004) these themes of decay and collage were fused into a large, flamboyant composition (Fig. 3.5). In his words, "There is something comforting about the old houses in New Orleans. I need no ruler to straighten any shutters, gutters, porches or wooden siding. My brush glides along perfectly with the warped lines and edges. . . . Houses are like people to me. Each has its own space . . . its own constitution. . . . I like to think of my work as ripe fruit and vegetables . . . edible in appearance."[9] The Hilton mural enlivens what was beforehand a forbidding, austere, concrete wall facing Convention Center Boulevard. From left to right, the mural depicts St. Louis Cathedral, the Vieux Carré, Harrah's Casino, the CBD and convention center (the scene of horrific footage transmitted globally in Katrina's aftermath), and a neighborhood comprised of frame shotgun dwellings. It is ironic that this urban collage is devoid of people—not unlike the evacuated state of the city in the aftermath of Katrina. In this sense, Osborne's mural foreshadowed the catastrophe on the horizon. Unfortunately, the siting and scale of the collage depicted in the mural would turn out to be highly ironic: its subject matter suddenly appeared as a mirror of a city in profound upheaval, because it would preside ominously above the misery that unfolded nearby along Convention Center Boulevard in the early days of the Great Flood. Regardless, through the artist's obvious passion for his hometown, this mural transformed a dull hotel-parking garage into a vibrant work of urban folk architecture. One wishes only that it were much larger in size, covering the entire wall.

Shrines and Other Places of Worship

People of all races and income levels in New Orleans are passionate about food, with Jacques-Imo's being but one of many memorable places to eat in an informal, folk-inspired architectural setting. It is impossible to think of New Orleans without thinking of food. It is a way of life. The adage "eat to live" is turned on its head: "live to eat." The entire city, in a sense, is a shrine to eating. From nationally known mainstream places such as Commander's Palace, Antoine's, Bacco, and The Upperline to little-known mom-and-pop places, the list is extensive. With regards to soul, funk, and hip-hop indigenous

3.1: *Dr. Bob's Airstream, Bywater, 2005 (pre-Katrina).*

3.2: *Dr. Bob's surfboard gate, Bywater.*

3.3: *UCM Museum filling station, Abita Springs, 2006.*

3.4: *House of Shards and Bottle House,* UCM *Museum, 2006.*

3.5: *Terrance Osborne mural on the Hilton Riverside, Convention Center Boulevard, 2005 (pre-Katrina).*

folk architecture, the most interesting eating and drinking establishments are generally in areas well off the trodden tourist paths. These informal places look and feel like natural extensions of the proprietor's home. It is almost as if one were eating at the chef's own family dinner table, engaged in lively debate on the performance of the New Orleans Saints after just having watched the game on his wide-screen TV. In various neighborhoods there were, pre-Katrina, dozens of such places, including Dunbar's, in Uptown, and the late Austin Leslie's Chez Helene (closed pre-Katrina), in the Upper Ninth Ward.

In these mom-and-pop places, a high priority on good food and the social aspects of eating are the main reasons one has the feeling of sitting in the chef's own home or at a church congregation's Sunday picnic. It is about the

conscious creation of what it means to be immersed in an unself-conscious atmosphere. This attitude and practice is in keeping with Glassie's definition of folk architecture. In the aftermath of Katrina, the local advocacy organization Common Ground recognized this important part of the city's folk culture and set out to construct an "urban farming" site in the middle of the city.[10] This "farm" is located adjacent to the site of a butter factory in a semiabandoned industrial corridor a mile from the central business district. This area was heavily flooded, and, to date, a number of schools and community groups have assisted in the effort. A mural was painted in April 2006 by the artist Dimitri (Fig. 3.6). This colorful mural's themes are rebirth, self-sufficiency, street marching bands and second lining, and the grassroots

3.6: *Common Ground mural, Earhart Boulevard, 2006.*

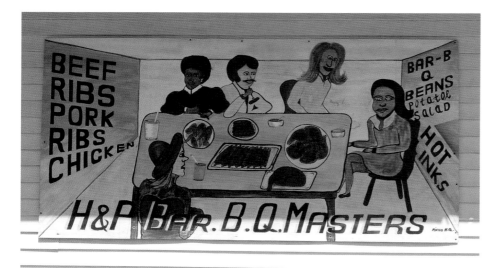

3.7: *Mural on H&P Bar.B.Q. Masters, Elysian Fields, 2005 (pre-Katrina).*

3.8: *H&P Bar.B.Q. Masters, 2005 (pre-Katrina).*

assistance being provided by Common Ground. (Second liners are the people who march alongside, in front of, or behind a parade, typically as an impromptu expression of sheer exuberance and joy.) Food is at the thematic epicenter: a large kettle and a fire are depicted in the lower-right corner. The mural is visible from the Earhart Expressway side of the site and from the nearby Broad Street overpass.

Home cooking is a theme taken seriously in the signage of these places. H&P Bar.B.Q. Masters, on the corner of Elysian Fields and North Rampart, is a small diner housed in a former dry cleaner's establishment. Upon first glance, its exterior is nondescript, but closer scrutiny reveals the great care and detail of a hand-painted sign. Near the entrance is a large painting of a family enjoying a meal of beef and pork ribs, fried chicken, drinks, and sides of barbecue beans and potato salad. The scene is convivial (Fig. 3.7). This sign, unfortunately, together with a second sign mounted nearby on the same face of the building, are overshadowed by a large Truck Stop Turn Left directional sign affixed to the roof (Fig. 3.8). The overall visual effect is jarring. Presumably, the owners received remuneration for renting out their roof. An ad hoc, mumbo-jumbo exterior is a theme in this and related off-the-path eating places. Sadly, the painting disappeared after Katrina, and the diner did not reopen.

At Big Cat Ernie Ladd's Throw-Down BBQ, on South Broad Street across the street from the Orleans Parish Prison and Municipal Courthouse, the gregarious Big Cat himself is shown in the sign. He is busy in his kitchen. He portrays himself as a member of the city's culinary royalty, occupying the throne of "B-B-Q Master" in New Orleans. Neighborhood restaurant owners in New Orleans such as Big Ernie and the H&P Bar.B.Q. Masters seek to establish their own reputational imprint. Sadly, the high-water flood mark of eight feet all but obscured his majesty at work (Fig. 3.9). Nonetheless, his pride and sheer determination to succeed, one hopes, will remain undiminished in post-Katrina New Orleans. At L.A.'s Café, at Josephine and Magnolia Streets, Uptown, the sienna exterior and bright blue awning are the first features that grab the eye. Its exterior color palette is based in Latin and Caribbean folk architectural precedents. For this reason, L.A.'s stands apart from its surroundings. A meticulously hand-painted mural on the front façade depicts a dinner-table setting. A large pot of crawfish étouffée is shown steaming on the table beside a bottle of wine, a wine glass, and a plate teeming with a variety of ingredients, or "dis 'n dat"—delicious home-cooked New Orleans soul food (Fig. 3.10).

Nearby, at the corner of Josephine and Clara, Shatlines Place beckons patrons. This bar and the adjoining lateral

3.9: *Big Cat Ernie Ladd's Throw-Down BBQ, Mid City, 2005 (post-Katrina).*

3.10: *L.A.'s Café, Central City, 2005 (pre-Katrina).*

shotgun residence are also painted a striking hue: sky blue. Similarly, this establishes an identity apart from the monochromic hues of its immediate residential neighbors of modest double and single occupancy shotgun houses. The art-deco-influenced round windows on both façades are of interest in this respect. The color scheme leaves no question about which part of the building is the bar and which is not (Fig. 3.11). Both the L.A. Café and Shatlines are proof that the traditions of mom-and-pop corner bars and hybrid corner bar–restaurants remained alive and well in the black neighborhoods of Uptown, pre-Katrina.

The tradition of family-run eating and drinking places dates from the city's earliest neighborhoods, in both black and white sections of the city. Liuzza's by the Track and Liuzza's in Mid City are venerable eating establishments, 1930s-era mom-and-pop neighborhood po-boy eateries, as is Frankie and Johnnie's Uptown, along with Mandina's on Canal Street. The interiors of these places are vintage period pieces, with classic memorabilia from local high school and college sports teams covering the walls and complementing the well-worn bars, stools, and bar trappings.

The sno-ball stand represents a unique New Orleans contribution to the American canon of commercial urban folk vernacular building types—a synthesis of the wit and entrepreneurial passion of New Orleanians. The sno-ball stand, as a type, is deeply woven into the social and architectural fabric of New Orleans's neighborhoods. A sno-ball is an ice cone draped with flavored syrup. The variety of flavors concocted seems endless. Before the invention of electric air-conditioning, the sno-ball was perfectly suited to New Orleans's oppressively hot and humid summers. Nearly every neighborhood in the city retains one or more of these places to claim as its own. Architecturally, these small nondescript structures may be one of three types: freestanding and autonomous; semiautonomous; or embedded within another structure. The freestanding stands are situated along sidewalks or roadways, most with modest signage. Semiautonomous stands typically project somewhat from a mother ship, be it a private residence or another commercial establishment, for example, a sno-ball stand joined to a check-cashing business. It is usually easy to discern one from the other, even though they are attached at the hip. Tee-Eva's

3.11: *Shatline's Place, Central City, 2005 (pre-Katrina).*

on Magazine Street (see Part 2) is an example of the semiautonomous type.

The embedded sno-ball stand is entirely within a larger commercial establishment, i.e., within a Laundromat, a mom-and-pop corner grocery, a mom-and-pop neighborhood gas station, or a currency exchange. Two noteworthy examples of the freestanding type are the sno-ball stands at Fourth and Derbigny (see Part 1) and the Red Rooster Snoball and Ice Cream, on Clara Street near Washington (Fig. 3.12), with its bright red exterior. These establishments are typically modest in scale, though the Red Rooster is somewhat larger than most sno-ball stands in the city.

With their modest operating budgets and slim profit margins, most sno-ball stands would not be taken seriously as eating establishments, let alone as works of architecture. Neither are they necessarily presented here as high design as judged against mainstream professional design standards. They are, however, culturally salient because they are well-known soul-, funk-, and hip-hop-influenced landmarks in their neighborhoods. Most are very modestly scaled and appointed, usually no more than fifty feet square

and constructed of wood frame.[11] The roots of this type date to 1900, when ice had to be shaved by hand. Interest in this part-dessert, part-refreshment product was flourishing by the 1930s. In 1936, George Ortolano, a neighborhood grocer and son of Sicilian immigrants, noticed a crowd of customers at a nearby sno-ball stand at a competing corner grocery market. He was inspired to start selling this inexpensive product at his struggling grocery store as a means to generate additional profits, and it worked.

He resolved to create a machine that would produce fine, fluffy shaven snow, similar to that made with blocks of ice and a handheld ice shaver. He invented a simple but ingenious machine he called the *SnoWizard* to transform ice blocks into mounds of delicate snowlike flakes, unlike the crunchy ice crystals from conventional snow cone machines. He took a respite from his new invention to build ships in a local plant during World War II, and then after the war he introduced the machine to other grocery stores throughout the city. He soon abandoned his grocery business to devote his total energies to his fledgling enterprise.[12] The business remained family-run, and SnoWizard machines are in numerous foreign countries in South America, Europe, the Middle East, and Australia.[13]

One visually striking sno-ball stand is located at the intersection of Arts and Franklin, in the Seventh Ward. It possesses most of the telltale attributes of the freestanding, autonomous stands—small, of modest wood construction, platform floor raised on concrete blocks, slightly pitched roof, small window, and an overhang to provide sun shading and protection from New Orleans's sudden downpours during the semitropical summer months—and little more. Accommodations inside this stand, as in most sno-ball stands, are spartan. The distinguishing characteristic of this stand is a hand-painted mural that adorns the façade facing the intersection. This mural depicts African tribal imagery: a pair of males appear to hold two warrior shields. These figures guard what at first seem to be a series of houses in the neighborhood, yet they simultaneously evoke the imagery

of decorative cemetery tombstones, as if to honor warriors fallen in the urban battlefield. Curiously, one residence-tombstone, in the lower-right corner, is rendered as a shotgun house, with a sole male figure (the artist) sitting alone on the front steps. The lights are on within the house, indicating evening (Fig. 3.13). At one time, this oddly shaped site was just grass, no structures. Over time, many residual plots such as this, the result of the city's colliding, irregular street grids, were reappropriated.

Another example, the mural on the exterior of the stand near the corner of South Robertson and Washington, depicted important figures in the local neighborhood. The theme of the murals was one of the empowerment and strength of the urban underdog—and, by extension, the urban underclass—against any and all odds (Fig. 3.14). This shuttered yet provocatively decorated sno-ball stand disappeared two weeks after this photo was taken (2006).

3.12: *Red Rooster Sno-balls, Uptown, 2005 (pre-Katrina).*

3.13: *Arts Street Sno-balls, Central City, 2005 (pre-Katrina).*

3.14: *Urban Warriors Sno-balls, Central City, 2006.*

3.15: *Mural on the South Claiborne Barber Shop, 2005 (pre-Katrina).*

As New Orleans became transformed by decades of white flight, many neighborhood shopping districts withered. The sno-ball stand has endured, almost in defiance, as a work of unself-conscious architecture while providing a place, a common ground, for socialization. Eventually, these older shopping strips, including those along Freret Street, Elysian Fields, North Rampart Street, Broad Street, and Orthea Castle Haley (formerly Dryades Street), came to resemble sad human faces with gaps caused by missing teeth. Within a landscape of poverty and despair, the local sno-ball stand endured as a timeless icon.

On South Claiborne Avenue between Napoleon and Louisiana Avenues, Uptown, one barbershop found an imaginative way to respond to the urban decay that surrounded it. In 2002, a mural was hand-painted on one side of the building. It depicted a typical day in the barbershop. The mural faces the foundation remnants of two buildings demolished years

earlier. Three barbers are shown cutting hair; people are engaged in conversation, with the shampoo girl nearby. A few customers waiting, chillin', are shown, and the figures, all rendered in silhouette, are African American. A large mirror is painted behind the barber chairs. Note the barber pole painted in the upper-left corner of the mural (Fig. 3.15). The overall effect is as if the brick wall were actually a large pane storefront running the length of the building, revealing (in cross section) the activity inside.

Hip-Hop

The hip-hop community has adopted this same strategy of using art and architecture as a means of staking claim to turf within the urban landscape—or what is widely referred to in the urban linguistic lexicon as "the hood." The rise of southern hip-hop and the subgenre of gangsta rap has its strongest roots in New Orleans. Gangsta rap is a subgenre of hip-hop music, and the culture it expresses centers on the lifestyles of inner-city thugs, criminals, and gangsters. Although crime and violence in the inner city have always been part of hip-hop's lyrical canon, before the rise of gangsta rap in the late 1980s, hip-hop echoed to a certain extent the tone of socially conscious soul music of the 1970s. New Orleans's brand of gangsta rap, by contrast, centers upon, embraces, and glorifies the extreme lifestyles of extremely violent street criminals. New Orleans gangsta rap has become the battle hymn of violent competing drug gangs on the West Coast and in the South.

The genre is regularly attacked in the mainstream American media for glorifying murder, violence, misogyny, homophobia, racism, and excessive materialism. However, gangsta rap and its offshoots by 2005 had become by far the most commercially successful strand of hip-hop in America, and had achieved considerable chart dominance during the 1995–2005 period. The rappers defend themselves and the themes portrayed in their music by pointing out that they are describing the reality of their inner-city ghetto lives and upbringings, and claim that when rapping they are simply assuming the role of narrator, merely that of the interpreter, or messenger.

Given that the audience for gangsta rap in America has become increasingly white, some commentators, such as the filmmaker Spike Lee, in his satirical film *Bamboozled*, have criticized it as being analogous to the minstrel shows and blackface performances of many decades ago. In blackface, performers, both black and white, were made up to look African American, acting in a stereotypically uncultured and ignorant manner for the entertainment of white audiences. Without regard to the possibility of being interpreted by "outsiders" as purveying caricatures of urban life, New Orleans rapper Percy Miller, aka Master P, and his label, No Limit Records, achieved immense commercial success in the past decade by exporting their themes far beyond New Orleans. Miller was born and raised in the Calliope housing project in Uptown.[14]

Cash Money Records, also based in New Orleans, achieved commercial success with a similar style. A Cash Money artist, Baby Gangsta, aka B. G., titled a single in 1999 with a catch phrase that epitomized the core message of this genre—"Bling-Bling" (from the album *Chopper City in the Ghetto*, 1999).[15] The term *bling-bling* refers to the glitter of large diamonds, and this phrase was recently added to the Oxford English Dictionary.[16] Although much gangsta rap of the past portrayed the rapper as being a victim of urban squalor, the persona of late-1990s mainstream gangsta rappers was far more weighted toward hedonism and showing off their finest jewelry, clothes, liquor, and women.[17]

The wall mural in memory of rising New Orleans rapper Soulja Slim (see Part 1) by Jessica Strahan (2003) at North Claiborne and Pauger epitomized the transformation of a nondescript wall into a powerful social commentary on the relationship between vernacular folk art, architecture, gangsta rap, and the violent realities of street life. James Tapp, aka Soulja Slim, was a local rap hero who was shot to death in 2003 outside his mother's house in the Gentilly neighborhood in New Orleans in broad daylight. He received the equivalent of a traditional jazz-cum-hip-hop funeral, complete with a marching parade, music, and second liners. Tapp had been involved in recent altercations in clubs in Mississippi, Miami, and New Orleans. He was shot five times point-blank in the head by a hitman wearing all black who had been waiting in the shadows along the side of his mother's house that afternoon. The mural reads "Soulja Slim R.I.P."[18] Similarly, the urban folk architecture of the Hip Hop Clothing Store on North Broad (see Part 1) depicted highly coded themes embedded in the city's indigenous hip-hop music and an attendant cultural lifestyle obsessed with "street cred" at any cost, misogynistic attitudes toward women, and death.

The well of hip-hop talent in New Orleans is vast as measured by the genre's accepted creative standards. New and established acts adopt commercial vernacular buildings and then paint murals on them as advertisements for their latest musical projects and as acts of self-empowerment. The Jackson Avenue corner grocery at Jackson and Willow, Uptown, was emblazoned with a mural of a group of rap promoters, 4 Kings Entertainment (see Part 1). This scene, from left to right, depicts a woman cleaning a front-porch stoop of a shotgun house; a young woman looking out from within onto a neighborhood scene of the nearby public housing project, C. J. Peete/Magnolia; and three figures, only two of whom, Ronald and Chev, are identified by name in the mural (Fig. 3.16). No artist credit was cited. As mentioned, this mural was eradicated six months after Katrina.

The hip-hop "Slack" mural on the façade of King's Fashion, on Jackson near South Claiborne, Uptown, conceived and painted in a blaze of fury in 2004, became little more than a backdrop for the widely publicized looting and destruction wrought in many neighborhoods after Katrina (Fig. 3.17). The smoking muzzle of the automatic assault rifle held in this hooded street warrior's hand cast an ominous pall over the scene. What was once a nondescript masonry block wall was transformed into a violent narrative of street life. The hip-hop cognoscenti embedded murals such as this and the one at the Jackson Avenue grocery with similarly charged, coded meanings that were generally not intended for widespread

3.16: *Mural on the side of Jackson Grocery, 2005 (pre-Katrina).*

3.17: *"Slack" mural on King's Fashion, Jackson Avenue, 2005 (post-Katrina).*

consumption, i.e., not meant for whites, or NWA (no whites allowed). Regardless of the message and its intended audience, the buildings themselves were often transformed into sophisticated works of urban folk architecture fully in keeping with Glassie's definition.

Black Mardi Gras and Placemaking

Carnival permeates the air and is a main reason why so many persons across all walks of life and all races choose to live in New Orleans. The pageantry of Carnival season is captured in murals in the black neighborhoods. A mural at the now-abandoned (and since demolished) C. J. Peete/ Magnolia housing project depicts the events of high Carnival,

and particularly those occurring on Fat Tuesday. Second liners, marching brass bands, food, and the Mardi Gras Indian processions through the streets of the neighborhood are collaged. It is located at Washington and Magnolia, inscribed in the lower-left corner "ReF.P.—Dec. The Legend Lives, 2800." From left to right, the mural depicts a second liner twirling a beaded umbrella, a Zulu parade marcher, a leader of the local street marching group, street revelers, and, at far right, a member of the Wild Magnolia Mardi Gras Indian tribe. Next to this figure, in the days after Katrina, someone spray-painted a plea: "Please Come Back" (Fig. 3.18).

The mural painted on the side façade of Jazz Daiquiri's, at South Claiborne and Louisiana Avenue, also aptly conveys

3.18: *Mural of second liners, abandoned C. J. Peete/Magnolia Project, Uptown, 2005 (post-Katrina). Demolished, 2008.*

the frenetic energy and syncopated rhythms of a street marching band. The figures, a percussionist with a big bass drum, a trumpet player, a sax player, a trombonist, and a tuba player, are shown parading in a loose formation. The five figures, all rendered as African Americans, are cleverly rendered as silhouettes against a white-walled backdrop, capturing the essence of street music processions (Fig. 3.19). Overall, this scene differs little from events ranging from Carnival second-line parades to jazz funerals. The jazz funeral itself is an internationally renowned New Orleans art form. This art form is depicted in one of the displays at the UCM Museum near New Orleans. In this miniaturized scene, a deceased musician's casket is marched through the streets

of the neighborhood to the nearby cemetery, accompanied by a brass marching band, friends and family, various second liners, and onlookers (Fig. 3.20). The jazz funeral is among the most sacrosanct, hallowed cultural traditions in a place where so many memorable moments in the rhythm of everyday life occur—in the street.

Before Katrina, the built environment was being reborn yet again as a canvas for urban folk expression. An outdoor museum being created was to highlight proud moments in the long African American history of the city. The Claiborne Avenue underpass that runs the length of the Tremé and Seventh Ward neighborhoods was in the process of being transformed into a vibrant expression of vernacular folk art

3.19: *Mural of a second-line brass marching band, Uptown, 2005 (post-Katrina).*

and architecture. The Seventh Ward is considered the quintessential Creole neighborhood in New Orleans. Many educated and accomplished people of color were born and raised there before the Civil War and throughout the time when the segregationist Jim Crow laws were in full force.

The Greater New Orleans Community Data Center (GNOCDC) notes that the Seventh Ward is opposite Esplanade Avenue from the Tremé. At one time it was the most prosperous African American business district in the entire country. The business district stretched along Claiborne Avenue from the Tremé into the Seventh Ward. In the 1960s, the area along Claiborne was deemed dispensable by the city, so it was destroyed to make way for the I-10 bypass behind the Vieux Carré. Four rows of beautiful mature live oak trees, over a mile long, were cleared from the neutral ground. Soon thereafter, the interstate heavy-handedly bisected the commercial strip. This act severely retarded future commerce and recreational activity in the area, and property values soon plummeted. Overnight, a once-prosperous area became undesirable. Homeowners moved away, and since homes were neither saleable nor rentable, abandonment ensued. Next, crime flourished. The irony of destroying a thriving neighborhood in order to facilitate faster access to the suburbs was not lost on the area's remaining black residents.

Although not as prosperous as at one time, this neighborhood remained identified with significant "social aid and

pleasure" meeting halls devoted to specific groups of black professionals, mechanics, or skilled laborers, or to benevolent societies or clubs. These halls are still used for business and social functions. The GNOCDC notes that the Autocrat Club on St. Bernard Street was one of the liveliest, having offered fish fries on Fridays and dances every Saturday night before Katrina. Several historic halls, such as Perseverance Hall on Villere Street and Frances Amis Hall, served as community churches. Many second-line parades devote a portion of their parading to the harsh cement surroundings of the Claiborne underpass in memory of this once-important commercial area. Every year on Super Sunday, the Mardi Gras Indians parade through the Tremé and down Claiborne, converging down at Hunter's Field in the Seventh Ward.[19]

Of the changes along the Tremé end of the avenue since the nineteenth century, none was more devastating than the cutting down of the live oak trees on the neutral ground in the mid-1960s, because it extracted something out of the spirit of the neighborhood. People had for generations embraced each other there in the daily rituals of life, and old ladies came out to the neutral ground to socialize. The neutral ground had also been square one for the rituals of Black Mardi Gras each year.[20] In 2003, local black artists on a mission to depict the people, places, and events that defined the area's soul set out to paint the large circular cement pilings of the elevated freeway underpass. New Orleans artist and community organizer Richard Thomas stated: "We are hoping that the project is creating awareness and keeping hope alive that something will happen. . . . when the trees were taken away, there were studies done that the city paid for . . . but those things never happened. This project is bringing attention to the neglect and the disenfranchisement of people. . . . Artists have a responsibility to be the shaman, the healers, the bearers of consciousness."[21]

A *Gambit Weekly* cover story in 2004 described the mural project: an open-air art museum with nearly forty full-scale murals covering columns from the Orleans Avenue intersection down to Hunter's Field. The column-gallery is shaded by the elevated interstate. This project, called "Restore the Oaks," was commissioned by the African American Museum, located in the nearby Tremé neighborhood.[22]

The murals collectively provide a glimpse into the world of Tremé, depicting everyday life without falling into the trap of nostalgia. Most local casual observers will easily recognize civil rights pioneer the Reverend Avery Alexander as well as a number of local musicians, including Jelly Roll Morton, one of the pioneers of jazz; Ernie K-Doe, who had a number one hit in the 1960s with his "Mother-in-Law"; and the legendary and highly influential rhythm-and-blues musician and singer Fats Domino (this last mural was painted by Fats's cousin Atlantis Domino). Facing downtown from Orleans Avenue, the first block of columns focus on Carnival experiences held on that spot, since in the years before desegregation, black celebrants were generally banned from the Canal Street and St. Charles Avenue parade routes.

Toots Montana was the subject of one of the first murals. He is depicted in full dress with large, brightly colored feathers. Other murals portray a number of well-known African American Mardi Gras figures: the Zulu krewe, the Skeleton Gang, a group known as the Million Dollar Baby Dolls, and other notable groups and individuals. Local chefs Leah Chase and the late Austin Leslie are shown in impressive murals in the block between St. Ann and Dumaine streets. Damon Reed painted Mahalia Jackson's mural. Local painter-teacher Prince painted a graphic rendition of a momentous event in the saga of the Freedom Riders. Near St. Philip Street, Johnny Payton painted a typical Sixth Ward house. In this mural, a horn player stands in the doorway of a house in homage to a

time when there were musicians in nearly every household in the neighborhood. Music was the lifeblood of the community, and these musicians played at jazz funerals and many other neighborhood events. This tradition is memorialized in the neon sign of the Jazz Funeral nightclub on Bourbon Street (see inside cover): beneath the neon letters, a brass band is shown marching in the street at a funeral. Joy Ebel's mural of brass-band players depicts a number of musicians from the past decades. For over two centuries, Tremé's second-line parades proudly took to the streets to celebrate various social events in everyday urban life.

The Claiborne mural project transformed a forlorn urban space into an outdoor enclosure, or room, its spatial qualities by definition quasi-architectural, since it provides sheltered protection from the elements. A harsh, inhospitable space was enlivened and significantly enhanced. In its totality, the setting became dramatic, even while temporarily used as a storage area for hundreds of uninsured flooded-out Katrina cars. In this regard, the pride expressed in the

3.20: *Jazz funeral diorama at the* UCM *Museum, 2006.*

3.21: *Mural,* Front Porch Gossips, *Claiborne Underpass, Tremé, 2005 (post-Katrina).*

3.22: *Mural of Mardi Gras Indians, Claiborne Underpass, Tremé, 2005 (post-Katrina).*

mural *Freedom* by Dwane Conrad (2002) stands in striking contrast to the flooded cars that surrounded it after Katrina (mural not pictured). The mural *Front Porch Gossips* by Labertha Dorensbourg McCormick (2003) depicts two ladies talking across the three-foot side lot separating their shotgun houses (Fig. 3.21).

Nearby, other colorfully rendered murals depict Mardi Gras Indians celebrating on what had been grassy neutral ground (Fig. 3.22). In each, the glory of celebration is clearly evident. Carnival provides a chance for generally friendly social competition and turf assertion, and is open to everyone who seeks to be a part of it. Furthermore, it is seen as asserting a New Orleans ethos that sets the city and its people apart from the rest of the United States. The persistence of what has been termed black street Carnival—as distinct from black elite Carnival—dates from 1823 and the "great Congodance." Here, the retention of African forms among African New Orleanians also continues to be clearly evident, as is their seizure of what otherwise would have become an exclusively white annual holiday. The late-nineteenth-century rise of the Mardi Gras Indians illustrated the power of the African–New Orleanian sensibility to purposefully and successfully integrate African elements into a unique African American social-folk art form.[23]

New Orleans was never exclusively French, and its cultural traditions were therefore not the product of French culture alone. The most important reason for this was the large African population of the original city. Africans came to colonial Louisiana as early as 1719. By 1746, African and African-Creole citizens outnumbered white New Orleanians roughly two to one. These Africans, imported as slaves, were largely Bambaras from the interior of West Africa. Africans and African-Caribbeans adapted well to the European festivity of Carnival, and eventually would shape these influences into the rituals of an indigenous subculture all their own. Hence, the birth of jazz.[24] In *Sinful Tunes and Spirituals*, Dena J. Epstein argues that this culture survived more nearly intact in New Orleans than anywhere else in mainland North America; only in Place Congo in New Orleans was the African tradition able to continue openly without fear of reprisal.[25] For this reason, the city remained in spirit the most African of all cities in the United States.[26]

In later years, the black population took advantage of Carnival to surreptitiously violate certain aspects of the stringent Jim Crow legal code and culture whenever possible. The Mardi Gras Indians, meanwhile, stuck largely to their own black neighborhoods. However, as far back as 1900, "respectable" white citizens worried that black people were boldly venturing into white areas of the city, particularly the central business district, to take part in white civic festivities. If Carnival helped break down forced segregation somewhat, it did little to end racism itself.[27] And by the late twentieth century, white citizens would use Mardi Gras, including its black folk traditions, as symbols of the city's racial harmony, despite any such claim's variance from the truth.

Urban folk architecture, New Orleans music, and the folk traditions of Mardi Gras powerfully converge at the Mother-in-Law Lounge on North Claiborne Avenue (at Columbus). This is the shrine to the late Ernie K-Doe, a flamboyant local musical legend who passed away in 2002. The lounge was purchased in 1995 and rechristened the Mother-in-Law Lounge, the name taken from his 1961 national number one hit of the same title. This two-level building houses a bar and a kitchen on the first level and an apartment on the second. In composition, it was not dissimilar from a camelback shotgun house. The exterior is covered with many murals painted by the artist David LeBatard (Fig. 3.23), who also muraled the exterior of Tee-Eva's (see Part 2). The bright colors of the murals evoke the costumes of the Mardi Gras Indians who parade across the street in the former Claiborne neutral ground each year and on a few other special occasions. The building was transformed, in effect, into a folk-architecture shrine to the late musician and his flamboyant legacy.

The mural on the east façade, by Fuslier, depicts K-Doe's life story, from his birth at Charity Hospital (lower-left corner) to his marriage and his relationship with his family, including his infamous mother-in-law (center, and center-left). "I'm Cocky But I'm Cool," one of his signature lines, is emblazoned at upper left. The eave proclaims, "A brave man is the one who walks in when the rest of the world walks out" (Fig. 3.24). The other side, nearest the main entrance, was painted with a mural by LeBatard, signed as LEBO, and was of Miss Pussycat and Quintron. Quintron is famed as the inventor of the Drum Buddy. Miss Pussycat is the owner and proprietor of Pussycat Caverns on Burgundy Street (Fig. 3.25). Quintron is shown holding his instrument while Pussycat second-lines.

A bronze plaque placed on the building soon after K-Doe's death reads as follows:

THE ERNIE K-DOE
MOTHER-IN-LAW LOUNGE
Sponsored by:
Marc H. Morial, Mayor
The Music and Entertainment Commission of
New Orleans
Jackie Harris, Executive Director
Badi Murphy, Chair

3.23: *Mother-in-Law Lounge, North Claiborne, 2005 (post-Katrina).*

3.24: *The mural* K-Doe's Story, Mother-in-Law Lounge, *2005 (post-Katrina).*

3.25: *Mural depicting Miss Pussycat and Quintron, Mother-in-Law Lounge, 2005 (post-Katrina).*

Besides "Mother-in-Law," K-Doe's other hits included "A Certain Girl," "T'aint It the Truth," and "Hello, My Lover." From the 1990s until his death in 2002, K-Doe jump-started his career with indispensable help from his wife, Antoinette. This lounge was the hub of his comeback and a gathering place for fellow musicians.

Ernie K-Doe was one of New Orleans's most flamboyant characters. He called himself "Emperor of the World," wore royal garb, and sought to be addressed as "emperor" wherever he went. K-Doe loved to meet and greet the public, and visitors to the Mother-in-Law Lounge were always welcomed with warmth, hospitality, and Antoinette's delicious home-cooked food. Although Ernie K-Doe has left this realm, his fans keep his spirit alive.

On Mardi Gras 2004, traditional Mardi Gras festivities returned to the Claiborne neutral ground. The Mother-in-Law Lounge was the epicenter for the event. Many of the iconic celebrants of the last forty years were there, including the Mardi Gras Indians (Chief Al Morris and Big Chief Alfred Doucet among them), the Baby Dolls, and Toots Montana. Well-known musicians, including the Baptiste family, performed as they marched through the Claiborne underpass-cum-museum. Al Johnson performed "Carnival Time," his 1960 hit and Mardi Gras anthem. The event was planned to reestablish the Claiborne neutral ground–underpass as the epicenter of the black folk-culture Mardi Gras. Montana recalled that "before they built that overpass on Claiborne, you would have all the maskers down here. Families would come and have picnics on sunny days on the neutral ground." Antoinette K-Doe recalled coming with her family as a child: "We would see the Baby Dolls, the Indians, the Moss Man. It was just great."[28]

The name Antoine Dominique "Fats" Domino is synonymous around the world with New Orleans popular music and folk culture. He achieved much in his life through his recorded music in the genre of classic rhythm and blues (R&B) and early rock and roll as a singer, songwriter, and pianist. He sold more records during the 1950s and early 1960s than any other African American musician. His piano style was grounded in the blues, boogie-woogie, and stride piano. He created a signature style, and with his warm, sincere personality, he endeared himself to audiences worldwide. He was so deeply rooted in New Orleans that he never left to live in Los Angeles or other more "glamorous" places. His first hit, "The Fat Man," sold over two million copies and peaked at number two on *Billboard*'s R&B charts. To date, Domino has sold more than 110 million records.[29]

As styles and tastes changed in subsequent years and his popularity waned, Domino continued to record and tour, though less often than when he was at the height of his fame. In the 1980s, he decided he would no longer travel, since he was earning a comfortable income from royalties. In 2003, he was honored in the aforementioned column mural painted by his cousin, beneath the overpass on Claiborne Avenue. This mural depicts Fats while at the peak of his powers in the world of popular music. Everything about it is classic—the color palette reminiscent of a two-tone 1957 Chevy, Fats's broad smile, his piano keyboard, and musical notes rendered with a spiritual reverence, symbolizing a joyous atmosphere filled with his upbeat, rollicking R&B melodies (Fig. 3.26).

Fats lived in a comfortable but modest home on Caffin Avenue in the Lower Ninth Ward. In the early 1960s, he began work on his home-studio-office compound, which consists of his home and two other structures adjacent to his original house. These structures now house a recording studio, a business office, and a shrine of his personal artifacts and mementos.[30] Throughout the years, he acquired additional adjacent property for his compound. He never left the neighborhood he grew up in, and for this he is greatly admired locally.

One of the buildings, facing Caffin, is an adapted double-shotgun house. It now serves as his business office. The roofline was altered to add a second gable, thereby making the front more closely resemble a bungalow. Above the steps leading to the porch and front door is a neon sign: Fats Domino Publishing. A single black star is displayed above this sign. To the right is a modified eave, sheathed in Plexiglas, with the initials *F D* in black letters. The structure is cream colored with conventional face brick, and the roof eaves are painted black with yellow inset panels (Fig. 3.27). He lives in an adjoining three-level pink-roofed house.

Fans from around the world visit Caffin Avenue to pay homage to Fats, just as Elvis Presley's devotees flock to Graceland. (Fats was a close friend of Presley, his peer atop the pop charts.) It is a testament to Fats's personality that he never sought to capitalize on his private residence by turning it into a folk "shrine," although it certainly could have become a highly profitable tourist attraction. Its architecture remains modest and completely authentic, just like its owner.

Domino elected to remain at home with his family because of his wife's poor health as Katrina loomed in the Gulf of Mexico. The Ninth Ward was heavily flooded when the levees broke, and his compound took on nine feet of water. On September 1, 2005, Domino's agent reported that he had not heard from him since the week before the hurricane. CNN reported that a coast guard helicopter had rescued Domino, and his daughter, gospel singer Domino White, corroborated the authenticity of a photo shown on CNN during the same

evening broadcast. It was not publicly known at the time that the Domino family had been taken to a Red Cross emergency shelter in Baton Rouge. JaMarcus Russell, the starting quarterback of the Louisiana State University football team, graciously allowed the family to stay at his apartment. The family first returned home on Saturday, October 15; their house had been looted twice in their absence.[31]

Grieving fans, upon hearing he was missing, had spray-painted "Rest in Peace" and "You Will Be Missed" on the upper-right front façade. Fats's compound sustained less damage than the surrounding houses, and he did his best to keep his battered spirits up after seeing his devastated neighborhood for the first time. "I'm still here, thank God. I'm alive and kicking," the seventy-seven-year-old musician said with a laugh. Domino's son-in-law, Charles Brimmer, helped the legendary musician salvage mementos from a career spanning over fifty years. The artifacts were quietly loaded into a car and taken away. The three surviving gold records (out of twenty-one stored in the house before Katrina)—for "Rose Mary," "I'm Walkin'," and "Blue Monday"—were found in very poor condition because of extensive mold and mildew damage. Domino said, "Well, somebody got the rest of them. . . . I don't know what to do, move somewhere else or something . . . but I like it down here."[32] In February 2008, Domino received the first "Hero of the Storm" award from the national civic-booster group Friends of New Orleans. The award was given to Domino and the Tipitina's Foundation for their efforts in the aftermath of Katrina to preserve New Orleans's unique culture.

The folk and pop-culture shrines of Ernie K-Doe and Fats Domino contribute much to New Orleans's soulful funkiness and charm. Each place has transcended its architectural limitations, becoming far more significant as funk and soul architecture than when they were first built. Both walk that fine line between self-conscious and unself-conscious architecture. These places completely personify the personalities of these two legends, and in the process have become extensions of their owners' idiosyncrasies and "outsider" aesthetic tastes. Though damaged by the brackish floodwaters, both shrines survived Katrina, and both will endure as urban folk-architecture icons.

Shrines to musical legends in some ways differ little from shrines devoted to religious icons. Such was the case with the United House of Prayer for All People (2001), located on the corner of Jackson and Willow, Uptown. This church was scaled similar to Fats's and K-Doe's shrines. It appeared, in scale and composition, like a large double-shotgun house that had been adapted into a church. The composition was symmetrical, with stairs leading to an entrance flanked by a

3.26: *The mural* Fats Domino, *by Atlantis Domino (2002), Claiborne Underpass, Tremé, 2005 (post-Katrina).*

3.27: *Fats Domino's residence-studio-office, Lower Ninth Ward, 2005 (post-Katrina).*

pair of glass-block columns. A pair of majestic white lions guarded the stairway. The inscribed entablature above the doorway bore the name of the congregation. Above this were three crucifixes. The exterior was of brick masonry of varying types. The brick coursing was variegated: red brick interspersed with beige soldier-course bands (Fig. 3.28). The most noteworthy architectural feature was the pair of ascending black angels draped in robes (Fig. 3.29). The church immediately became a landmark in the neighborhood. It was located diagonally across from the Jackson Avenue Grocery, the site of the 4 Kings Entertainment mural (Part 1). Suffice it to say, the hip-hop mural stood in sharp juxtaposition to the United House of Prayer for All People.

The geographic and racial lines of demarcation that exist between adjoining neighborhoods dramatically influence

how a city is perceived and conceptualized by its residents. A neighborhood, defined as a discrete entity within a city, is composed of edges, landmarks, grids, grains, figure-ground relationships, age and condition, and boundaries. Some of these features are purely spatial, some are architectural, and others are purely cultural. All the elements of this spatial syntax are nonetheless intertwined. Often, a neighborhood's expression vis-à-vis this syntax is very subtle. For instance, how does someone know when he or she is leaving one area and entering another? If a freeway bisects two neighborhoods, one residential and the other industrial, there may be little question about which is which. Similarly, it may be simple to discern a residential neighborhood that is directly across the street from an auto-assembly plant. One is perceived as a workplace, the other not.

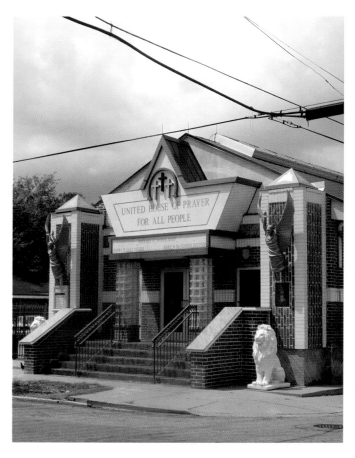

3.28: *United House of Prayer for All People, Washington Avenue, Uptown, 2005 (pre-Katrina).*

3.29: *Black angel on the United House of Prayer for All People, Uptown.*

The functions of race, class, income level, and social structure are detectable in a city if one takes the time to observe closely enough. In New Orleans, one can learn quickly in most cases whether one is in a black, white, or mixed neighborhood by reading a combination of blatant as well as subliminal codings in the vernacular of its soul, funk, and hip-hop urban folk architecture. The black angels adorning the United House of Prayer for All People might lead one to infer that that neighborhood was primarily comprised of black residents. The congregation's church was not so subliminally coded to reinforce this fact: "for All African American People." Similarly, in the case of the Budda Belly Bar, on Magazine Street no more than a mile away as the crow flies, all the patrons depicted in the exterior mural are white (Fig. 3.30). Is this mural's not-so-subliminal message the same, only in reverse: "Budda Belly Bar is for Caucasians"? Another example, on the side façade of a masker building also not very far from the church, the Bluebird Café, a logo of a "white" bluebird is painted on the side of the mask-façade (Fig. 3.31).

Is this coding entirely a coincidence? In these two examples from Uptown, one may infer that some degree of subliminal coding is in effect. Coding in the urban landscape is used in many ways everywhere, although it may perhaps be deduced that the last two examples, one a bar and the other a diner, are, by and large, by and *for* whites.

Architecture and Insularity

In New Orleans, the residents of the poorest neighborhoods have been shown here to produce architectural narratives of significant ingenuity, vibrancy, and resourcefulness. It is a body of work, unfortunately, that has evolved nearly entirely outside the notice of the architectural mainstream. And because it is considered "untrained," outsider vernacular architecture—folk architecture—it naturally has failed to garner serious attention from either the local professional architectural establishment or its regional and national counterparts. Ironically, the world of popular culture—music in particular—beyond New Orleans has by no means dismissed

3.30: *Mural on the Budda Belly Bar, Magazine Street, Uptown, 2005 (post-Katrina).*

3.31: *Mural on the Bluebird Café, Prytania Street, Garden District, 2005 (pre-Katrina).*

these shrines of urban folk and popular culture. This has certainly been the case with regard to the musical devotees of the folk-pop shrines of Ernie K-Doe and Fats Domino, and to a lesser extent, the bars and outdoor places where the Mardi Gras Indians have gathered for generations to engage in their fascinating rituals. The evidence for this rests in the tens of thousands of Internet inquiries, post-Katrina, regarding the status of New Orleans's pop-music legends, the city's musical traditions both new and old, and the state of the physical shrines associated with these creative artists. This alone is irrevocable proof that black popular and folk culture continues to endure, continues to remain relevant.

Unfortunately, the soulful, funky, and hip-hop architecture and artworks in black neighborhoods remain unknown for the most part beyond the black community, yet this condition cuts both ways. In these places, the architectural landscape remains a narrative about neglect, suppressed rage, rage itself, tempered hope, despair, and, above all, intense fear and uncertainty. At the same time, it is an urban culture

increasingly centered on striving for empowerment and self-actualization. The inspirations for these creators' places and artworks were deep-rooted and at the heart of the black experience in New Orleans, dating from the period of slavery and, later, Reconstruction. Restaurant owners, corner-grocery-store owners, bar owners, proprietors of sno-ball stands, church groups, rappers, members of the social aid and pleasure clubs, and others all have continued, each in their own way, to find a way to do so much with so little through sheer will and determination. Resources have been scarce for architecture per se. Moreover, financial limitations have been real: property owners have been very limited in what they could afford to build on their own. Private investment from outside the black community has been little to nonexistent, and public-sector grants have usually been too few and too small. As a result, seldom has it been possible to hire an architect, and there are only a handful of black architects in the city to select from anyway.

Meanwhile, on the high ground in the oldest sections of

3.32: *Katrina's devastation, Lower Ninth Ward, 2005.*

the city, and in particular on the strip of dry ground referred to earlier as the "sliver by the river," an almost paradoxical attitude of racial indifference prevailed prior to Katrina. New Orleans had indeed reached a critical turning point, and the Mardi Gras establishment had reached its apotheosis in many ways. The subculture of Carnival was showing signs of stagnation as the demographics of the city shifted to a black majority and the long-dominant white-centered power structure showed signs of waning. Perhaps the defining moment—the high point, architecturally—for this subculture of the Mardi Gras elite was the period immediately

preceding the 1984 World's Fair. Not surprisingly, the fair's central aesthetic themes were rooted in the annual rituals of white Mardi Gras. In addition, the Piazza d'Italia, an internationally praised work of urban design and architecture when it opened in 1978, next to the fair site in the booming Warehouse District, had fallen into ruin; the city and private civic groups, although they had tried from time to time, were unable to afford its upkeep, and it subsequently suffered from looting and vagrancy (see Part 1 and Part 4).[33]

Throughout New Orleans's history, when whites were in the majority, they assimilated only those aspects of the local black culture that they found particularly entertaining or rewarding, i.e., music, food, and dance. It was this process that made the place so fascinating. Katrina, however, exposed the other side of this coin, and architecture was not immune to these critiques. In contrast to this broader tradition of selective appropriation, why did so few white architects meaningfully assimilate key aspects of New Orleans's black folk culture, specifically its Mardi Gras and hip-hop subcultures, into their own work? The city's elite white architects (and their clients) dismissed outright folk, funk, and hip-hop expressions of urban culture. Worse, as already noted, the white architectural elite's dismissiveness remained off the radar screen of civic discourse. This lack of interest further insulated this group of professionals from the changing demographic and cultural realities of the city. The notable exception to this elitist attitude was perhaps the populist sensibilities in non–New Orleanian Charles Moore's Wonderwall at the 1984 World's Fair (see Part 4). There, Moore sought to appropriate, assimilate, and draw from divergent sources, and not to isolate or perpetuate false social or racial myths.

Katrina's floodwaters exposed much. The catastrophe afforded a rare chance to pause and take note of why so little serious attention had been devoted to diversity or to the function of race and class in New Orleans's *insider* architecture and urban design. Direct references made by insider architects rarely sought to draw parallels between racial subcultures, and usually occurred only when referring to the decades-long migration of whites out of the city for the blissful, supposedly tension-free (i.e., safe) pastures of suburbia. The problems caused by unabated suburban sprawl and its corrosive effect on the urban neighborhoods of New Orleans were unwittingly foisted upon those (the poor) who were left behind.[34] Meanwhile, any fissure between white and black subcultures was the last thing the tourist industry wished to discuss, either pre- or post-Katrina. This is because it remained an industry that relied on large numbers of low-wage workers—the urban poor—a sizeable percentage of whom lived in the now-destroyed Lower Ninth and in nearby neighborhoods.[35]

It took a national catastrophe for Americans to wake up to the social and racial condition of America's cities, and New Orleans became the poster child for this realization. The devastation in the Lower Ninth Ward instantly conveyed this reality to the world (Fig. 3.32). The sudden dislocation of an entire city and metro area, nearly a million people, would have profound outcomes and ramifications that would be felt for decades (Fig. 3.33).

Unfortunately, even after Katrina too many in the wealthy white establishment (architects included) quietly went about

3.33: *Walking to New Orleans, September 1, 2005.*

their own business in an often-desperate personal search for normalcy. And to some extent this was understandable. On the other hand, once again the danger lurked that they would ignore the burst of visual creativity taking place in the poor black neighborhoods, if and when they revived and creative activity resumed in earnest. The possibility of the resumption of this cultural disconnect remained real, and glaring. Would the white and black creative communities grow even more distant from each other, sharing even less common ground than before? The case could be made that a further drift would have occurred even if Katrina had not occurred. As mentioned, racial and cultural alienation was being fueled by a crime epidemic. The continuing crime problem, post-Katrina, served only to further confuse matters that threatened to polarize repopulating neighborhoods.

In recent years the crime epidemic had thrown the city's neighborhoods, both black and white, into a state of delirium. Perhaps whites' fear of crime influenced their decision not to go out and learn about the positive attributes of black urban culture.[36]

Despite the persistence of race- and class-based inequalities, benign urban neglect, and rampant crime, residents of poor black neighborhoods endeavored to accomplish what they could on their own, by themselves, for themselves. Usually, as mentioned, funds allowed for only superficial interventions—the repainting of an exterior façade of a frame structure, or a hand-painted sign or mural on the side of a corner grocery store or tire-repair shop (see Part 5). An ad hoc construction and renovation work crew—consisting of cousins, parents, friends, and church groups—typically donated labor and supplies. Before Katrina, the everyday commercial and residential vernacular architecture in the black neighborhoods was vibrant and vital. The city's folk, funk, and hip-hop expressions in the built environment had reached a turning point—the question now was whether roots architecture could survive in post-Katrina New Orleans.

Illusion, Delusion, and Folly

Nobody around here wants to talk about the really important things, but if you're gonna make an omelet, you gotta break some eggs.

—VINCE MARINELLO, 2006

A Seductive yet Perilous Place

AS ONE APPROACHES NEW ORLEANS FROM the east or west via I-10, or from the north via the twenty-four-mile Causeway Bridge, the skyline of the city appears above a carpet-like expanse of water, live oaks, and, finally, rooftops. There is something almost surreal about the city's skyline, as if these high-rise structures should be someplace else, such as Houston or Atlanta. It is as if one expects not to see any architectural references to a modern American city, although the majority of the skyline was built during the oil boom of the 1970s or during the frenzy of speculation before the World's Fair of 1984. The mind's eye of tourists, anticipating vistas of old New Orleans, may attempt to suppress the gleaming towers from view. Even the living and the dead occupy their strata in New Orleans differently from the way they do elsewhere. Since corpses buried in the city's spongy, moist soil tend to rise to the surface, the dead are interred aboveground in conspicuous necropolises; these are often referred to as cities of the dead, and thus always appear to reside next to the living as their neighbors. Even these lifeless neighborhoods are highly conscribed by race, religion, social class, and, to some extent, political ideology.

A deeper reading of New Orleans's urban vernacular landscape and its commercial architecture requires one to explore its necropolises as well as its living neighborhoods, from uptown to downtown, from Kenner to New Orleans East, from present to past to future, from white Uptown enclaves to Vieux Carré and Bywater retreats, to the street corners, bars, clubs, and small grocery stores in the black neighborhoods of Gert Town, Carrollton, Mid City, central city, and the Lower Ninth Ward. Although the essence of truth remains elusive, the essence of Carnival is expressed in these places—the commercial establishments—where people congregate on a steamy summer night because they cannot afford to air-condition their cramped apartment or shotgun house.

New Orleans, constructed between a lake and a river, with swamps on the other two sides, is situated in a precarious—even perilous—location. Its citizens drink reprocessed water flushed from the entire Mississippi Valley. Yet many consider it a cultural mecca. As the Vieux Carré goes, so goes New Orleans.[1] This has been the case since the city's inception. Other white neighborhoods built on the high ground along the Mississippi—notably the Garden District, in the American section; Uptown, farther upriver; and the faubourgs built on the downriver side of the Vieux Carré—were traditionally the domains of the city's ruling cognoscenti.

Whites had begun to migrate decades before Katrina struck. Census figures from 1990 showed that whites composed only 34.9 percent of the population of Orleans Parish, compared to 42.5 percent in 1980 and more than 50 percent in 1970. In the 1960s, when the city desegregated its schools and lunch counters, the white population had been nearly 70 percent. New Orleans, which ranked in 1900 as the nation's fifth-largest city, had fallen to twenty-fifth by 1990, and thirty-second by 2000.[2] By 2000 the city's population was nearly 70 percent African American. New Orleans's population shrank by 150,000 between 1960 and 2000, and pre-Katrina, 28 percent of its people lived below the federal poverty line. Before Katrina, 89 percent of black New Orleanians were native-born.[3] The city's pre-Katrina population stood at 484,000 and was neither holding its own nor attracting many transplants.[4]

In New Orleans, appearances are almost always deceiving. The city's bifurcated cultural traditions manifest in a layered, fragmented, and illusive physical landscape rarely found in other American cities. It is nearly impossible to understand the complex meanings embedded in the everyday vernacular architectural landscape of New Orleans without some understanding of the critical functions of race, class, and politics.

New Orleans is ancient by American standards. It will not suffice for one to look merely at the surface of anything; deeper investigations are necessary to uncover the prior "lives" of a given site or building as well as its genius loci. Archeological approaches to urban and architectural inquiry in New Orleans often yield a wealth of information about previous incarnations of various buildings and places, commercial and otherwise, and their past inhabitants. New Orleans is a center for the study of the deep cultural significance of architecture in the truest sense.[5] It offers opportunities for in-depth fieldwork, and much can be learned from archival sources, such as the history of land transactions, as well.[6]

The swampy land near the mouth of the Mississippi River was a harsh, forbidding place to build a city. It was on average six feet below sea level, squeezed between a giant river

4.1: *Panorama of the Vieux Carré, 1906.*

and a huge lake. Some of the French engineers who advised the city's founder, Bienville, told him, in vain, that his vision of a future settlement on this spot would be no less than an act of folly (Fig. 4.1). The French initially called this location Le Flottant—the Floating Land. Others named it La Prairie Tremblante—the Shaking Prairie. And the English dubbed it the Wet Grave. Incredible quantities of water proved a double-edged sword. The place was strategically located at the general confluence of three navigable waterways: Lake

Pontchartrain, the Gulf of Mexico, and the Mississippi River. Important primarily as a trading depot for French fur trappers, the city evolved into one of the most significant ports in America, providing a gateway for the nation's agricultural and, much later, petrochemical industries.[7]

Water was and remains the source of the city's predicament, but also its raison d'etre and the means of its salvation, since the Mississippi is the most vital water transportation link in the United States (Fig. 4.2).[8] Human transformation

4.2: *High water at Mississippi River levee, Vieux Carré, 1903.*

of the physical environment enabled the city to grow and prosper. To reduce the risks of episodic flooding, the physical environment was reengineered, spawning an era of river-control interventions designed, implemented, and overseen by the U.S. Army Corps of Engineers. This system eventually proved unsustainable, even feeble, when judged against best practices internationally in the field of civil engineering.[9]

Against this geographic and civil-engineering backdrop, the privileged class in the city, from its inception, sought to set itself apart. Separation was achieved by means of position, lineage, education, political orientation, and race. This last factor would become predominant in shaping the built environment throughout the twentieth century and up through Hurricane Katrina's devastating outcome. The ruling classes, so to speak, sought to construct barriers marked off by these factors, the result being acute class inequalities fueled by a lingering racism, and the decline of a separate-but-equal (meaning unequal) political order.

According to LaNitra Walker:

When Hurricane Katrina bombarded the Gulf Coast . . .
she blew open a Pandora's box of race and class issues that
Americans thought they had packed away. In the wake
of the destruction of the hurricane, we simply weren't
prepared to see how poor Americans in the South really
are, and how many of the poorest are black. The media
focused on the tired and desperate victims in the Superdome and the New Orleans Convention Center pleading
for aid in the hours after the storm, and television audiences could see that they were almost all black . . . after
much footage of Army helicopters plucking entire black
families off of rooftops, the questions turned to whether
or not the victims' race played a role in the slow relief
response . . . the amount of poverty in New Orleans is
astounding . . . the median family income in New Orleans
is estimated to be just two-thirds of the national average.
An estimated 80 percent of those living below the poverty
line are black.[10]

In the South, poverty transcends racial lines, to be sure.
But the 2005 catastrophe once again reminded Americans
that poverty is an unforgiving reality for a disproportionate
number of blacks. The dual southern legacies of slavery and
segregation mean that it remained difficult to talk about
class without also talking about race. As noted by Walker,
many of the interviewed hurricane victims, black and white,
denied that their suffering was solely due to their race, but
claimed that it was rather due to their class. As the hurricane
approached, wealthy blacks, like wealthy whites, were able
to flee the city in their cars. Sadly, most of those who stayed
behind stayed because they were poor, and so many also
happened to be black.

Geography has also mediated this relationship between
class and race throughout the city's history and its patterns
of growth. Specifically, land elevation has always determined
one's susceptibility to flooding, and Katrina proved no exception. The flooding of 80 percent of the city in Katrina's aftermath revealed much about the city's history and geographic
landscape. From the city's inception, most of the wealthiest
inhabitants have always lived on the highest ground. Over
time, a combination of racism, classism, and the need to be
close to jobs led to the draining and settlement of large tracts
of unsustainable land. Because of this, the Lower Ninth
Ward, New Orleans East, much of Gentilly, and virtually all
low-lying districts of the city, which had a high percentage
of minority residents, were devastated by Katrina's flooding.
Of course, this was not an absolute pattern: the hurricane

destroyed white neighborhoods of all income levels as well,
including Chalmette, in St. Bernard Parish, and the Lakeview
area of New Orleans proper. And the policies of private-
sector institutions were at the root of the problem. For
generations, land covenants restricted the sale of property
to "coloreds," meaning that the land could not be sold to coloreds, and real estate firms practiced a form of discrimina-
tory selling known as redlining.

The earliest settlement by Europeans was the Vieux
Carré. This area was the highest ground, built up from silt
deposited by the Mississippi over the course of nearly seven
thousand years. Soon, canals, including Bayou St. John, were
built to connect the downtown with Lake Pontchartrain.
Residences and business were built out on the water until
this practice was outlawed by twentieth-century zoning
laws and public health statutes (Fig. 4.3). The river's natural
levees and their associated high ground extended upriver
and downriver to a certain extent. As the number of settlers increased, they built first on this relatively high land,
creating the neighborhoods known as the central business
district, the faubourgs, the Garden District, and the early
sections of Uptown. It logically follows that these neighborhoods would constitute the 20 percent of the city's east
bank that did not flood after Katrina. In a view of Milneburg
from the air, a photo from 1921 shows about one hundred
camps built on stilts out over the water. This Little Venice

4.3: *Living on Bayou St. John, New Orleans, 1910.*

was demolished when lakeshore development took place in the 1930s (Fig. 4.4). It had been a sign of wealth and social status for a family to own a camp of this type.

By the late nineteenth century, development pressures resulted in the draining of swamps further from the Vieux Carré and the naturally elevated areas, while others had already built out in such adjoining neighborhoods as Tremé. As discussed in Part 2, Tremé is one of the oldest black neighborhoods in America, and was the first place where blacks were allowed to own land and build homes while slavery still existed. Adjacent to Congo Square, it later became the birthplace of jazz, as discussed in the previous section. This was an area where slaves working on the river would congregate during their off time. Rich blends of diverse cultural influences—dances, food, and music—were eventually assimilated into the dominant Anglo-European culture, yet kept at arm's length.

In the Tremé and the adjacent neighborhoods along St. Claude Avenue and Rampart, these streets marked a division between the higher, more valuable ground closer to the river and the lower, less valuable ground on the "lakeside" of St. Claude. Affordable land, housing, and access to jobs were of utmost concern. The area's propensity for flooding mattered far less. People were more concerned with destruction by wind or fire than by floodwaters. Nonetheless, the structures in this area were built on "raised" foundations. The architectural ramifications of this were numerous. They were elevated as much as five feet above the ground on proportionally spaced masonry piers. From the nineteenth century up to World War II, white residents generally continued to build on the highest, most secure ground. Correspondingly, blacks lived in communities nearby in order to be near their workplaces. And black cemeteries were mostly built on the lowest ground. Even the better-off black business owners, who catered to whites, often operated in the lower-lying areas. Poorer blacks built in neighborhoods such as the Lower Ninth Ward because land was cheapest there. The city's vernacular architectural landscape was driven by these determinants.

This pattern gave rise to the checkerboard city, where segregated white neighborhoods, differentiated by geography and architecture, were positioned close together, yet were interspersed with black enclaves. But most importantly, this pattern gave the city its cultural vibrancy. As white residents fled the core city that hugged the river's natural levees, they too moved to undeveloped areas on highly vulnerable land. These areas included Metairie, in neighboring Jefferson Parish; Lakeview, in Orleans Parish; and Chalmette, in St. Bernard Parish. All three areas are low lying; Chalmette is

4.4: *Milneburg "aqua-hood" on Lake Pontchartrain, 1920s.*

the lowest. Worse, in an unimaginable display of collective urban topographic amnesia, the homes built in these areas in the post–World War II decades were usually built directly on a *concrete slab* at grade. It seemed that all the lessons learned from previous floods in the city, including one from the wicked 1915 hurricane whose eye-wall passed just twelve miles west of the central business district, and especially the devastating 1927 flood, had been forgotten.[11] There are two possible explanations: the developers' greed, or the opinion that it was unnatural to be able to look under a raised house clear to the other side. The attraction of these neighborhoods, and of the earlier-developed Gentilly neighborhood, was their convenient proximity to the central business district and the port, where many of the highest-paying jobs were.

By the time a sizeable portion of black residents in New Orleans arrived at something beginning to resemble equal economic footing with the white middle classes, in the 1970s, they looked for new areas in which to build their own homes, schools, and other civic institutions. The only remaining undeveloped land was in the far east end of the parish. This area soon prospered and became known as New Orleans East, or simply "The East." Metairie and Chalmette, the white communities, are at about the same low elevation as The East, but The East is on far riskier land. It projects out into the end of Lake Pontchartrain and Lake Bourne and their large marshes. It is therefore surrounded by water on three sides, and therefore immediately became the most vulnerable, unsustainable part of the entire city. This, in turn, rendered it cheaper land and allowed upwardly mobile black residents the opportunity to build relatively large homes on larger lots, including in upscale neighborhoods, where more than 90 percent of the structures were built on slabs. In 2005, cultural artifacts of great historical significance within the African American community were lost when The East took on as much as fifteen feet of water in some areas.[12]

A Paradoxical Place

Order and decay are inherent dichotomies in any built environment, although these attributes are especially pronounced in New Orleans. It is a place in a perpetual state of physical decay. This has been due to the climate as much as anything else.[13] What many outsiders view as picturesque, romantic, and even poetic are qualities, for locals, impossible to comprehend in the same terms. After the Civil War, which left New Orleans demoralized and defeated, the Reconstruction era was painful. The city's civic architecture suffered from benign neglect. In 1884, less than a decade after the end of Reconstruction, the city attempted to restore its honor as "Queen City of the South" by hosting an extravaganza known as the World's Industrial and Cotton Centennial Exposition (cotton had first been exported from the United States in 1784).[14] The fair was touted by its backers as the dawn of the economic renaissance of New Orleans, but the exposition, not unlike the World's Fair a century later (held in 1984), turned out not to be the answer to the city's problems. Visiting reporters mocked the slapdash exposition buildings and exhibits, which included a Statue of Liberty made of corn, a cathedral made of cracker boxes, and a large wreath woven from the hair of Confederate generals, and they ridiculed in print the city's muddy streets and primitive sanitation system.

The main building covered thirty acres; the Horticultural Hall, a 600-foot-by-194-foot house of glass, was the largest conservatory in the world. There were a number of other buildings, and for the first time at a world's fair, electricity was used to light the buildings and grounds. In the Horticultural Hall were displayed more than twenty thousand pieces of fruit in a setting of tropical and semitropical plants, flowers, and shrubbery. The hall is shown in a sketch by T. de Thulstrup and Charles Graham (Fig. 4.5). Partly because of the bad press, less than one-fourth of the expected six million visitors attended.[15] When the exposition was over, the city was left with losses of nearly half a million dollars, and the flamboyant, politically connected director of the fair, Major E. A. Burke, slipped out of the country. Shortly thereafter, the state treasury, of which he had been in charge, was found to be short $1.7 million.[16]

4.5: *Horticulture Hall at the World's Exposition in Audubon Park, 1884.*

4.6: *Comus Parade, 1867.*

Oddly enough, it may well have been follies such as the city's two world's fairs and their unfulfilled illusions of grandeur, as well as its overall poetic decadence, that have preserved the city's unique culture and ambiance. Since the 1850s, New Orleans had experienced a glacially paced decline, buffered from reality by a combination of self-depreciating humor, illusion, and delusion. It has somehow shielded itself from the mainstream of American progress, for the most part, while concurrently exerting a profound influence on mainstream American culture. The city, encased like a cocoon in its Old World Napoleonic legal code, perceives itself to be an outpost in a Yankee republic. Throughout its history, the city has observed its own rites, moved to its own syncopated rhythms. As with any city, its cultural attractions—the food, rituals, music, and architecture—remained vulnerable to external influences.[17]

Time was not on New Orleans's side even before Katrina. Delusion, disillusion, and civic uncertainty existed long before the recession that followed the oil boom of the 1970s and early 1980s, long before the folly of the 1984 World's Fair, long before the U.S. government deferred maintenance on the metro area's levee system, long before the rise of the drug epidemic that threatened the city's neighborhoods, and long before the invasion of the Formosan termites in the 1950s. Many born-and-bred locals and adopted transplants openly admit to an irrational attachment to the place, regardless. This is the common ground that attracts returning natives and visitors alike, because for all its flaws, its distinctive culture remains its most alluring and enduring contribution to America.

Mardi Gras and the Commercial Vernacular Environment

It is impossible to understand to any reasonable degree the inner life of New Orleans's culture, geography, commercial vernacular and folk architecture, and patterns of land development without some knowledge of the underlying influence of Mardi Gras. Carnival's influence has been profound since its earliest days, as an annual festival of paganism, and the built environment was to a large degree shaped by its rituals. The culture was wrapped around Mardi Gras. Its inner profundities extended far beyond social, racial, and political spectrums, and this culture and its influences were expressed in subtle and not-so-subtle ways in the urban and suburban landscape. Historically, Mardi Gras was premised on the perpetuation of racial and class inequalities, screened— masked—through a process in many ways brilliantly conceived and executed; it was a nomenclature based upon civic illusion, delusion, and folly (Fig. 4.6).

How did New Orleans arrive at the confluence of natural and social vulnerabilities that were laid bare to the world by Katrina? It is a long and winding story, but here is one short version: Nearly two decades before New Orleans was founded in 1718, by Jean-Baptiste Le Moyne de Bienville, Mardi Gras had become part of the local geography, for it was on that holiday (Fat Tuesday) in 1699 that Iberville rediscovered the Mississippi River and camped for the night on the embankment of a little bayou that he appropriately named Bayou du Mardi Gras—the first place-name in Louisiana. Early in the city's history, French settlers celebrated Mardi Gras. When Governor William C. C. Claiborne inaugurated the American regime in New Orleans in 1803, he was impressed by the passionate love of the Creole population for dancing and holding masked balls. In the early nineteenth century, the Crescent City's reputation as a carefree city was further enhanced. As early as 1837 the first organized masquerade parade in carriages took to the streets, where it was witnessed by a delighted crowd of spectators.[18]

"The Missing Links" was the first parade float to be entirely constructed in New Orleans. Previously, the big masks and animal figures had been imported from France, but in 1873, local artisans found ways to make them stronger, and no doubt cheaper, and a new industry was born. The illustration depicts the interior of the "den" where carnival masks and costumes are being prepared for Mardi Gras in 1880 (Fig. 4.7).

Mardi Gras is synonymous with New Orleans, and it occupies a permanent place in the American national consciousness. Since the mid-nineteenth century, travelers have participated in the city's forbidden pleasures. The Pavlovian response of a conventioneer upon arriving, even today,

4.7: *Frantically working to meet the deadline, Missing Links' den, 1880.*

4.8: *Waiting for a parade, Canal Street, 1880.*

is to rush toward the sultry commercial establishments of Bourbon Street. For Middle America, Mardi Gras, New Orleans, and its architectural and spatial experience endure as an escape destination from mainstream American Puritan traditions of solemnity, deferred gratification, and assiduous, undeterred self-actualization. To the casual observer, there is little distinction between the oldest Carnival parades, put on by the city's social elite, and the newer extravaganzas, such as Orpheus, designed to entrance tourists. Behind the public spectacle of Carnival and the seeming chaos on the streets on Mardi Gras, and set against the architecture of the commercial establishments that line the parade routes, however, are rigid rituals and an articulated social structure (Fig. 4.8). It is a protocol defined by kinship, money, and strong familial affinities with neighborhoods, and one that has evolved over a century and a half.

New Orleans, through its history, has been profoundly contradictory. Its vernacular and folk built environment is largely expressive of the culture of Mardi Gras, with its peculiar social hierarchies, pockets of byzantine traditions, bawdiness, spectacle, and partiality to drama and the unexpected. The floats themselves are often a concoction of thematic innovation, political commentary, racism, and architectonic dexterity, such as two floats in the parade of the Krewe of Momus in 1878 (Figs. 4.9 and 4.10). Many of the more than thirty thousand active participants (pre-Katrina) who worked, often clandestinely, on the planning and staging of this annual festival were involved year-round. It was estimated to generate $150 million in economic activity in 2004. The civic-oriented events of Carnival extend over a four-month season, ranging from debutante balls and luncheons for Carnival royalty to a costume contest for drag queens and the chants of the Mardi Gras Indians.

Carnival has endured amid the built environment of New Orleans in its current civic form since 1857, an eternity in a nation of disposable popular culture. In various guises, it extends back even further, at least to the days of French rule in Louisiana, and perhaps back to medieval and ancient pagan festivals.[19] According to Carol Flake:

The damp tropical heat, the permissive colonial regimes, the pomp-loving expatriate royalty, the human flotsam and jetsam washing up from the Mississippi, the enclaves of practical nuns and worldly priests, the pirates and prison escapees, the influx of Caribbean planters and slaves, the *gens de couleur libres* [free people of color], the floods, the fevers, the voodoo altars, the madams of Storyville, the ragtime professors, Louis Armstrong, the spastic bands, the shot glasses of absinthe, the spices in the market, the iron-lace balconies, the jazz funerals, the Mardi Gras Indians, Tennessee Williams . . . made new Orleans a place like no other in America. If carnival had not existed, surely New Orleanians would have invented it. Even the broad avenues of the city, divided by tree-lined neutral grounds, seem to have been designed with parades in mind.

Sold up the river by the French, undefended by the Confederacy, New Orleans nevertheless never really gave in to its Yankee occupiers. Losses, retreats, disasters, plagues, decay, and pestilences did not bring more than passing clouds of gloom and pessimism to a city literally sinking, day by day, further below sea level . . . the permanent plague of locusts, the tourists, who flock to New Orleans to feed on its oddities, are also its last source of sustenance. . . . How can a city so ostensibly Catholic celebrate with such pagan gusto? How can a city so poor concoct such extravagant displays, year after year? How can a city with a majority black population so proudly proclaim the reign of bewigged white pseudo-royalty? . . . New Orleans is still a stratified city, constrained by secrets and social codes and double lives . . . it is (still) a crushingly poor provincial outpost burdened by corruption and a petrified elite. . . . Parades, parties, spices, and even music aren't enough to save the soul of a city, although those things may make a city worth saving.[20]

For many, Carnival is sacred, a virtual religion whose rituals cannot be tampered with without injuring the city's fun-loving spirit and image. For others, however, it is "the altar of

4.9: *A float from the Momus parade, mocking African Americans, 1878.*

4.10: *A float from the Momus parade, mocking General Orville E. Babcock, 1878.*

the golden calf, the glittering idol of the idle rich, blinding the city to its sins and shortcomings."[21] In 1992, these undercurrents erupted into open confrontations over the adoption of the city's Mardi Gras Anti-Discrimination Ordinance. Dorothy Mae Taylor, a black city councilwoman, introduced a long, complicated ordinance that, in effect, prohibited discrimination on the basis of race, gender, or religion in Carnival organizations. The initiative garnered much momentum in the black community and stirred much resentment and defensiveness among the city's white minority. In 1992, New Orleanians for the first time openly faced the realities of race

4.11: *Rex parade on Mardi Gras Day, 1905.*

and class prejudice that had remained concealed by the grand civic and architectural façades of Carnival.[22]

Just one month before, David Duke, a former Klansman and something of a cryptic neo-Nazi, was soundly defeated in a nationally covered race for governor of Louisiana by Edwin Edwards. The brief, heady alliance of blacks and whites that defeated Duke, holding him to less than 15 percent of the vote in the city of New Orleans, proved to be an illusory bond. The images evoked in the campaign were reminiscent of those of the Klu Klux Klan, and the KKK itself was eerily reminiscent of the maskers of the most elite krewes, dating from long

before the Rex parade in 1905 (Fig. 4.11). During both the Duke campaign and the intense debate over the Mardi Gras antidiscrimination ordinance, blacks spoke out angrily.

Privately, whites threatened to "secede" from Carnival rather than comply with the new ordinance. There was something inevitable about this symbolic showdown, whose roots could be traced back to the Louisiana Purchase, the Napoleonic sellout that set Creoles against the Yankee new-comers; to the slavery era, which reinforced the multitiered caste system in New Orleans; to the Reconstruction years, which fueled provincial paranoia and preceded the golden era

4.12: *Rex parade on Mardi Gras Day, 1952.*

played out in private clubs, restaurant backrooms, and the krewes' *dens*, the places where the floats are constructed. Before the newer sections of the city were built, the Vieux Carré, Garden District, and Uptown provided the main civic stage and architectural backdrop, linked by the main parade route, St. Charles Avenue, its gently winding streetcar line running along its green neutral ground.[27] For their part, krewes do all they can to perpetuate myths, including using mystifying themes for their parades, such as the theme of the Rex parade in 1952, "Panorama through the Magic Sugar Egg." The float depicted was titled "The Bees Build the Magic Camera" (Fig. 4.12).

By the 1990s, Mardi Gras, with the built environment as its stage, had become, for cynics, the epitome of decadence, snobbery, dispassion, and thinly veiled racism. Moreover, it was increasingly becoming a financial drain on a city with a structurally inadequate tax base that had reduced its 128 public schools to a shabby and forlorn architectural tradition.[28] Above all, to critics, the annual event was the cause of the city's malaise, not merely a symptom, and it symbolized everything that was wrong with New Orleans. In truth, the Mardi Gras syndrome had largely perpetuated, architecturally or otherwise, a fatalistic, escapist view of the city's prospects and, by tragic default, a general disinclination toward alleviating the plight of the less fortunate inhabitants in the less fortunate neighborhoods.[29]

of Carnival; to the civil rights movement, which challenged the tenets of exclusion; and to the Reagan and Bush years, which left New Orleans, like other cities in America, resource starved. The conflict over Carnival was symptomatic of larger forces reshaping the city as well as pulling it apart. David Duke and the divisive governor's race had reminded New Orleanians that despite their romantic self-sense of isolation, they were still living in the South. New Orleans's well-preserved bubble of civic-sanctioned escapism had been broken. And like the rush of Katrina's storm surge through broken levees, nothing could hold it back.[23]

Trouble and care, the two worst enemies of Carnival, and of life in New Orleans in general, finally caught up to present-day realities.[24] New Orleans had always been a haven for odd enclaves and subcultures. It remained a place of last resort, a place for restive spirits, for those seeking freedom from ill-fitting identities elsewhere and the bland Wal-Mart milieu of faceless, placeless mainstream America. The city's elusive, soulful essence, having survived for so long amid all the strangeness and decadence, remained rare and fragile.[25] The word *carnival* itself is derived from the Latin *carnelevare*, first appearing in Roman Catholic Church writings in the year AD 965. Literally, *carnelevare* means to lift up, or remove, flesh or meat. In Italian, the term evolved into a hailing of meat and a letting go of meat. In English there is a tie with the word *carnivore*. The *Catholic Dictionary* insists that the word was derived from *carnem levare*, meaning the taking away of flesh or meat, in this case at the start of Lent.[26]

There is really no architectural or geographic "center" to Carnival in the strictest civic sense, though its rituals are

Let's Have Another World's Fair

Taken further, this illusion or delusion was rationalized by accepting tourism as the best economic hope for the city's future. In reality, the city had become paralyzed by its byzantine political power structure and by the bifurcation of competing constituencies across its various neighborhoods, e.g., Uptown versus New Orleans East, Lakeview versus the Lower Ninth Ward. These competing political interests tended to cancel one another out. Tourism emerged as the preeminent civic income generator that could conceal the structural defects in the economy and political process. And this is precisely what the deliriously optimistic proponents of the 1984 World's Fair emphasized in their arguments for holding the exposition during an era when such events had already become passé—little more than follies—from an economic-development or technological standpoint, and a huge challenge to stage without any promise of financial success. As noted, the prospect of success proved to be illusory.

Past world's fairs, such as Chicago's Century of Progress Exposition in 1933, had celebrated the triumph of technology. More recent fairs had touted geodesic domes and towering "needles" with observation platforms at their pinnacles. But the 1984 New Orleans fair was a postmodern tribute to the city's past and its culture of decadence, escapism, and fatalism. One entered the gate's portals—a threshold guarded by scantily clad mermaids amid alligator figures. The main attraction was the Wonderwall, which resembled a frozen Mardi Gras street procession. With its scaffolded mélange of turrets, towers, figurines, and gilded cherubs, the Wonderwall, designed by Charles Moore, the late renowned architect, with Perez Architects, came off as a theatrical, postmodernist parody of Carnival. This wall, with its twenty-foot-high pelicans, appeared to be leaping toward a nearby giant Ferris wheel (Fig. 4.13). The wall was the fair's most unifying element, the pin that held the toy together. Its main theme was literature and theatre—appearance versus reality—illusion and folly. It ran for three blocks to Bayou Plaza. The content was highly ironic: brightly colored twists on local icons and local urban myths. The double entendre inherent in the Wonderwall represented a midpoint between classical references and pop-culture references that anyone could relate to on some level. For example, the wall was punctuated with royal palms, but here, reality was inverted, for the palms were constructed of concentric layers of green metal tubing crowned with potted palmettos that appeared to be growing out of the crown. Alive, yes; true palms, no. At night it was far more effective than during the day, when the raw scaffolding was spatially overpronounced and dominant.

The fair was forced to file for bankruptcy, and many vendors, including Perez, the lead architectural firm, went bankrupt (it has since rebounded under new management). However, the cloud had a silver economic lining: the Warehouse District, the neighborhood surrounding the fair site, entered a twenty-year boom period of adaptive use conversion to thousands of apartment and condos. Its future appears even brighter in Katrina's aftermath.

In the end, the 1984 World's Fair functioned to perpetuate the city's Mardi Gras syndrome because the poorest neighborhoods were completely left out of the civic-improvement equation yet again. Concocting yet another tourist attraction seemed to be the best solution that civic leaders could devise to solve the city's chronic problems. Unfortunately, the more tourism was promoted as an industry, the less chance there was for fundamental economic structural diversification. In one national survey after another, New Orleans scored near the bottom for attractiveness as measured by CEOs asked to judge the quality of life in the nation's major cities.[30]

By the 1990s, many neighborhoods were changing, and the poor ones were becoming even poorer and more desperate. The chasm between the haves and the have-nots became

4.13: *Wonderwall at the World's Fair, 1984.*

significantly wider than it had been only ten years earlier. How did this affect architecture? The ornate houses of the haves, in the best (almost always white) neighborhoods, had not been designed for the intense level of protection from intruders that was now needed. Most Uptown mansions, for instance, with their generous verandas, French doors, and tall windows, had not been built for this new age of heightened security. Visual screening from, and surveillance of, the street from within one's home became a prerequisite in architectural renovations and additions in the neighborhoods now under siege. It was as if the middle class had gone underground. The aforementioned checkerboard that characterized the city's traditional pattern of development, a crisscross pattern of black-white enclaves within approximately one-square-mile superblocks, further exacerbated the problem.

Not surprisingly, there were black civic leaders who shared many of these concerns, and who had similarly taken to arming themselves in their own declining neighborhoods. Some resided in the Lower Ninth Ward or in the Pigeontown section of Carrollton, where crime worsened dramatically in the 1990s. The guardians of African American culture, concerned about personal safety and neighborhood cohesiveness, were just as nostalgic as whites for the vanishing social order of the past. In an interview conducted at the time, a prominent member of the African American community, Edgar Chase III, known as Dooky Chase, mused:

People in New Orleans are not looking for a savior. Just someone to bring the city back to where it was—the city in their memory. In the Inter-Business Council, we talk a lot about keeping the essence of the city alive. The architecture of our buildings, the beauty of the people, our way of celebrating is inborn. When I was a child, people would sit on the stoops every evening. You'd take a bath and come out on the porch until mosquitoes made you come inside. You'd turn on the fan and cool things off. Life centered around your neighborhood. We've lost that idea of being safe and free in the neighborhood . . . we've lost the days of the sno-ball man, the watermelon man. We want to be a world-class city, but we have to be careful not to change our culture. We're different. We're not as plastic as other places. We want to be hospitable . . . we like to sin, but we don't want to be known as sinners. Sticking to our roots is how we should grow and evolve—not trying to be like someone else. . . . Mardi Gras was never a civil rights thing for black people. Maybe the other 364 days. But on Mardi Gras, we really didn't care. Mardi Gras was the one day when people accept one another and put down all disputes.[31]

As long as people from all walks of life, i.e., all races, social classes, and neighborhoods, continued to accept the faux royalty of the Carnival krewes, the tradition, i.e., myth, persisted. That is, as long as people continued to be willing to suspend their value systems, thereby preserving the bubble that separated folly and illusion from reality. Otherwise, it was feared within the business community, the year-round culture of Mardi Gras would simply collapse. The Carnival attitude seemingly remained impervious to external realities of race, class, and politics.[32]

Ironically, the civil rights era largely bypassed Carnival. Blacks had developed their own Carnival hierarchy and traditions, centered on Zulu, the parade over which Louis Armstrong reigned in 1949, and the Mardi Gras Indians. Before the interstate destroyed the neutral ground along Claiborne Avenue in Tremé in the 1960s, the Indians celebrated Mardi Gras day on the Claiborne neutral ground, seldom venturing into the Vieux Carré or onto other turf dominated by the white Uptown krewes. These traditions persist to this day; no one wants to "rain on anyone's parade." This "live and let live" mentality may make it difficult to rebound from Katrina.

Even in the aftermath of the Mardi Gras antidiscrimination ordinance, and despite the yet unknown long-term effects of Katrina on Carnival culture, the motto of many remains *Laissez les bons temps rouler* (Let the good times roll). What has endured is an attitude toward Mardi Gras that treats it as a disconnect, as an event in suspended animation, in an in-between zone. In this space, this vector, there are few rules, allowing people to break away from unwieldy ties and excessive restrictions found elsewhere (or at least that is

how they behave). In New Orleans, it seems, marginal, "on the edge" behavior often dominates the middle ground. In fact, many live out their everyday lives in parallel realities—secret relationships, activities, places, and the like—wholly unrelated to their primary reality, or "home range." This explains why in a recent national exposé, an upscale Mid City whorehouse's list of clients was never made public: doing so might have ruined "proper" families and the careers of prominent men in civic life.

Meanwhile, many of the children of the Carnival ruling classes have migrated to other cities to pursue more promising careers. Job opportunities have been increasingly scarce in New Orleans for both blacks and whites since the early 1980s. This migration has had a profound effect on the memberships of old-line organizations such as Comus. They had painted themselves into a corner by closing their membership to "outsiders" over the generations, and the past was catching up to the present.

Uptown whites were not the only New Orleanians under siege. Nor were white Carnival celebrants the only group fervently clinging to their rituals as a way to keep the festive spirit alive and to hold their families and neighborhoods together. Black citizens of New Orleans had a head start in all these concerns. Historically, black residents had demonstrated as strong a predilection as whites' for clubs and societies, pomp and ceremony. Brass bands and "social and pleasure" clubs, both of which originated in the flowering of black folk culture in New Orleans following the Civil War, had been around for at least as long as the Mistick Krewe of Comus. Long before 1900, brass bands dressed in bright uniforms were a common sight. The black community, barred from using white banks, traditionally avoided charity from whites and turned to their own to provide a sense of belonging and social status, in life and in death. During Reconstruction, the mortality rate for poor blacks was very high, particularly for men, and the streets resounded with the mournful dirges of brass bands, hired to follow horse-drawn hearses to the cemeteries, where young men who had died before their time were laid to rest in tiers aboveground. Behind or alongside the band, the parade of mourners, which, as mentioned earlier, came to be known as the second line, would follow, carrying umbrellas, good for sun or rain. Once the body was interred, it was time to celebrate.[33]

In terms of architecture and urbanism, no city seemed to possess a more promising future than New Orleans in the 1850s. In James Gill's words:

The magnificent French Opera House, designed by James Gallier, opened on Bourbon Street in 1859, when political differences with the northern states were the only blot on the horizon for a vibrant, polyglot city of 170,000 people, including 25,000 Irish and almost as many Germans. It was a sporting town with plenty of horse racing and boxing matches. Men played cricket and raquette, a game resembling lacrosse, or took their sailboats out into the lakes. The mood of the city was buoyant and secure, and few doubted its superiority to anything the North could offer or had any qualms about slavery . . . the railroad was now spreading through the state, bringing the prospect of faster transportation between the port and the plantations and even greater accumulation of wealth. The streetcar was introduced in 1860, and New Orleans seemed safely established as a great metropolis of the modern world. Then, however, the blue cockade, emblem of the secessionists, began to appear on lapels all over the city.[34]

In 1860 a statue of Henry Clay (1777–1852) was proudly erected in the middle of Canal Street where it intersects St. Charles Avenue. The great southern statesman (from Kentucky) became the symbol of the prevailing social and political order as well as a rallying point for Mardi Gras merrymakers (Fig. 4.14). In 1900, it was relocated a few blocks away to Lafayette Square. While monuments to white supremacy were being erected in the streets, the long-established old-line clubs, such as the Boston Club on Canal Street, were solidifying their power base in New Orleans society and political life. The Boston Club, the third-oldest such club in the United States, was founded in 1841, only five years after New York's Union Club. The Boston Club was not named after the city, however, but after a card game called boston that fascinated its members.[35] Eventually, improvements to the streetcar line required the Clay statue to be

4.14: *Henry Clay monument, Canal Street, 1893.*

4.15: *Belknap's Fountain, Canal Street, 1888.*

relocated a few blocks away to the center of Lafayette Square, where it resides today.

At the time, statues and fountains were being built frequently. Maybe the most bizarre fountain ever built in the city was on Canal Street, Belknap's Fountain. It featured miniature steamboats, swans, ducks, and cupids, all set in motion by waterpower. A very strange composition and sight to behold, its style was "arabesque-circus," although this folly functioned also as a memorable civic advertisement (Fig. 4.15).

By the late nineteenth century, the visual and civic spatial dominance of Carnival was firmly fixed in the cultural life of the city. Visitors from afar came to witness this spectacle in the streets, and Canal Street became the epicenter. To view a parade on Canal during the Jim Crow era was to witness a highly choreographed portrayal of social and racial status hierarchies publicly displayed on an unprecedented scale. The wealthy ruling class of white uptowners perched in viewing stands along the parade route, safe from the fray on the street below (Fig. 4.16). These temporary scaffolded edifices, along with architectural, permanent outdoor viewing galleries, were festooned with bright banners and provided with specially designed latrines for ladies. The white lower classes, including the Sicilians, Irish, and other Caucasian immigrants, could view the parade only from street level. Blacks were kept away from Canal Street, in their own neighborhoods, removed from the civic and commercial center.

At this time the streetcar lines were being greatly extended outward from the city center to such far-flung points as West End Park, with its whites-only pavilions (Fig. 4.17), and the adjoining New Orleans Yacht Club and roller coaster, which extended far out on a boardwalk over Lake Pontchartrain (Fig. 4.18).[36] For active diversion, the pleasure resorts—West End, Spanish Fort, Milneburg—were not far away from the chaos and grime of the city. New Lake End, later known as West End, opened in 1871 when the city took over the partially built embankment erected about eight hundred feet from the shoreline in Lake Pontchartrain. It was near the terminus of New Basin Canal and the Seventeenth Street Canal. It raised the hundred-foot-wide bank to a height of eight feet above sea level. In that year, the New Orleans City and Lake Railroad started its steam "dummy" and cars, and soon on a large wooden platform constructed over the water, a hotel, restaurant, and various structures intended to house amusements were built. A garden was laid out along the embankment. By 1880, the palace had become popular with white pleasure seekers (Fig. 4.19).

Some thirty years earlier, in the 1850s, a wondrous spectacle was Spalding and Roger's *Floating Palace*. This

4.16: *Mardi Gras Day "Red Pageant" on Canal Street, 1903.*

4.17: *West End pavilions, 1900.*

4.18: *Roller coaster at West End amusement park, 1901.*

4.19: *Pier at the West End amusement park, 1885.*

4.20: *The Floating Palace on Lake Pontchartrain, 1858.*

4.21: *Interior of the Floating Palace, 1859.*

two-hundred-foot-long vessel, which had been built in Cincinnati in 1851, was a super-showboat (Fig. 4.20). It could accommodate 3,300 spectators and more than a hundred staff members. The crew consisted of trainers, performers, and the horses and other animals of the menagerie. A daily newspaper was even published aboard. Besides the circus performance, there were minstrel and dramatic performances and a museum that the proprietors boasted contained "100,000 Curiosities." The circus wintered in New Orleans for several years, performing at the Academy of Music, at St. Charles and Perdido. When spring came, the performers and animals were loaded aboard for the trip upriver. The *Floating Palace* was converted into a hospital in 1862 by the Confederate Army. The interior of the *Floating Palace* is depicted in a lithograph by A. Forbriger. One of the chief attractions of the circus was its performing horses, shown in the center view and in the side-panel vignettes (Fig. 4.21).

The Spanish Fort, on the Lake Pontchartrain shore, was originally built to protect the city from invaders from the North. It later became a place of amusement and included such attractions as a concert hall, the massive Over the Rhine pavilion restaurant, and unusual attractions like an alligator pond (Fig. 4.22). New Orleans's rich tradition of amusement parks extended into the twentieth century. On May 4, 1907, a promoter named Charles C. Mathews advertised the opening of White City. This was to be the best of the new generation of amusement parks in the United States (Fig. 4.23). It was modeled on Coney Island, in New York. On opening night, it featured a performance of *Kismet* by the Olympia Opera Company. The grounds were illuminated by 1,500 electric lights, and one could ride on the Flying Horses or the Figure 8, play the Japanese Ball Game, or view Katzenjammer Castle. It was built on the site now occupied by a Burger King and the former Fontainebleau Motor Hotel at Tulane and Carrollton, where Pelican Stadium once stood. White City closed in 1914, when Heinemann Baseball Park (later Pelican Stadium) was built on the same site. Perhaps the name White City carried a double meaning; one doubts the reference was solely to the white electric lightbulbs.

Fourteen years later, in 1928, the Pontchartrain Beach amusement park opened. It was built on filled land reclaimed from the lake by the Orleans Levee Board, directly across from the Spanish Fort. It had rides, bathhouses, and a boardwalk. The main attraction was the Big Dipper roller coaster. The park survived the Depression, remaining open until 1938, when it was relocated farther east along the lakeshore. The new site was at the end of Elysian Fields Avenue in Milneburg. Only the lighthouse remains today. Rides at the new location included the Wild Mouse, the Smokey Mary, and an immense Ferris wheel. The most memorable icon was the popular Zephyr roller coaster. The park closed in 1983. In the era of segregation, a separate-but-(un)equal park for blacks, called Lincoln Beach, after the president, was created nearby. It operated from 1939 until 1964, when segregation "officially" ended.

Seventeen years after the second Pontchartrain Beach amusement park closed, yet another amusement park opened. This one, Jazzland, was built in the far eastern swamps of Orleans Parish, and many claimed it was a folly from the outset. The $135 million park opened in 2000, and was financed by a group of local investors and by federal loans backed by the city. The park went bankrupt only two years later. In 2003 it reopened as Six Flags New Orleans. Six Flags, a prominent national chain, purchased the park for the bargain price of $22 million and promptly invested $25 million more in upgrades, including dramatic new roller-coaster rides. Ironically, plans for a themed water park were underway when Katrina struck and submerged the entire park in up to ten feet of water. Six Flags abandoned the site entirely in 2006 amid veiled claims in some quarters that (white) locals never embraced the park because of its location. The place now appears destined to become a ruin.

The most intriguing sights during the period of 1920–2005 were for amusement, but places of worship also were admired as sources of spiritual "escape" of a different sort. After all, fifty-six streets in New Orleans are named for Catholic saints. One of the most revered places of high architecture is a cemetery built in 1875 at the end of a new streetcar extension in the New Marigny neighborhood. It was modeled after the Campo Santo dei Tedeschi (German Cemetery) in Rome. Inside the cemetery's walls was constructed a miniaturized Gothic cathedral, named the Chapel of St. Roch.

St. Roch was born in Montpellier, France, around 1295. It is said that he was marked at birth with a red cross on his chest. According to "Blake Pontchartrain," the trademarked moniker of an anonymous local historian who writes a weekly column in *Gambit Weekly*:

As the story goes, he was orphaned at age 20, gave all his fortune to the poor, gave the governorship to his uncle, and went on a pilgrimage to Rome. On the way, he stopped at a town stricken by the plague. The young man healed the people and moved on. Everywhere he visited in Italy, he cured all those he touched. Then he himself was stricken at Piacenza.

Rather than be a burden, he hid himself in a hut in a forest. And here comes the best part. A dog found him,

4.22: *Alligator pond at the Spanish Fort, 1898.*

4.23: *White City, Carrollton and Tulane avenues, 1909.*

4.24: *St. Roch Chapel and Cemetery, Ninth Ward (New Marigny), 1910.*

4.25: *St. Roch, New Marigny, 2006.*

licked his wounds, and brought him a small loaf of bread each day until he recovered.

Eventually he made his way home to France, but his relatives did not recognize him, and he refused to reveal his identity. In his disguise as a pilgrim, he was taken for a spy and thrown into prison by order of the governor. There he died five years later in 1327.

The red cross on his breast and documents in his possession proved his identity, and 100 years after his death he was canonized.[37]

The inherent folly of the structure, which is beautiful in its own right, rests in its diminutive scale. It was built after an epidemic of yellow fever in 1868 as a thanks offering by Father Peter L. Thevis (Fig. 4.24). The priest promised he would build a chapel to the saint. Legend has it that not a single parishioner died, and Father Thevis kept his promise. Soon thereafter, the shrine gained fame as a place where cripples shed their crutches (leaving them behind on permanent display) as evidence of newfound physical abilities thanks to sacred intervention. The cemetery and shrine stand today, having weathered Katrina remarkably well, although many of the artifacts were looted (Fig. 4.25). It apparently was designed with periodic floods in mind. The crypts and graves were safe, resting slightly above the reach of Katrina's high floodwater mark. The chapel appears to have been designed to withstand repeated flooding as well. And Claremont, California, is home of the St. Roch Dog Rescue, an organization dedicated to saving abandoned and homeless dogs.[38]

St. Roch's was to miniaturized cathedrals what another church of the same period, the Second NME Church of the South, was to miniaturized medieval castle fortifications. This church, completed in 1907, was designed by M. B. De-Pass, and stands near the corner of Music and Burgundy in the Faubourg Marigny (Fig. 4.26). The façade contains what appear to be gun turrets, shielded behind a rusticated wall with few openings.

Other unusual structures built during this period include the Doullut Houses, popularly known as the Steamboat Houses. Built in 1905, these residences are situated prominently along the Mississippi River levee in the Bywater neighborhood, a few miles downriver from the Vieux Carré (Figs. 4.27 and 4.28). These houses, which resemble each other like fraternal twins, were built by a determined individualist, steamboat captain M. Paul Doullut, for himself and his son. Heavily influenced by a Japanese precursor, the Kinkaku, or Golden Pavilion, at the St. Louis–Louisiana Purchase Exposition of 1903–1904, they were constructed the following year. Oriental motifs occur throughout the

4.26: *Second* NME *Church of the South, Faubourg Marigny, 2005 (pre-Katrina).*

three-tier configuration of each house, as well as on the dipping roof overhangs and deep eaves. Motifs derived from the vernacular architecture of steamboats were incorporated, including narrow interior halls, decks, squared corners, and a pilothouse at the top. Especially at night, the illuminated pilothouses atop steamships passing by can be easily seen from each house's pilot perch, and vice versa, as if to convey the illusion of a landlocked ship. The immense wooden Mardi Gras–like beads that give a distinctive accent to the galleries are graduated in size and loosely strung between the columns on steel wires.[39] The vernacular high architectural synthesis of illusion and deliriousness exhibited in the Chapel of St. Roch, the Second NME Church, and the Steamboat Houses indicates deeper undertones in the city's culture of escapism.

Speaking of escapism, the invention of motion pictures was embraced with enthusiasm in New Orleans, just as it was everywhere else in America, but until the late 1960s, nearly every movie palace was segregated.[40] The wealthy white elite went to their theaters on Canal Street, while the poor blacks had their own in the "back neighborhoods." In 1896, the first motion pictures shown in the city were projected from an elevated wooden booth in the center of the West End amusement area. They were shown outdoors on a large canvas screen that was unrolled in front of a viewing stand. A five-hundred-volt current was rigged from the nearby streetcar line; the current was reduced with a water

4.27: *Doullot House (Steamboat House #1), Lower Ninth Ward, 2005 (pre-Katrina).*

4.28: *Doullot House (Steamboat House #2), Lower Ninth Ward, 2005 (pre-Katrina).*

rheostat, and was attached to a Vitascope machine. Canal Street movie palaces included the Triange, the Dream World, the No Name, and the Alamo. Later came the Globe and the Trianon. By 1940 there were nearly fifty movie theatres in New Orleans.[41] By 1970, more than two-thirds had been destroyed. Drive-in theatres included the Airline Drive-in in Metairie; it was destroyed in the late 1960s.

Meanwhile, Louisiana remained, in the view of outsiders, backward. African Americans lived in neighborhoods where it remained common to see buildings completely overgrown with vegetation. These odd places were taken for granted because "That's just the way it is," in the words of Bruce Hornsby from his 1993 hit song of the same title (Fig. 4.29).[42] In 1993, when the old-line white Mardi Gras krewes reluctantly agreed "to seek to become racially and ethnically inclusive in their membership policies and not to discriminate on the basis of race, color, creed, or religion," the effect of the city council ordinance was the reverse of what had been intended. Unfortunately, the white Uptown social elite was by then more isolated than before.[43] A climate of mutual mistrust prevailed. The civic pride based on being "different" has unfortunately been the city's undoing, for it cuts both ways—cultural uniqueness too often impedes economic advancement. In the case of New Orleans over the past twenty-five years, and especially since the 1984 World's Fair, these two civic goals have often been contradictory.

As discussed previously, the social status, race, and political orientation of an architect in New Orleans determined the course of his or her professional career. These factors figured prominently in what might be referred to as an architect's acceptability factor in the eyes of potential clients. This has also been true, of course, in other American cities, although in New Orleans this pattern appears to have been more pronounced because of the Carnival syndrome. Not surprisingly, the old-line Uptown social order that historically dominated Carnival also dominated architectural commissions. This continued to be the case in both the private and public sectors, as it had been since the antebellum era of the 1850s, the halcyon period of the architect James Freret and his contemporaries. In the private sector, white clients tended to hire white architects, usually men. In public-sector commissions, joint white firm–black firm ventures came to be undertaken more and more frequently, and this was a sign of progress, although the results met with varying degrees of success.

Caucasian architects, a significant percentage of whom were raised in the area and had studied locally, provided a core group of architects who met these criteria.[44] Many of the post–World War II generation of young architects, having been fully inculcated in the International Style, and led by the talented firm of Curtis & Davis, returned to work for their clients on a wide variety of building types, ranging from small private residences and oceanside villas to churches to public libraries—including the main library in the central business district (1955–1957)—to the New Orleans City Hall, the State of Louisiana Office Building and state Supreme Court Building complex at Duncan Plaza (1955–1957, both scheduled for demolition in 2008; see Part 5), and the Louisiana Superdome (1972–1977). The modernist Rivergate Convention Center in the central business district (1963–1965), also destroyed (1996), was perhaps the most noteworthy postwar downtown civic building; it even housed an anticipated (but uncompleted) four-lane highway beneath. In New Orleans, large-scale federal public-housing experiments, many of them inspired by Le Corbusier's iconoclastic plan for Paris, La Ville Radieuse (1922), and his later Unité d'Habitation housing block in Marseilles (1945–1947), were nearly always built in or adjacent to traditionally black neighborhoods. The Guste housing project was a prime example of the latter.

Overall, however, the black community in New Orleans was left to its own devices when it came to architecture. After white flight reduced the economic bases of many neighborhoods to vestiges of their former selves, the new residents of these old neighborhoods were poorer and less educated than their predecessors. They inherited a vernacular building stock that was, by and large, built by whites for whites. By 2005, the pool of licensed black architects could not come close to meeting the demand in a city that was by now 68.7 percent black.[45]

The treatment of blacks by elite white architects was based, for the most part, on noblesse oblige. This code of genteelly patronizing the "less fortunate" was bound to fall short as the level of meaningful social engagement remained superficial, by and large. It remained, in many ways, an intractable situation for everyone involved. The relatively few architects who seriously engaged black clients' and community groups' neighborhood redevelopment goals and agendas often felt bewildered and betrayed whenever their efforts were received with skepticism by black community groups. To the white architect, it was as puzzling as a string of beads tossed from a float during a Mardi Gras parade being thrown right back.[46]

As discussed in the previous chapter, with comparatively few economic resources at its disposal, the black community was reduced to a limited range of architectural options. Tight construction and renovation budgets usually allowed for only the minimal reworking of a structure, limiting the scope

4.29: *Central City "vegi-tecture," 2005 (pre-Katrina).*

of intervention. Intervention consisted mostly of modest facelifts—although many a white-built and formerly white-occupied dwelling was culturally recoded in this manner. This pattern was shown to be particularly evident among locally owned commercial establishments in black neighborhoods, such as masker buildings and corner food stores (see Part 3). Architectural interventions, folk or otherwise, remained illusive, impermanent, and fleeting, lacking a strong sense of place proprietorship due to financial constraints, but certainly not because of any lack of will. African Americans nonetheless would continue to struggle to achieve self-actualization in post-Katrina New Orleans, especially

4.30: *Fleeing the Great Flood, 2005.*

when measured against the taste standards of the entrenched mainstream establishment.

Before the diaspora caused by Katrina, much remained unsettled in New Orleans. In the 1980s and early 1990s, as mentioned, the city underwent a metamorphosis in the political balance of power. This balance had precariously held the city's business and social fabric together. In this era of transition from white to black political control, long-established power bases were dislocated. In an expanding economy, the fallout from such changes can often be absorbed successfully, even transparently, since alternative means exist to compensate for such losses of control. But in a *shrinking* economy, as was the case in New Orleans, forced dislocation from the status quo was of vexing concern and anything but transparent. Racial, social, and political tensions therefore remained high right up to the morning of the hurricane.[47]

In Katrina's aftermath, comparisons between the Iraq War and the crisis in New Orleans were inevitable, and the city's mayor, C. Ray Nagin, openly decried the distorted priorities of the Bush administration.[48] Soon thereafter, T-shirts appeared in the city with the slogan "MAKE LEVEES NOT WAR." As the city sat flooded, its exiled residents could only watch the horrific events on TV, shocked to the core by the vastness of the destruction. The unfortunate souls left to fend for themselves were reduced to living on freeway overpasses (Fig. 4.30). As the scope of the devastation unfolded, it became clear that the rebuilding of New Orleans would be long and arduous. The flood-level-depth maps released by the U.S. Geological Survey were bone chilling, especially when rendered in full color (Fig. 4.31). Tens of thousands of ruined refrigerators were discarded on the streets, soon becoming blank canvases for witty slogans, most of which were

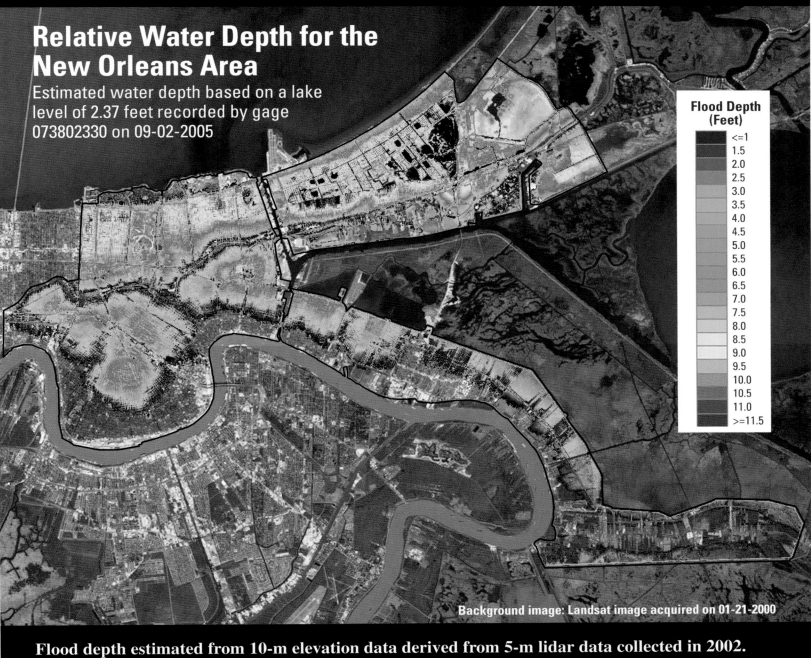

Relative Water Depth for the New Orleans Area

Estimated water depth based on a lake level of 2.37 feet recorded by gage 073802330 on 09-02-2005

Flood Depth (Feet)

	<=1
	1.5
	2.0
	2.5
	3.0
	3.5
	4.0
	4.5
	5.0
	5.5
	6.0
	6.5
	7.0
	7.5
	8.0
	8.5
	9.0
	9.5
	10.0
	10.5
	11.0
	>=11.5

Background image: Landsat image acquired on 01-21-2000

Flood depth estimated from 10-m elevation data derived from 5-m lidar data collected in 2002.

U.S. Department of the Interior
U.S. Geological Survey

4.31: *The worst-case scenario becomes a reality: USGS map, post-Katrina, 2005.*

painted with epithets lambasting the Federal Emergency Management Agency (FEMA), New Orleans Saints owner Tom Benson, President Bush, and various local officials. Others simply forewarned looters of the consequences of their actions (Fig. 4.32). In the most deeply flooded sections of the city, such as the Lower Ninth Ward, the situation was a matter of life and death. More than 200,000 vehicles were ruined citywide, including those at this used-car lot on Airline Drive (Fig. 4.33).

As for the fate of the city's historic inventory of twentieth-century commercial vernacular architecture, signs, and artifacts, it was hit as hard as everything else. The "big guys" did all right, but the little guys suffered: many of the largest national chain hotels, such as Marriott, Hilton, and Sheraton, possessed the fiscal resources to quickly make repairs and get back online. This enabled them to house first-responder disaster workers and various federal officials, often for months. Establishments featuring vintage commercial vernacular architecture did not escape flooding, and these places were left to fend for themselves. Mom-and-pop businesses such as the vintage Capri Motel (1952) on Tulane Avenue were ruined (Fig. 4.34).

It was bound to happen. Disaster planners had considered two specific scenarios: a major hurricane with a twenty-foot-plus storm-surge inundation affecting the Gulf Coast region, or a hurricane-induced levee failure in New Orleans. Hurricane Pam, a fictional FEMA-funded emergency exercise for federal, state, and local officials in Louisiana, was conducted just one year before, in 2004, and planners tested both scenarios. Katrina, sadly, played them out in real life.[49] The negative outcome of poor decisions by the federal government would prove much worse in New Orleans than in other places ravaged by hurricanes in the nation's history. This is because the city was below sea level, virtually surrounded by water, and because the federal levee system was unsustainable. With 80 percent of the city under water, tragedy swallowed the privileged and the poor alike as well as persons of all creeds and races.[50]

Status hierarchies persist in the built environment, and the landscape of social inequality continues to further divide rich and poor in America. The increasing vulnerability of the urban poor, especially those who live in hurricane alleys, is but one outcome. Strained race relations and the skewed responses to the disaster suggest that in planning for future catastrophes, Americans need to look not only to the natural environment in the development of mitigation programs, but to the social environment as well.[51] It is these transactions between nature, humans, and place that result in the vulnerability of places.[52] Most experts agree on the fundamental

4.32: *"I Will Shoot Looters,"* 2005.

measures needed to encourage the rebuilding of New Orleans: functional levees and drainage systems, affordable housing, jobs that pay a living wage, a functioning public school system, the availability of shopping and services, and the assurance of safety and public services.

Mardi Gras versus Remembrance
The push to celebrate Mardi Gras only a few months after Katrina prompted angry outcries from displaced residents around the nation. An op-ed piece in *USA Today* underscored the costs and benefits as well as the possibility for civic

folly that a delirious New Orleans confronted in Katrina's aftermath:

The Place. In the French Quarter, the ridge of high ground that made New Orleans famous, you can almost pretend Hurricane Katrina never happened. The smell of chicory coffee wafts onto the sidewalks. Jazz spills from the clubs. The storied streets bustle. But that veneer of normalcy is deceiving, even dangerous, to the city. With its short attention span, the public could easily latch onto this portrait of plenty and forget that large and less-visited swaths of New Orleans remain without. Without light and power, without jobs and a tax base, without inhabitable homes and without working schools. The city also lacks a singular vision of how to rebuild and a take-charge leader. The chaos of Katrina has given way to a different kind of turmoil, a desperate and fragmented push to rebuild. There is the Governor's Louisiana Recovery Authority, appointed to set the course; the Mayor's Bring New Orleans Back Commission; and a myriad of civic groups teeming with proposals. President Bush has named Texas banker Donald Powell as a sort of federal recovery czar. But no one is in charge . . . the American Institute of Architects recently recommended that New Orleans' rebuilding effort "speak with one voice" through a consolidated entity. That's good advice. If the French Quarter's glimmer is ever to spread, New Orleans needs a vision.

The People. Three months ago they were on the run from Katrina's winds and surges, watching as water swallowed up their pasts. Now, they are the future. . . . The fate of the Big Easy depends on where ordinary people . . . decide to live. For New Orleans, characterized even more by its twenty-five percent poverty rate than by its Cajun flare, how many return and who they are could influence the city's fate more than all the planners combined. New Orleans can rebuild, but they might not come.

The Party. Some folks scoff that a city in ruins, mourning hundreds of deaths, has no business throwing a bash. But Mardi Gras is New Orleans' essence and its chance to shine. The 2006 Mardi Gras (marks) the 150th anniversary of this pre-Lent bacchanal. It was been cancelled for only thirteen years, and then generally when the nation has been at war. There is a practical draw—the tourist revenues. City studies have shown that Mardi Gras produces $900 million in annual spending and nearly $50 million in tax benefits. And an emotional one: residents need this one for themselves. Think of New York City celebrating New Year's Eve in Times Square less than four months after 9/11 . . . perhaps this undertaking provides a model

4.33: *Quality Used Cars, Airline Drive, Metairie, 2005. Demolished, 2008.*

for the city's (New Orleans') more daunting challenges. Scale back on dreams of re-creating a pre-Katrina city. Seek creative financing. Be flexible. Above all, don't lose what is quintessentially New Orleans.[53]

To proponents, this striving to move forward was far preferable to striving to remember. Some argued that it would have been wiser to take the Carnival investment and build a memorial to the more than 1,800 who died because of the more than one dozen major federal levee breaches.

Since communities across the country were so welcoming and generous to Louisianans displaced by the storm, it remained bizarre that anyone in New Orleans could be any less so.[54] The key to drawing people back is based on reestablishing the social connections that had held together neighborhood, kinship, religious, and ethic networks. Long-simmering institutionalized inequalities in New Orleans indicate this will be an uphill struggle. People naturally connect to the place where they live, emotionally as well as pragmatically, and the experience of place—its genius loci—gives meaning to life. In New Orleans, it is arguable that place attachment is significantly stronger than in most other parts of the United States. However, critics howled that the federal bureaucracy overlooked this reality. The higher up the food chain of government bureaucracies, i.e., HUD, FEMA, the SBA, and others, and the farther decision makers were from the daily rhythms of the city, the harder this illusive connection would be to attain.

4.34: *The devastated Capri Motel, Tulane Avenue, 2005. Rebuilt, 2007.*

Cities have proved to be resilient after disasters only if they have the resources at hand to lift themselves up. An example of the wrong approach was the delusion and folly exhibited by FEMA's ill treatment of New Orleans's Vietnamese community. As the first few hundred Vietnamese returned to New Orleans East, they relied on local institutions such as Mary Queen of Vietnam Roman Catholic Church as a base around which to reorganize their lives. They requested FEMA assistance to set up trailers in their neighborhood, hoping to create a core group of settlers who would encourage others to return. But FEMA is used to dealing with individuals, not communities. FEMA gave priority to people in shelters. For local leaders, it made more sense to take exactly the opposite approach—to seek out and support the neighborhood associations, ethnic institutions, and other organizations essential to community life. These are the networks through which absent residents can be reached, and they are the support structures they will rely on to reestablish themselves if they opt to return.[55] When churches, athletic leagues, and other associations show signs of life, this is a strong signal that recovery is under way.[56] This will be of utmost significance in New Orleans.[57] Americans must not be allowed to forget either the horrific images of the tens of thousands of people fleeing rising floodwaters, or the abject poverty so many left behind.[58] Generations of racial- and class-based wounds were laid bare by Katrina.[59]

As the hurricane raged through the night and early morning of August 29, the monsignor assigned to guard St. Louis Cathedral on Jackson Square witnessed what to him was a magnificent sight. He watched in awe as one large tree after another slammed to the earth in the courtyard immediately behind the cathedral, each accompanied by a loud thud. Somehow, the destruction in that courtyard spared the marble statue of Christ, atop a pedestal, at its center; it sustained the loss of only two fingers. To the monsignor, this was a divine sign of hope for the future of New Orleans.

Roadside Nomadicism
and a City's Rebirth

*The better question is whether New Orleans has the will to recover. Business as usual—
even disaster relief as usual—will not suffice.*

—WITOLD RYBCZYNSKI, 2005

▌N THE FIRST YEAR AFTER KATRINA, LOCAL LEADERS in New Orleans experienced problems in rising to the challenge of the large-scale urban planning that would be essential to the city's resurrection. Mayor C. Ray Nagin formed his Bring New Orleans Back civic commission in the weeks immediately following the catastrophe by assembling an impressive array of specialists and community and business leaders. By January 2006 this multiracial body had drafted a multivolume set of reports on issues encompassing urban planning, education, tourism, and health care. The various reports were presented in public forums, and by far the most controversial report was the one that focused on urban planning and redevelopment.[1]

The mayor constantly contradicted, and thereby undercut, his stance on land-use planning and planning-process protocol when he spoke to groups with different agendas.[2] He immediately rebuked the most controversial, racially charged aspect of the commission's work—the recommendation to shrink the city's physical footprint.[3]

Meanwhile, tens of thousands of austere trailers provided by the Federal Emergency Management Agency (FEMA) rolled into virtually every residential neighborhood, commercial district, and industrial and recreational area. The public was told that these temporary housing units were the federal government's best solution to providing emergency housing for returning evacuees. At one point FEMA claimed to be delivering nearly five hundred units daily. Unfortunately, although not unexpectedly, Nagin was ill prepared to cope with the controversy that erupted over the trailers and their placement. Soon, one subset of trailers, the roadside nomads, dotted the city's main commercial arteries and those of the surrounding parishes. To the chagrin of the relatively few unscathed residents and business proprietors, as well as for the homeless occupants of the trailers, they posed myriad problems. These centered on the design and manufacture of the units; their cost (approximately $70,000 each, including delivery and installation); the level, or lack thereof, of commodity, firmness, and delight they afforded inhabitants; and their pattern of installation across a delirious and devastated urban landscape.

As politicians bickered about rebuilding strategies and who would be responsible for what, an armada of FEMA trailers quietly conquered the landscape. These trailers, with their flimsy stark white vinyl-sided exteriors and their cutout doors and small black wheels, became an omnipresent sight. Though they arrived inauspiciously, often under cover of darkness, their impact on the urban landscape became unmistakable. The adage "Life is what happens to you while you are busy making plans" comes to mind when thinking of how oblivious the local so-called decision makers were to the profound ramifications of the trailerization of New Orleans. The politicians appeared to be little different from fish unable to see the water surrounding them. To them, the trailer armada was a necessary evil.

The few planners who managed early on to attempt any community planning acted as if they were oblivious of the trailer armada. Few spoke of it, at least publicly. Perhaps this was because they were focused on the "long term" rather than anything temporary, ephemeral. This applied to the out-of-town New Urbanist planners who came into the area—such as Andres Duany, apt to be referred to by his critics and admirers alike as the *high priest* of the movement—as much as to notable, respected local architects. The New Urbanists brought with them their brand of heroic postmodern romanticism. A series of four one-week charrettes (intense design and planning meetings) were conducted by Duany and his Miami-based firm, DPZ and Associates.[4] The two charrettes (attended by this author) in St. Bernard and Gentilly took on a delirious, surreal atmosphere of their own.[5] How was a homeless, shell-shocked audience to take seriously, especially in the case of the charrettes, the romanticized images of canals, idyllic footbridges, and pastoral town squares presented to them by Duany and his team?[6] Any vital sign of life along the sprawl of the roadside strip, even if only a trailer dispensing hot dogs, was warmly welcomed by returnees. Despite everything, people never lost their sense of humor. As difficult as things were, even an abandoned rescue boat beached on a neutral ground could be transformed into a somewhat humorous spectacle (Fig. 5.1).

The FEMA Trailer: Lifesaver or Folly?

FEMA, post-Katrina, in accordance with the convoluted policy of its parent organization, the Department of Homeland Security, ordered its travel trailers from a list of approved U.S. manufacturers. Trailers were designed, built, and manufactured according to a stringent set of specifications provided

5.1: *Stranded rescue boat, Broadmoor, 2005 (post-Katrina).*

by the agency.[7] The prime installation contractor was responsible for delivering the unit, blocking and leveling it on the site, securing it with anchoring and strapping devices, hooking up sewer lines to the unit aboveground, hooking up water lines to the unit at grade, wiring the trailer to the external power source, filling the propane tanks, installing steps and ramps for ingress and egress, and taking any additional measures necessary to prepare the unit for immediate occupancy, or what in the lingo is referred to as RFO (ready for occupancy).[8]

The push was on by October to get as many trailers to where they were most needed on the devastated Gulf Coast. By February 2006, there were 18,336 units positioned in staging areas in the region. A total of 79,798 units were already on site and RFO, and a total of 26,160 units were positioned but not yet approved for occupancy. In Louisiana, the figures were 1,606, 48,428, and 8,742, respectively.[9]

Despite their exorbitant cost and the great effort expended in installing them, the trailers had an anticipated life expectancy of only eighteen months. The preoccupancy phases consisted of manufacture, procurement, routing, transportation to a site, and installation. At the end of eighteen months, the designers' intent was for the unit to be disposed of. This was planned obsolescence at its best (or worst). The Keystone Corporation's *Fifth Wheel and Travel Trailer Owner's Manual* stated:

> Remember, your trailer is not designed, nor intended, for permanent housing. Use of this product for long-term or permanent occupancy may lead to premature deterioration of structure, interior finishes, fabrics, carpeting, and drapes. Your recreational vehicle was designed primarily for recreational use and short-term occupancy. If you expect to occupy the coach for an extended period, be prepared to deal with condensation and the humid conditions. . . . The relative small volume and tight, compact construction of modern recreational vehicles means that the normal living activities of even a few occupants will lead to rapid moisture saturation of the (indoor) air.[10]

The manual also stated:

> Allow excess moisture to escape to the outside when bathing, washing dishes, hair-drying, laundering and using appliances and non-vented gas burners. . . . Do not hang wet clothes in the coach to dry. . . . Keep the temperature as reasonably cool during cold weather as possible. . . . Use a fan to keep air circulating inside the vehicle so condensation and mildew cannot form in

dead air spaces. Allow air to circulate inside closets and cabinets. . . . The natural tendency would be to close the vehicle tightly during cold weather. This will actually compound the problem.[11]

Soon, FEMA subcontractors set up trailer villages for their workers all over the metro area, with little oversight. It was inevitable that fires would erupt in the trailers. The general public quickly learned that their little shoebox could prove dangerous: "As he pulled up to Dow's temporary housing site in St. Charles Parish, where a travel trailer sat engulfed in flames, Hahnville's Fire Chief Reggie Gaubert recalled feeling a sudden swell of apprehension as he realized the predicament facing his firefighters. 'There was no provision to provide us with firefighting water,' he said. The blaze incinerated the trailer and damaged two others, all within a matter of minutes."[12]

As it became evident that the trailers would be occupied for far longer then the expected eighteen-month life span, locals began referring to them as "little matchboxes" (Fig. 5.2). Propane-tank gas leaks would emerge as the number one fear in the short term. The number of inspectors in New Orleans had plummeted from their pre-Katrina numbers. Corporate "angel" sponsors, and even FEMA itself, failed to apply for required construction and inspection permits in many cases. This further exacerbated an already untenable situation. Newspaper accounts began to appear on the deplorable living conditions in the trailer encampments. The so-called Renaissance Village opened to house 1,600 displaced New Orleanians in 573 units installed on a disputed, desolate, sixty-two-acre patch of open land in Baker, north of Baton Rouge.[13]

The FEMA bureaucracy did not want to add anything that might somehow create an appearance of permanence. Six months after the hurricane, FEMA stopped providing food service at the park, leaving residents to fend for themselves. The neediest were referred to Meals on Wheels for assistance. Although most residents could afford to buy groceries on their own, the cramped quarters of the trailers made cooking a chore. The minuscule standard-issue refrigerator and freezer unit did not provide much storage, a particular problem for larger families. Since residents were also required to purchase their own propane, the handwriting was now on the wall, although most continued to have no viable housing alternatives because of the tedious pace of recovery in New Orleans. Families able to return to the sites of their disemboweled homes and apartments in the New Orleans area fared slightly better. The six members of the Howard family shared two FEMA trailers installed side by side in the front yard of their ruined home in Slidell:

Inside Judith Howard's FEMA trailer, a thin, blue curtain divides her bedroom from the rest of the living area, offering the appearance of privacy without actually providing it. "This is our door," she said, pulling the curtain taut, as though extra tugging could make up for its lack of width. "It doesn't even shut all the way." Howard misses privacy most, but she misses other things too, like 15-minute showers, indoor storage space and a refrigerator that can hold more than one gallon of milk. After Katrina upended the contents of her home . . . the family has made the best of it, slapping hooks onto trailer walls to hang clothing, keeping pots and pans and other bulky items on a table outside and stacking cereal boxes on their sides so they'd fit into the too-short cabinets. . . . There are moments when life feels like a "camping trip that never ends," as Judith put it. Welcome to life in a FEMA trailer . . . an inconvenience that has become as much a part of the post-Katrina era as contractors and gutted homes.[14]

By April 2006, more than 63,000 travel trailers and mobile home units had been delivered to southeastern Louisiana. But while trailers have offered a number of residents the chance to return home, start over, and rebuild, critics charge that the trailer units—poorly designed, too small, and flimsily constructed—functioned as a major source of stress and health

problems to their inhabitants. They confronted occupants with an unprecedented array of safety risks.[15] Meanwhile, FEMA officials stressed that the units were designed and built for temporary use, not as long-term housing. As returning residents battled the stresses of rebuilding, trailer dwellers vacillated between relief and frustration: relief, because a shoebox trailer was better than nothing; frustration, because in the richest country in the world, it still wasn't much.[16]

Worse, the negative stereotypes associated with trailer parks in general were difficult for many to overcome. Manufactured housing, the trade name for trailer homes, had its origin as affordable dwellings for blue-collar World War II veterans and their families. They were grouped together into "parks" on the edge of town, near enough to places of employment that could be reached via a private auto or public transportation. The epithets are well known, "trailer trash" being the most common pejorative term in use today. Post-Katrina, as the months passed, more and more occupants used their trailers only as places to eat, bathe, and sleep. Few opted to use the gas oven. Most returnees considered their FEMA trailers a mixed blessing at best—for without them they could not have returned at all.

By January 2006, five months after Katrina, FEMA trailers had begun to roll into town in ever-increasing numbers. Recipients received their trailers, but utilities were not being

5.2: *Typical FEMA trailer enclave.*

hooked up until many weeks later. FEMA attributed this to a lack of coordination among its various subcontractors. The problems behind the delays were many: a bankrupt public-utility company (Entergy), an understaffed city inspector's office, and FEMA subcontractors who failed to explain the multistep process homeowners had to follow to activate their units. The net result was mass confusion. Residents were baffled. The layers of seemingly endless red tape were enough to make residents wonder why they had bothered to return home in the first place. Many families had to wait as long as six weeks for power to be turned on.[17] As for the plight of the utility company, it had filed for bankruptcy shortly after the hurricane, when it became clear that nearly all of the utility's customers would be lost for months, and some perhaps for years. The company faced storm-related damages of up to $325 million and had no money for repairs. These constraints severely limited the number of repair workers deployed in the field.

In the frantic days after Katrina left 66,000 homeless in St. Bernard Parish, parish president Henry "Junior" Rodriguez ordered 6,535 travel trailers, even though he knew his devastated parish would never be able to afford the nearly $90 million price tag. It took five long months for FEMA to agree to pay for the trailers.[18] In places such as St. Bernard Parish, the devastation was so complete that no neighborhood was intact. As more units appeared on the scene, whispered epithets discreetly voiced by neighbors soon turned into vocal public outcries. The trailers were being demonized and the message was always the same: not in my backyard (NIMBY) (Fig. 5.3).

Perhaps the most public battle was fought in the Lakewood Estates gated community in Algiers, an affluent suburban neighborhood on the west bank. Algiers is located across the river from downtown New Orleans. Carrying signs that rebuked FEMA for "raping" their neighborhood, about one hundred Lakewood residents staged a protest

5.3: *Demonizing the homeless in New Orleans:* NIMBY, *2006.*

in April 2006. The protest was incited by the construction then underway of a FEMA trailer village to house displaced women and children. It was targeted by the NIMBY faction solely because it was being built immediately next to their gated enclave, called Park Timbers, an area within Lakewood Estates.

Calling the site "illegal and illogical," residents of adjacent neighborhoods accused FEMA of refusing to consider their demand to shut down the construction site now and erect a new one elsewhere. As property owners in one of the few parts of the city not flooded by Katrina, the protesters, interestingly, said they were not simply echoing the chorus of unscathed residents throughout the region who were expressing wholesale opposition to the interloping FEMA trailer parks. Nagin had agreed in January not to authorize any group trailer sites in a district except those supported by the district's city council representative. However, only two weeks earlier he had approved ninety-eight locations for FEMA trailer installations all across New Orleans. These sites were to hold anywhere from six to as many as a thousand trailers.[19] FEMA continued to maintain its innocence in the Lakewood Estates matter. Construction had begun, $2 million had been spent thus far, and FEMA did not plan to stop now. Despite residents' protests, construction was nearly complete on the day of the protest and sit-in.

The trailers sat high on cinder blocks along several blocks of Tullis Drive. Several of those along the tract's northern edge were only a few yards from a brick wall that enclosed Lakewood Estates. Residents whose properties abutted the wall on the other side said the proximity threatened their privacy and safety, and that the trailers' windows overlooked their bedrooms, bathrooms, and living rooms. For some residents, most infuriating was the notion that the site might have been developed without proper city building permits. When they heard the grind of heavy machinery along Tullis Drive, they quickly formed a human and vehicular chain that pressured about twenty-five FEMA workers to leave. They then set up a picket line nearby to prevent the workers' return. About four in the afternoon, the crowd homed in on a pack of sport-utility vehicles clustered at the edge of the trailer site. Men wearing hard hats accompanied by members of the Federal Protective Service, which protects federally leased facilities, then entered the site.[20]

The flare-up in Algiers ended only when New Orleans police showed up and threatened to arrest the federal security guards. Under a front-page headline three days later that read "Nagin Halts Trailer Site Work," the tale of the battle of Lakewood Estates was recounted.[21] After much public acrimony between FEMA and Nagin, the mayor agreed to rescind his shutdown of all trailer-construction sites. By April, only 11,555 trailers were occupied, and almost all of these sat next to flood-ravaged single-family homes.[22]

Because of Katrina's widespread and indiscriminate destruction, it would have been foolish for anyone to assume that all FEMA trailer inhabitants were poor. Unless those who lost their homes were degenerate compared to those whose homes were spared, it remained entirely unjustifiable to object to temporary trailer parks for returnees. The vocal NIMBY factions protested nonetheless, thereby slowing the pace of progress by working against the returnees. Instead of defending the interests of evacuees—referred to officially as IDPS (internally displaced persons) by the United Nations—who wanted to return home, local politicians chose to meekly defer to the NIMBYists' racist and paranoid rants. Jarvis DeBerry wrote:

> The New Orleans area has plenty of parks and other wide open spaces that could accommodate large numbers of the travel trailers being provided by FEMA. What the area seems to lack, though, is the requisite hospitality . . . we lack even the compassion needed to comfort our own. Not foreigners, mind you, but people who want to come home, people who have no options. . . . More than 200 people attended a meeting to discuss the recent construction of a temporary trailer park near the intersection of Ames and Lapalco boulevards. "Our crime rate is not as bad as New Orleans," a woman said. "If they want to take in Jefferson Parish residents only, that's one thing. But outsiders, no." . . . (politicians) insist on having a say in the placement of trailers in their districts, but their intentions are (equally) clear: they don't want trailer parks at all. They ought to know that returnees don't want trailer parks, either. No more than they wanted the storm that made the trailers a necessity.[23]

By June 2006 there were more than 100,000 evacuated households living in FEMA trailers in the areas devastated by Katrina. Of these, more than 68,000 occupied units were in the New Orleans metro area. Soon, collateral concerns would emerge.[24] What chaos would ensue, for instance, if tens of thousands faced with another direct hurricane hit decided to hitch up their trailers and evacuate all at once?

A Typology of Interventions

The FEMA trailerization of New Orleans was a sight to behold: banal, shiny white shoeboxes sprang up on neighborhood streets across the city, and large aggregations appeared on parks, football fields, playgrounds, and industrial sites,

5.4: *FEMA residential village, Central City, 2006.*

attached umbilically to a vast assortment of commercial vernacular roadside establishments along the roadways. Five broad types of installations occurred, characterized by density, site planning, and infrastructural support amenities. This typology is as follows:

1. RESIDENTIAL VILLAGES

The residential village, together with its one-off autonomous installations (see below), was the most pervasive of all intervention types in the New Orleans area in the first year after Katrina. The village aggregations of temporary living units typically ranged from four or five units on a single site to as many as two hundred; the numerous examples erected throughout New Orleans represented many variations in scope within the basic theme. They were, without exception, configured in rows, forming, whenever possible, a matrix in plan. The number of units in a row might be as few as two or three and the number of rows as few as two. The smallest aggregations, two rows of three units, for example, were set up in parks, in vacant lots, and as infill units installed beside existing permanent houses. Residential villages, in infill settings, often housed the relatives of people who had returned to repair and reoccupy nearby houses on the same lot, block, or street.

In the case of larger villages, open lots on school sites, athletic fields, and abandoned fields were deployed. The largest residential village was erected in City Park (680 units) and on the campus of Southern University in New Orleans (400 units). Smaller villages were erected also. A sixty-unit village was erected on South Claiborne Avenue and Jackson, near the downtown area (Figs. 5.4 and 5.5). The Carver Playground residential village across from the Mississippi River levee Uptown housed twenty units on the site.

2. CORPORATE VILLAGES

The scale of the devastation required that the private sector in New Orleans adopt a first-responder stance as a provider of emergency housing. In the first weeks after the hurricane, a number of corporations with operations in the New Orleans metropolitan area made a compelling case to their superiors at the national corporate level to initiate the process of securing temporary housing for their employees. FEMA supported this movement for a number of reasons, including the fact that the agency quickly learned that relatively few large open parcels of land were available in the area for emergency housing. FEMA reasoned that the development of corporate villages would reduce the burden on the federal agency as the first-line housing responder.

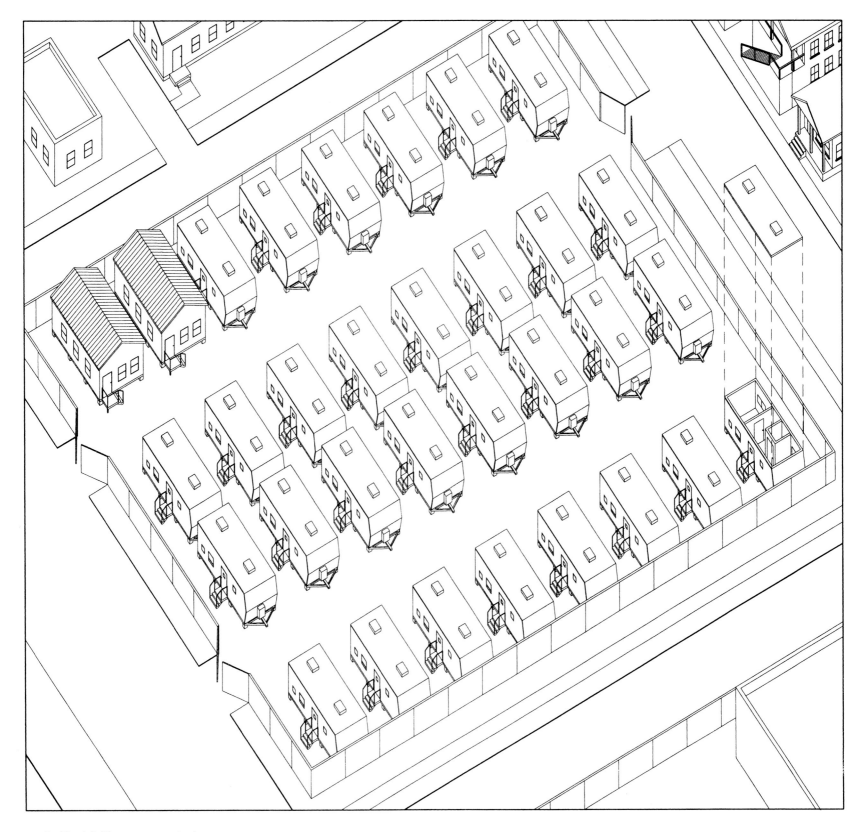

5.5: *Residential village, axonometric view.*

5.6: *FEMA-USDA residential village, City Park, 2006.*

Early corporate villages were installed at the Exxon refinery in Chalmette (200 units) and at the Coke Bottling Plant in suburban Harahan (75 units). Soon, FEMA corporate villages appeared beside factories, warehouses, and office buildings across the metro area. A particularly interesting installation was at the Southern Regional Research Center of the Agricultural Research Service (part of the U.S. Department of Agriculture, or USDA). Forty-five units were installed for USDA employees and their families in a park-like setting on the edge of the mammoth City Park (Figs. 5.6 and 5.7). Children here, unlike those at the urban encampments, could play on the grounds and be in contact with nature, nor was the village visually sequestered from its surroundings. As with the aforementioned residential villages, corporate villages ranged in size from a few units to the hundreds, on one or more contiguous parcels near a mother ship (a plant, an office building, a research lab, etc.). Top management and their families in many cases lived in downtown hotels, whereas rank-and-file workers and their families typically occupied FEMA trailers.

3. COMMERCIAL ENCLAVES

Large corporations were not alone in seeking temporary housing for the hundreds of people they employed before Katrina. Small-business owners and local franchise outlets affiliated with national chains were equally determined to provide housing for workers and their families. Some installations were linear in their siting, others more concentric. Very few of these enclaves were walled off from the street or surrounding buildings. As a result, they appeared far more informal, even randomly placed in some instances, than their large-scale village counterparts.

Cary's Furniture & Appliances, located on South Broad Street in Mid City, took on six feet of water in Katrina. This enclave personified the informal appearance of small-scale commercial installations across the city. Three units were installed for use by family members and employees, tethered behind the mother ship. They mediated the space between the commercial side of the block and the adjoining residential side street insofar as their siting corresponded to the narrow shotgun houses immediately next door. The exterior space between these units was cleverly deresidualized by the occupants. An outdoor laundry "room" and activity area was created between two of the units on the side cloaked with shade provided by a large tree (Figs. 5.8, 5.9, and 5.10).

Turner's Tire Repair, on Felicity Street in Uptown, and a neighboring business had four units installed on their adjoining open space in the midsection of the block. The units were placed along the outer edges of the site, thereby creating a courtyard in the center. They were screened from the street with a wood fence built by FEMA. Largely because of the damage sustained from the hurricane, the ramshackle appearance of Turner's starkly contrasts with the outward image of uniformity conveyed by the adjoining trailer enclave (not pictured).

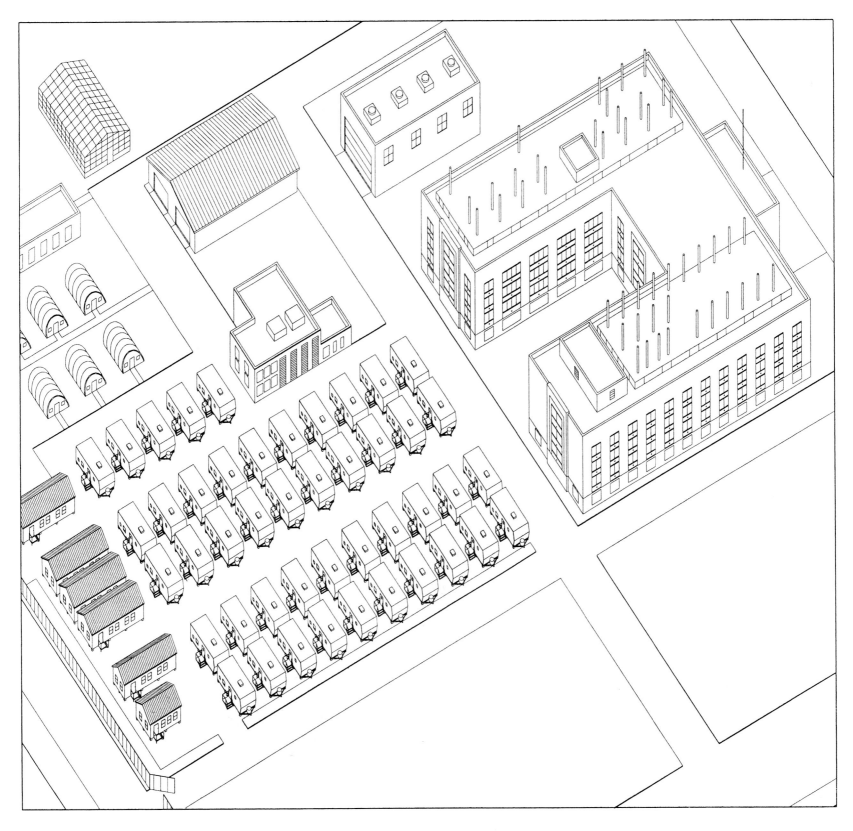

5.7: *Residential village, axonometric view.*

5.8: *FEMA trailers in a commercial enclave, Mid City, 2005.*

5.9: *Commercial enclave, Mid City, 2005.*

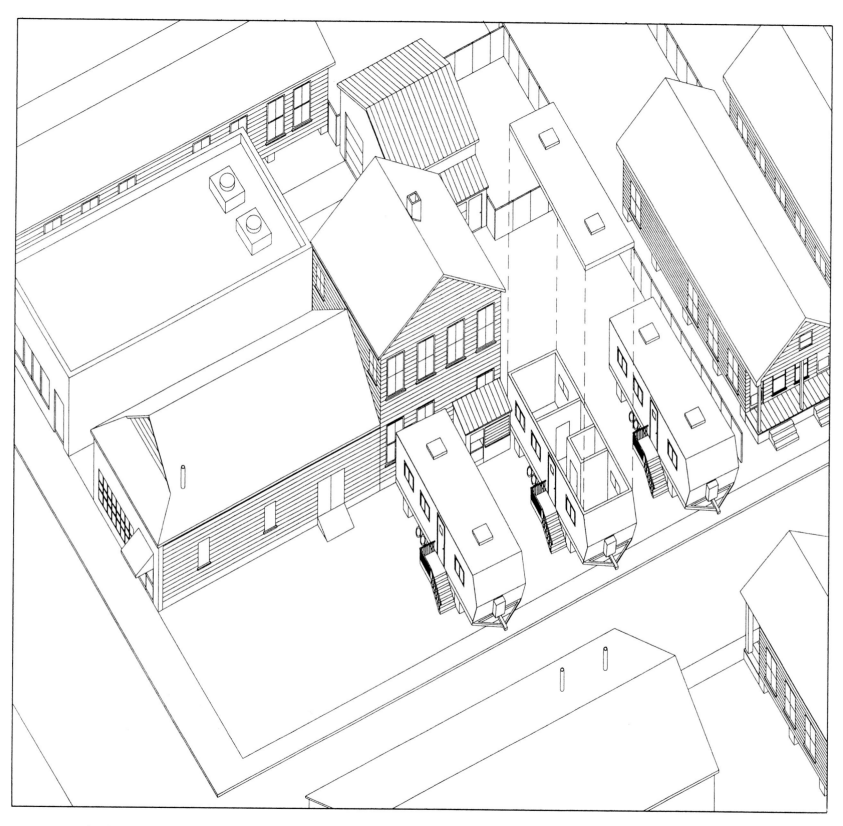

5.10: *Commercial enclave, axonometric view.*

5.11: *Platinum Auto and Beauty Salon, Broadmoor, 2005.*

5.12: *Church's Chicken, St. Claude Avenue, 2005.*

Platinum Auto Detailing and Beauty Salon, on Washington and South Galvez, in the Broadmoor section, epitomized the type of FEMA enclave associated with an adjacent mom-and-pop business. Here, four units were arrayed as two rows of two units in a parking lot. In contrast to Turner's, however, they were not walled off from view. The policy of FEMA in this regard was very inconsistent: in some situations it insisted on some sort of screen, while in other situations this did not appear to be a priority. This enclave was adroitly installed between a single-family residence and the family business (Fig. 5.11).

In post-Katrina New Orleans, mom-and-pop businesses and local franchise outlets of national chains were in equally desperate straits in their quest for emergency housing for their employees. Church's Fried Chicken, on St. Claude in the Seventh Ward, installed two units on its site. This outlet is located on the main route to the Lower Ninth Ward and was the first franchise to reopen in this part of the city. The bright colors of the mother ship stood in sharp contrast to the stark imagery conveyed by the pair of FEMA trailers tethered to its backside (Fig. 5.12). Mother's restaurant is a landmark, located on the corner of Poydras and Camp in the heart of the tourist zone in the central business district. A small enclave of ten units was installed on the parking lot behind the restaurant. These housed cooks, waitresses, managers, and their families. Mother's worker village was dwarfed by neighboring buildings (Figs. 5.13 and 5.14).

The largest examples of the three types of villages described above were in most cases served by on-site support facilities that provided central security, laundry services, sidewalks, lights erected on telephone poles, and access drives constructed of crushed aggregate stone. Some even provided day care on site for young children. These services were housed in separate trailers on the site. Second, a key feature of these places was that access to the site was controlled: one had to present photo identification to gain access. This policy was enforced around the clock, 24/7. During the site-prep stage of construction, chain-link fences were erected around the site perimeter. The result was unfortunate for both habitability amenity and visual aesthetics: from outward appearances, it was difficult to tell whether the overriding intention was to keep the dislocated residents in or unwanted intruders out. These intrusive wire-mesh barriers gave the village a cold, cage-like, walled-off, even hostile appearance.

4. AUTONOMOUS INSTALLATIONS

These places stand in sharp contrast to the FEMA villages built across the metro area, defining the opposite end of the range. This type of installation is one-off, autonomous. It is

5.13: *Mother's Group Catering, Poydras Street, 2006.*

5.14: *Employees' trailer enclave at Mother's, 2006.*

the individual unit installed on the site of a small business. Weegee's Tavern on Jefferson Highway in Jefferson Parish was built in the 1930s. Jefferson Highway and Airline Highway served as the two major East-West thoroughfares linking Baton Rouge and New Orleans before the construction of Interstate 10 in the 1970s. A roadside fixture for generations, it has achieved the status of a classic roadside attraction—despite the intrusion of a generic McDonald's that was built next door in the 1980s—with its rounded art deco windows on the front façade and its neon signs. The trailer at Weegee's blends rather seamlessly into the larger commercial context in appearance and composition; it and the mother ship share similar colors, massing, setbacks, site orientation, and silhouettes (Figs. 5.15 and 5.16).

The operator of Charley's Sweet Shop, on Elysian Fields near the Vieux Carré, had his unit installed on the site of the sno-ball stand. The housing unit and the stand appear engaged in a dialogue, sharing a similar outward orientation toward the street (Fig. 5.17). A vintage filling station at the corner of Washington and South Galvez, in Broadmoor, was built in the 1920s. The gas station was converted in the 1970s to a car wash and an auto-detailing business. The housing unit appears to have been barely inserted beneath the overhead canopy, between the now-defunct gas pumps and the front door of the former gas station. This tight fit was a testament to the proprietor's determination to get back to the city as soon as possible (Fig. 5.18). The proprietor of the used-car lot on the corner of St. Claude and Elysian Fields, near the

5.15: *Autonomous trailer installation at Weegee's Tavern, Jefferson Parish, 2006.*

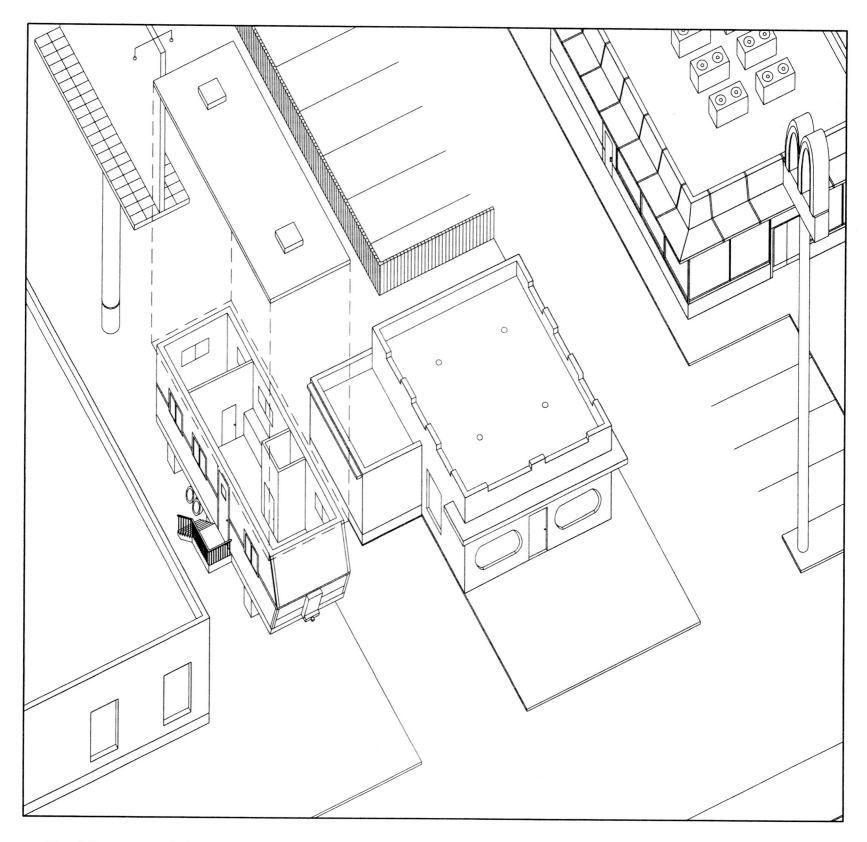

5.16: *Weegee's Tavern, axonometric view.*

5.17: *Charley's Sweet Shop, Canal Street, 2006.*

Vieux Carré, proudly displayed his FEMA trailer. In this case the trailer doubled as a business office and a private residence. Whether by design or through mere serendipity, the trailer and the residence to its rear appear to be coordinated, as if both formed a single composition, one framing the other. In addition, both express horizontal siding, rectangular windows, and sloping rooflines converging into one as they cascade to the ground (Fig. 5.19).

5. UNTETHERED NOMADS

These are the ad hoc entrepreneurs—squatters who relocate from site to site, sometimes during the course of a single day or week. There are two types of untethered nomads: sanctioned and unsanctioned. Sanctioned nomads apply

for their municipal operating permits and make an effort to "do the right thing." But the others are outlaw enterprises, at least as judged by conventional standards in "normal" times, and may move frequently in order to keep one step ahead of the law. Perhaps the owner of a roadside tamale stand did not apply for a commercial retail food license, or maybe the business is outlawed by neighborhood zoning laws. Boldness and rapidity are the nomads' trademarks. They set up shop along well-traveled streets and parish highways in order to be clearly seen by passing motorists. Some of these entrepreneurs are more territorial than others, even going so far as to set up their own picnic tables, strings of lights, and neon signs near the roadway as a means to attract attention. The unsanctioned nomad might set up shop on the front lawn

5.18: *Auto-detailing shop, Broadmoor, 2006.*

5.19: *Used Cars, St. Claude Avenue, 2006.*

of a single-family house, as was the case along Paris Road in Chalmette. These are usually mom-and-pop operations, so much so that dining at them feels like enjoying a picnic at a friend's house (Figs. 5.20 and 5.21). After speaking with a number of employees and owners of these places, I realized that they were no less passionate than their sanctioned counterparts in their determination, commitment, and even sense of mission to create a place, an oasis, for their customers amid the devastation. It is about the noblest qualities of placemaking, qualities expressed in European cultures of the nineteenth and twentieth centuries in the aftermath of war.

In the weeks after the receding of Katrina's toxic floodwaters, at a time when the community was virtually depopulated, a number of ad hoc roadside food establishments quickly popped up. The most interesting of these places quickly began dispensing hamburgers, catfish po-boys, beer,

and other much-craved local food for first responders and a vast array of disaster-relief workers. Many such places were set up weeks before the city's health department could regroup and restart its "normal" inspection enforcement protocols. One example, the Hot Food roadside stand set up ad hoc in the parking lot of a Lowe's home-improvement store, on Elysian Fields Avenue near the I-610 interchange, thrived in Gentilly. Food was prepared and dispensed from a modified mobile home, which was festooned with Christmas lights and sported a motley assortment of cookers, signs, tables, and chairs in front. It was impossible to miss. It was sited at the entrance to the parking lot, adjacent to the roadside (Fig. 5.22).

Other examples, such as the New Orleans Sno-Balls trailer, were poised to be deployable anywhere at short notice. The location may change five times in a single week.

5.20: *Untethered roadside nomad, Paris Road, Chalmette, 2006.*

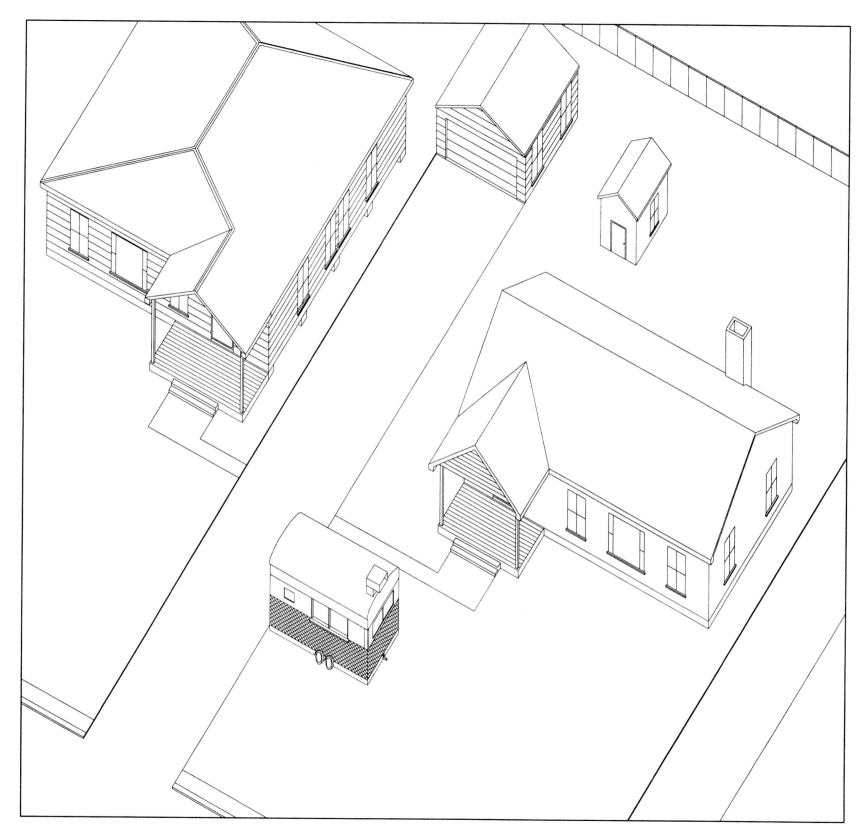

5.21: *Untethered nomad, axonometric view.*

5.22: *"Hot Food" nomad, Elysian Fields Avenue, 2005 (post-Katrina).*

The sno-ball stand, as discussed in Part 2, is deeply woven into the fabric of daily life in New Orleans. The typical sno-ball stand, while extremely basic in its scale and imagery, is deeply rooted in its neighborhood. It is a gathering place for people of all ages throughout the long humid New Orleans summer. This tradition persisted in the post-Katrina roadside milieu, where brightly colored stands, both fixed-site and portable, were a comforting sight to those who had returned to reclaim their homes and neighborhoods. Whereas pre-Katrina one frequented the same sno-ball stand for years, as one would a favorite corner bar, now such allegiances were cast aside. What mattered most was that the institution itself had persevered. Territorial rights had been cast aside. In this example, it is almost as if the house trailer and the sno-ball trailer are competing for a hitching spot on the first vehicle to approach (Fig. 5.23).

5.23: *Sno-balls nomad, Chalmette, 2006.*

The nomadic Smoothie King stand set up in St. Bernard Parish was a most welcome sight to returning residents in the aftermath of Katrina. This rapidly deployable roadside version of the fixed-site franchise restaurants was created in (and for) better times and was intended to travel to sporting events, food festivals, school demonstrations, and other civic events (Fig. 5.24). The bright fruit-like colors and the trademark logo depicted on the Styrofoam Smoothie King to-go cup emblazoned across the front of the trailer functioned as the only signage necessary to attract business along this busy roadway. As mentioned in Part 2, this chain of more than 350 fixed-site franchises across the United States was founded in New Orleans. The first outlet opened in the New Orleans central business district in 1989.

Some occupants chose, either from indifference, necessity, choice, or some combination thereof, to defy the law when it came to self-expression: FEMA banned trailer inhabitants from making any external physical alterations to the trailer unit. This ban on personalization prohibited residents from painting, attaching objects to the exterior (except for ramps and stairs), or modifying the trailer structurally or spatially in any significant way. Despite such bureaucratic authoritarianism, the decorated FEMA box was a renegade occurrence to be found randomly at autonomous fixed-site installations as well as among other untethered nomads. In the former category, for instance, numerous occupants in residential areas decorated their trailers at Christmas and at Mardi Gras with brightly colored lights and banners festooning rooflines, windows, and side panels.[25] In roadside commercial contexts, others applied neon signs and related advertisements to the banal, characterless trailers. An altered trailer thus resembled what Robert Venturi and Denise Scott Brown described in the early 1970s as a classic "decorated shed."[26]

5.24: *Smoothie King nomad, Chalmette, 2006.*

Memory, Place, and Authenticity

These autonomous, nomadic shelters symbolized, above all else, the heroic intentions of their occupants to push on. This demonstration of determination, grit, and sheer will to return were at the core of the movement to repopulate New Orleans. For this reason, these early pioneers often acquired a folk-heroic stature in their communities. Roadside nomads, in their defiant, inimitable style, led the way in resuscitating a delirious city when it was down. The sight of these places along the otherwise bleak, lifeless roadside landscape gave people hope. The sense of gratitude was palpable, genuine, and heartfelt. For these reasons, the unheralded everyday roadside-commercial nomads deserved much praise.

The power of place in the everyday environment is at the core of human existence. Through the millennia, societies have existed and evolved in the pursuit of common goals in everyday life. When neighbors and relatives are torn apart, the sense of shared purpose or collective mission in a community is lost, since deeply rooted values and traditions fracture, or worse, and become threatened with extinction. The shared values and traditions of a community constitute the core of its basic reason for existence. When the social fabric is torn, the social ecologies formed by interpersonal relationships become radically transfigured, as occurred in the aftermath of Katrina, when the social capital diligently accrued and nurtured over many generations disappeared overnight (Fig. 5.25). *Katrina profoundly tested the fragility (and durability) of the construct of place*. This predilection to reconnect in order to reestablish place was a part of a deep-seated effort to mitigate the opposing condition—placelessness—that characterized the earliest days after the catastrophe. One story is recounted below.

Ronda DeForest, age thirty-six, is the proprietor, with her husband, Doyle, of Flour Power, in Chalmette, located on Paris Road near St. Bernard Highway, in St. Bernard Parish (Fig. 5.26). Flour Power is near the main entrance to the Port of St. Bernard, and is situated on some of the highest ground (3.5 feet below sea level) in the parish. They began their mom-and-pop business in 1998, working out of the garage of their home in nearby Meraux. Their coffee house–restaurant and account-based catering business specialize in pastries and assorted bakery goods. Chalmette is a suburb ten miles downriver from the New Orleans central business district. I interviewed Ms. DeForest extensively on May 22, 2006. Excerpts from our conversation follow.

We bought this building in 2002. Before that, it had been a florist for twenty-five years. They were the ones who added on the back part of the building. The front part—the part that is raised—actually was a residence built in the 1920s. So we made all sorts of renovations to add the kitchen and the café. Before the storm, Paris Road in general was not the commercial hub it is now. The hub was definitely along Judge Perez [Drive]. But because this part of the parish got the least amount of water—we only got three and a half feet in the back and about six inches in the inside of the front part of the building. But it was enough to knock out a lot of our equipment. We lost our freezers, a refrigerator, a prep table, and a cooler, but nothing major. Luckily, most restaurant equipment is built with the motors on top because of the cleaning and the floors, so most of that stuff was OK. So we were very fortunate. We came back December 5. It took us until January 24 to get the place up and running. We are still fighting with insurance companies. We have gotten no money from homeowner's or from business-interruption insurance—the same situation as everybody else.

So we had no money to hire someone to come out and gut it, so we did all of that ourselves. That was after we came back. When we evacuated, we first started in Houston for the first three days, then we went to north Louisiana. And then when we realized that we weren't coming back, then we needed to find something a little more permanent. So we were in Bastrop. My husband is from Bastrop—that's where his grandmother and father are. They took us in. I'm from Chalmette originally. We have lived all over New Orleans and in Colorado over the years. But we always came back. My mom lived maybe two miles from here. Grandparents, everybody, was in this general vicinity. My mom and sister are in Thibodaux, which is not too terribly far from here. Cousins are in Pontchatoula, Hammond—other cousins live nearby. My dad passed away three years ago, and I don't know if he would have done so well with all of this.

He had worked for Entergy, so he would have been one of them in the middle of all of it. My mom and sister live in a FEMA trailer in Thibodaux. I have elderly grandparents—rather, my grandfather passed in January. That is what's been happening with the older people (Fig. 5.27). At least once per week we host a funeral reception here. It's really hard. It has been terrible. The elderly can't cope with it. It's terrible. It's understandable, because there is nothing to come back to [and] because it looks nothing like it looked before. And that's the thing about our place. I've had grown men come in and stare at my pastry case and begin to cry—you can see the tears streaming down their faces—because this [is] just about the only place that reminds them of before. The curtains are the same, there-

5.25: *Mountains of debris, Slidell, 2005 (post-Katrina).*

5.26: *Flour Power, Paris Road, Chalmette, 2006.*

5.27: *FEMA trailer, residential installation, Jefferson Parish, 2005.*

fore it looks like maybe nothing happened. And outside it's not all that different. The oak trees are sparse compared to before the storm. The trash is bad, but we try to pick it up. People just don't respect it as much as before. You know, we've had to put up this yellow caution tape because they roll their trucks up all over the grass and plants. You know, those are some of the issues we deal with now.

We lived in Meraux. It was much worse down there. We lost the entire house and will end up having to bulldoze it. We lived there eight years. Since my son was born, we lived there. It [the devastation] was the same for most of our neighbors. In our subdivision, which was an older one, there were either mostly older people or starter homes for younger people with families. But there is a very large subdivision right next to us. That whole subdivision seems to be coming back—they have big two-story homes, and about a third are back in their homes, living on the second floors while they work on their first floor. There are also quite a few [FEMA] trailers there. What I'm thinking is that somebody's going to come along in two, three, four, five years and knock down the house and build a big house there anyway.

We have two children, ages eight and nine. Our son is in second grade and our daughter is in the third grade. That was really the catalyst for our coming back—the [opening of the] schools.

We came back at the end of September. I guess they allotted my husband a special pass because we had a business here. It was look-and-leave at that point. It was terrible, horrible to see. Then we came back again to see the house in the beginning of October. And it was like, wait a second, when you've got water over your roof at home and only three and a half feet in your business, you begin to frame everything around your business. You can begin to wrap your mind around the business. And this area was minimally damaged by comparison. We were very fortunate: we are in a very small group [among St. Bernard residents]. It did not make it any easier. It was still terrible: the smell, mess, when you have water over your rooftop and nothing—I mean nothing—is salvageable. . . .

We were still not sold on the idea of coming back. We continued to drive back and forth to Bastrop every week or so [a five-hour drive each way], and a friend of a friend called and asked, "What are you doing with Flour Power?"

5.28: *Trailer configuration, Flour Power, Chalmette, 2006.*

I said, "We don't know. Why, do you want to buy it?" She asked if she could put a trailer for her sister on our property, because she needed a place, and I said, "Fine, go ahead." We did not know her personally. But at that point, I told friends, "If you need it and we've got it, it's yours. If you've got a trailer or an apartment, take our tables and chairs, because they're just going to sit here or get looted, you know?"

It was the first day the school was reopened, and it was wonderful to see the principal and all the teachers and the kids so pumped up. My husband said, "We can't stay away from here." North Louisiana, it's lovely, the people are wonderful. But don't think you can drink a beer around any of 'em. And believe me, after all we've been through, I mean, you NEED it [alcohol]. They didn't get it, and still don't get it. Because they don't see the enormity of it [the devastation]. Pictures don't tell the story at all, mile upon mile [of devastation] . . . [Her voice trailed off.]

We decided to come back, and would have come back sooner but we were waiting for our [FEMA] trailer. Ours came through the Louisiana economic development program. We went back and forth with FEMA. Fighting hap-

pened. Finally, FEMA said, "Take 'em. Do what you want with 'em, but don't call us until we come out [to activate them]." We got the trailers in December but had no idea that we had no water, no electrical, no nothing. Nobody helped us, and there was no one to call. You are responsible for everything yourself. We did the primitive camping thing in the trailer for about a week until we got a plumber and an electrician (Fig. 5.28).

We made our decision [to return] early on compared to most. We were the first sit-down restaurant to reopen in the parish. Imagine, a place where you could actually come in and sit down and eat with silverware on real dishes. And that was amazing to everyone. They loved us, and people still come in to just say, "Thank you so much." And I say, "Why?" I didn't understand at first [but] . . . I just didn't want to be anywhere else. It was so emotional. It was a good thing. It didn't take long for the parish to inspect and recertify the kitchen. In fact, now he [the parish sanitarian] comes in here to eat every morning.

On the status of Flour Power's restaurant business in post-Katrina Chalmette:

In fact, before the storm we never did a breakfast or dinner buffet. Most of our business was just in catering pastries to businesses. We had the Hyatt Regency [as an account]. It was one of our hotels. Also, the Audubon Institute and Martin Wine Cellar. It was all pastries. Here [in the coffee house–restaurant], it was just lunch for three hours daily from Tuesday through Thursday. It was just a side gig, because we served goat cheese and provided something different for [people], and that was cool. And now the Hyatt is gone, you know [*laughs*] . . . and you know they aren't coming back for a while, and the aquarium just reopened—they just got their penguins yesterday—so their business isn't much right now. For one thing, we don't have a delivery van. This is a big problem because we lost our delivery van. We left our delivery van behind. It did not have liability coverage. Yeah, I learned a lesson. We had $125,000 in business-interruption insurance, but did not have flood insurance. We have yet to see a penny. If we had lost everything, we wouldn't have come back either.

I've got a staff of five people now compared to sixteen before the storm. They work hard. Everyone had to evac [evacuate]. I've been putting flyers around everywhere. I put the word out everywhere. Usually it's a friend-of-a-friend kind of thing, and I say, "Oh, you know somebody who wants to work? Send them in." High school students, college students, for the summer, for sure. I need them full-time. Absolutely. And you know whom I get a lot of help from? The emergency-aid community, what they [others] call the hippie tents [locally known as the emergency community]. They are separate from the Common Ground base camp, but they are over in the same area on Judge Perez Drive [a mile and a half away from Flour Power], across from the [now shuttered] Wal-Mart. [As mentioned in Part 3, Common Ground is a national activist political action organization, and its post-Katrina base operations were in Orleans and St. Bernard parishes.]

They come from all over the country. I've got two or three of them working at any given time, and they are awesome people, especially if you've got a family. They won't take anything from you. You don't have to worry about any of that. They are just trying to help. They may stay for two days, two weeks, even two months. And I pay them daily, so if they have to go, whatever, you know? And they say, "OK, I'm leaving, but I'm going to send so-and-so over to take my place." And that is really great. Most of them live in tents [in a tent city], so it is really nice for them to be able to come inside and be in air-conditioning. [*laughs*] I don't know how they do it.

On the subject of the recent (March 2006) week-long parish-wide design charrette conducted by the high priest of New Urbanism, Andres Duany:

I didn't go to any of those [charrette] meetings [in the fabric-sheathed tent bubble behind the Chalmette civic center, the work site for the charrette]. I did go to the big one at the parish courthouse on that Wednesday night. You know, the plan with the streetcars running down the street and all of that. I think it's a dream, a wonderful dream. But we just got our landline phone last week. He [Duany] did not want to deal with any of that. I mean, it is great to make all of the green spaces. And oh, "We're going to buy you out of your house to make it happen" [quoting Duany]. The people say to each other, "Where are we going to live for the next five years, in the meantime? When will we be able to move back from Hammond? And how will we pay for all this? We need a place now to live." It's a big issue. But because we were near the river, all he [Duany] said was he wanted to convert the [St. Bernard] Highway into some sort of interstate kind of thing. And it would affect us because there is a stoplight right there at the corner and it's wonderful. And people can look over here and say, "Hey, there's a restaurant." So at this particular juncture in time, do we really need that? This is the main thoroughfare, right here [*points out the front window toward Parish Road and its intersection with the St. Bernard Highway*].

On the harrowing early days of the family's return home:

The hub of the parish is right here. This is it. The Merabeaux Food Store [across the street] was the first to reopen. They were open on the first of December. And of course the bars [across the side street from Flour Power], they never closed, and they were there before we were. And all the construction people here for the debris removal. All of that awful stuff. It's gotten much better since we first got back here, because [*pauses*] . . . it was all hours of the night, all hours of the night. We had drunk people actually try to walk into our trailer, then say, "Oops, I'm sorry, I didn't see y'all." Others would bump into our trailer in the middle of the night. Usually [there were] drunken persons walking down the street, you know, [it was] noisy all hours. It's gotten better from when we first got back here [post-Katrina] and since the population has increased. It really was anarchy when we first got back. There was nothing. We tell the kids, "We're pioneers, we're pioneers." That's the way we had to live. Getting the kids back in school was the most important thing. That was a really positive thing. Everything else remains weird.

On the adjacent FEMA trailer and the main building's restored kitchen:

I'm really glad that we have this kitchen. We can cook and eat in here and then use the trailer mainly for sleeping, reading, TV, watching movies, and for office paperwork. We try to get the kids out as much as possible on the weekends, especially. We go downtown to a hotel, and they get to use the pool, and they can swim. And they're so cute about getting in a bed, and they say, "It's so cool to be able to sleep in a real bed again." But they're troopers. We have a double bed [in the trailer] and they have a bunk bed.

When we first got here, we used the trailer's kitchen a little bit, because when we first got back we had to completely redo all the wiring in the building. So we had a temporary generator for the trailer. We keep the A/C on all day, and leave it on 75. They don't have much insulation. The shower is very small, and there is no tub, so that is another exciting thing about going into the city [to a hotel]. We do that every couple weeks to maintain sanity. We're taking the kids to Universal Studios [in Orlando, Florida] right after they are out of school. Our vacations used to be where we closed the shop on January 1 every year because everyone gives up sweets for their New Year's resolution. So our vacation was always to go skiing over New Year's Eve [through] the first week in January. And of course this year we're pioneers. [*laughs*] This year it will hopefully be just a false-alarm evacuation.

On the spirit and outlook of the relatively few who have returned home to Chalmette:

The people who are here are pumped to be here. The people who are not here cry at night because they are not here. And of course there are the people who say, "The hell with the place." They just aren't up to going through all that again. They are throwing in the towel, absolutely [*pause*] . . . Absolutely. They made their mind up back in October [2005]. But many people who made up their mind [not to return] have changed again and again since, and still are [confused].

On the profound dislocation and loss of community experienced by the 67,000 exiled residents of a parish where all but six of the buildings were ruined by Katrina:

5.29: *Burger Orleans, St. Claude Avenue, Ninth Ward, 2005 (post-Katrina).*

For example, my sister, who was dead set [against returning] bought a house in Thibodaux. She didn't want to stay there, and then moved to the north shore [of Lake Pontchartrain, in St. Tammany Parish]. So after living on the north shore and realizing that she's not finding Chalmette anywhere [else], she had already sold her house in Chalmette. It was near the Murphy oil spill, which is a whole different can of worms. Her home was covered with muck [she and her husband are among the plaintiffs embroiled in a class-action lawsuit against the refinery]. Now they are looking in the subdivision behind me [in Meraux], where the bigger homes are. So, you know, no one knows [what to do]. Some seem to go through three or four changes in the same week. [*laughs*]

A strong bond exists in the parish. It is heartbreaking to see what has happened to the city (Fig. 5.29). It's very sad. We had my son's birthday party here on Sunday. So of course I don't have anyone's addresses anymore, so I just e-mailed out invitations, which was just mortifying to me. I was always the party person—you had to have a theme, you know, the whole thing. And I even called people on the phone who were living wherever to try to find out where the kids were in school, and the party turned into a big crying session. We had a cry session here on Sunday. One mother sobbed that she now had a beautiful house in Madisonville, and the kids were in such a wonderful school, but it wasn't Chalmette. You know, someone else bought a house in Abita Springs, but it wasn't Chalmette. Another was up in Ponchatoula, and although they may on the surface appear happy, they're not happy at all. They are all homesick [for Chalmette]. We are talking about people who are in their mid-thirties; my cousin, who is forty-eight; my mom, who is fifty-eight; and my grandmother.

They were all here [at the restaurant–coffee house], and they all feel the same way.

I am the fortunate one, in their eyes, because I am here. I'm living in a FEMA trailer, but I'm here. People make it a point to get together often. They are always here. They drop in to eat lunch. They hang out. My personal opinion is that many people are waiting to decide if they'll return until this first [post-Katrina] hurricane season passes, because if everything turns out fine, it will instill in them the trust that they can live here once again. If something happens, or even a close call [occurs], that will be it for many. We unfortunately have no knowledge of what Mother Nature has in store for us. The prediction for this year is not encouraging. I was listening to the TV the other day, and they said we are in a twenty-year cycle. It will be an active period, and we're only in the tenth year. That was all I wanted to hear. I mean, I don't need to hear it. I've got enough to worry about.

On the controversial subject of the closure of the flood-prone Mississippi River Gulf Outlet channel, commonly referred to as MR-GO. MR-GO has been widely blamed for the massive storm surge that destroyed St. Bernard Parish and much of eastern New Orleans. It was built by the U.S. Army Corps of Engineers, and opened in 1964:

If you drive back to the 40 Arpent [canal levee], which is not too far from my mom's [former] house, and she was there this past Saturday afternoon. The water [caused by multiple breaches in the levee] just picked up those houses right off of their foundations. And we're talkin' about brick houses. Even whole foundations moved, just like my grandmother's house. My take on it is, you can't do the [Katrina disaster] tour in one day. I'm still driving—today I drove past my kids' school because I was told yesterday that they had to tear it down. The first time I drove past, I couldn't see anything wrong with it. Then they told me, drive around, look at the other side. So when I picked up the kids from school, I drove down, and, sure enough, although this school is only five years old, the water took a big chunk

out of it. So my take on it is, I don't want to see it all right now [nearly nine months post-Katrina], because everything starts to look like everything else. It all needs to be appreciated in its own right. And, yeah, OK, I haven't been to Lakeview [in Orleans Parish], or Waveland [Mississippi] yet. I couldn't get there, but I'm not going to look at it all in one day, because it was somebody's home, too. I don't want to walk past this stuff and say to someone, "Oh, hello."

We had a [fishing] camp on Lake Catherine, and I haven't been there either. It's the same story; everything's hard [all the structures along Lake Catherine literally vanished in Katrina's thirty-foot storm surge]. You just have to take it in gradually. You have to absorb it in sections, because I don't want to dismiss any of it as "Oh, yeah, that was . . ." I want to take it for what it is. I will need to absorb [the loss] of every single bit of it, in time. The stories people tell are the same way, because so many are so similar.

But at the same time, each person wants so desperately to tell their own [story]. I respect that. This place has definitely seen its share of tears. That's what kills me—it's the men, to see those men and the tears rolling down their face. I think that happens because they remember the Chalmette that was. That's part of it. Because when you're in here, if you close your eyes to everything outside, that is all you see, you think it is all like this. And someone asked me, actually, the other day during an interview I was doing for NPR [National Public Radio], "When do you think it will be normal again?" I don't even know what normal is anymore. I don't know what to expect. No one ever expected any of this. Normal has been completely redefined. A grocery store would be nice.

That would give me some level of normalcy, even a drugstore. Family Dollar has made a real presence. Which is great, because the kids need socks. There were three gas stations open when we got back. The gas stations and bars were first. There are [still] no franchises, and they are being leveled left and right. I guess they figure it is easier to start from scratch. I never thought I'd miss McDonald's. We do have one Home Depot. People need building supplies.

On whether the St. Bernard Parish government is doing all it can to encourage rebuilding, given the near-total scope of devastation:

I am so confused on that issue, because I am in the loop so much here [at Flour Power] and I am out of the loop at the same time. Everyone, every [parish] politician, every construction person, is in here talking, but I can't keep up with what is being decided or who is doing what, or not. I am so caught up with so much other stuff to deal with that I am out of the loop. My take on it is that, looking at this parish, and comparing it to the Lower Ninth Ward, in Orleans [Parish]—we're doing a fantastic job. The real issue is, who is doing the job. And I think it's because a lot of the people who were back first were, of course, the politicians, their families, et cetera, so they said, "Oh, wait, we need a waste disposal company? Well, we'll finance that." Because there was nobody else here to do it. So they did it, and now it's all coming back on them, because it's all being awarded through politicians' families or through people who know so-and-so—volunteers, whatever—but they were the only people who were here getting it done. Now FEMA is giving them flak, and I'm sure, you know, that things probably could have been done in a more professional way, possibly. But there was no time to do that. And now I'm between FEMA, with these trailers, and all the stuff you deal with [with FEMA]. If our parish, or any other parish, had as many problems with FEMA as we as individuals had in getting things done, then we would all still be stuck back exactly where we were on August 29 [the day the levees broke].

CNN broadcast daily reports by correspondent Anderson Cooper in the aftermath of the catastrophe and the inexplicable FEMA-trailer debacle in St. Bernard Parish:

Oh yeah, he was down here a long time. He asked, "Why are all these FEMA trailers just sitting here? Why won't FEMA just pay for them to get them out to people's houses?" And let me tell you, we are still waiting for our personal trailer at our house. These are business trailers [beside the building]. In our trailer, we have all of our business stuff, the business computer, as well as our family stuff. It would be nice to just have a trailer at the house so we at least could get away from the business for a while. But that's OK. I can't complain, because we at least have this one. I know so many people who are still waiting and don't have anything. No job. No home. Nothing.

On the slow return of life:

We have one church open. They were holding mass outside on the lawn on Sundays, down the street from here, until they got the main church [building] back together. The Catholic school is also open. I am a little bit—I don't want to say upset, with them, because when we came back, we were told by the archdiocese they decided that

the school would not come back until they knew it was safe, because of all the chemicals and the contaminants. Basically, I felt like they were taking a shot at the local public school for already being up and running. And personally, I cannot say enough about how fantastic that has been. I commend all those teachers from pre-K up to the twelfth grade. These people have put their personal lives on hold. They're there from six in the morning until seven at night. They are amazing.

A portable intermodal-shipping-container-cum-commercial-store squatted on the site:

Another friend of a friend called and said, "We wanted to start a business [in Chalmette] pre-Katrina, and we couldn't find a spot anywhere for a trailer due to codes, permits, and all that stuff." They wanted to open a business to print up signs, business cards, and now [post-Katrina] there were no laws or codes about putting [such] signs up everywhere. So somebody gave them a laptop and the equipment. But I said to them, "There are already two trailers here, and there's no parking to speak of as it is." Frankly, the guy was starting to piss me off, so I said no. Two or three days later, the guy shows up here, with the building on the back of a truck. He said, "Look, let's make a deal here. I need a place to put it. We can put it right there [*pointing*]. It only takes up one of your parking places." Then he said, "I'll tell you what. I'll set you up with WiFi for free. Anything else you need—faxes, copies, signage, anything like that—we'll take care of." So here's this guy with this trailer, he's waiting. It's there. And, you know, it's not as if it's going back to Baton Rouge, where it came from. And he's going to have to pay to return it. So we're like, you know, the circumstances are such that you've just got to wing it these days. That's how it is with everyone. No one has a place to go. It's the same with these things [the two on-site FEMA trailers and the portable shipping-container-cum-business] as with everything. He was from here, so I just said, "We'll just make it all work. It'll be OK" (Fig. 5.30).

Dozens of funeral receptions and similar "reunions" were being held at Flour Power because in the aftermath of the storm, the parish lost virtually every public place where social intercourse had occurred:

We had two receptions [this past] Friday, and one today [Tuesday]. We have lost so many elderly people since the storm, it's unbelievable. Last week it was two who were in

5.30: *Sign shop, intermodal-shipping-container nomad, Paris Road, Chalmette, 2006.*

their eighties, and this week it was somebody else's dad. Everybody is saying the storm is the reason why. Absolutely. I too believe it is. When you pull an older person out of their element and they don't know what's going to happen next and they're living in an apartment somewhere, after living in their house for thirty or forty years, it's just too much for them. It's too much for *us* [referring to middle-aged and younger persons]. Yeah, it's been hard.

Their community is gone. All of their friends are somewhere else. My grandmother, for instance, she's eighty-three, and now living in Thibodaux. She can't drive her car around Thibodaux. She's wary. She doesn't know where anything is. She can't just get in the car and drive to Wal-Mart. But here [Chalmette] she could go to Wal-Mart, shop, and do her little thing. She can't do that now. She's extremely skittish and nervous as it is about everything. And she doesn't try to put the best face on it either, not at all. No way. She does not hide anything. Oh, she is a gem. [*laughs*] She says, "I'll never live to see this place come back to the way it was before." She was born in the French Quarter. She grew up there and later in the Ninth Ward, like so many [in Chalmette]. It was all about suburban sprawl then.

Flour Power became the de facto social center of the parish in post-Katrina Chalmette, serving as the pulse of a faltering community:

This place is just like the parish community center. Absolutely. And I certainly didn't volunteer for the job, but this is where we find ourselves, and we adjust. I'm glad I'm in the middle of it, because I wouldn't want to be anywhere else. I was somewhere else, and, you know, another reason we came back was that each time I came back here [from Bastrop, in the weeks following Katrina], I didn't cry. I only cried whenever I left. Whenever I got back to northern Louisiana, I would cry for days, and I'm not a crier. Finally I said, "You know, if I'm crying when I leave that [devastation], and I'd rather be in the middle of all that, compared to here in a nice comfortable house with a grocery store and lovely people and normalcy, then something's wrong." I needed to be back here to see what we could do to help. My husband needed to be convinced more, but he soon remembered why he left north Louisiana.

We needed to be back where we were appreciated. Halloween in north Louisiana made us realize, "Oh, we need to be back." [*laughs*] It was the costuming that did it. It was too conservative. The Bible Belt, you know? There

was a Mardi Gras parade here this year. My husband actually rode [on a float]. It started here on the corner [at St. Bernard Highway], passed by on Paris Road, up to Judge Perez past the Wal-Mart, and the whole FEMA area, then made a U-turn by the emergency community. We got our apartment every year like we do, on St. Charles Avenue [during Mardi Gras in New Orleans], and it was wonderful, just wonderful. It was the same with having held the Jazzfest. If we can come back from this [devastation] and stage those events, then we're good. We'll be just fine.

A tour of the kitchen was provided, then the family's personal FEMA trailer:

The trailers have wheelchair ramps because—well, that's a long story. Remember I mentioned earlier that this is a business trailer, so they just dropped it. There's a 2101 Paris Road, New Orleans, on the other side of the parish. That's by the bridge where you go over the MR-GO channel. We told them, "This is not the address where you want to build the ramp." We were told, "These are our orders, now we have to comply. Now step out of the way. I'm going to build the ramp. We have to build the ramp." I told them, "I do not want a handicap ramp if you're going to impede me in any way, shape, or form." So they built it however we wanted, which was very nice of them.

On their trailer's minimal amenities:

We have an office set up. The priority was to just get in everything we need [to run the business]. Plus, I don't want to put too much in there because, you know, the more space you have, the more you fill it up with. The shower is small, but it works. In a rainstorm, it really gets crazy. [*laughs*] We had a rainstorm recently, and my daughter was in the top bunk, and when the rain hit the roof of the trailer, it sounded like when you're frying something and you throw water on it and it goes POP, POP, POP, POP—that's what it sounds like in here. The wind also is funny, because we are right next to an oak tree. And the acorns in the wind hit with a BING—and you then hear them roll down the side of the trailer. So, that was a challenge with the kids. It took them a while to get used to it. They would much more prefer to be in a real bed. I can't say enough about how wonderful they've been with all of it.

Ronda concluded:

All you can do is make the best of a bad situation. That's all. Or you can be miserable someplace else. As hard as it is—we work fifteen hours a day—still, I'd rather be here, in the middle of all this, working hard, versus not being home. Nobody has dealt with anything like this before. How do you know what to do? It's overwhelming. There are so many lessons to learn from Katrina.

Reflections

In a 1956 essay titled "Other Directed Houses," the landscape historian J. B. Jackson, mindful of a recent spate of harangues on the aesthetic and moral failings of the emerging American highway strip, wondered if the critics' drive-by denunciations were not missing the mark: "In all those streamlined facades," Jackson wrote, "in all those flamboyant entrances and deliberatively bizarre decorative effects, those cheerfully self-assertive masses of color and light and movement that clash so roughly with the old and traditional, there are, I believe, certain underlying characteristics which suggest that we are confronted not by a debased and cheapened art but by a kind of folk art."[27]

He posed the question "Why not have a built landscape that jumbled forms and spaces much as the evolving American culture mixed regional dictions and stylistic variation?" What critics of the post–World War II strip typically failed to note was that the built environment of the everyday roadside landscape, rather than having its meanings and contours safely circumscribed by history, represented a landscape embedded in motion. It could not be considered with the same criteria used to assess the typical "static" pastoral or urban setting. This distinction certainly applied in the case of New Orleans, with the fine collection of pre–World War II commercial vernacular architecture and signage that lined its urban commercial districts along Claiborne Avenue, St. Claude Avenue, and Tulane Avenue, and along such pre-1945, pre-interstate classic strips as Airline Highway (now Airline Drive) and Chef Menteur Highway. He termed this incipient architecture "other directed."

This was not architecture intended as a self-justifying work of art, but was meant merely to please and attract passing motorists. Nor was it meant to supplant the civically inspiring neoclassical public libraries, churches, or pedestrian-scaled courthouse squares that had dominated towns across America before World War II. It was about the currents and crosscurrents in contemporary life. It was about the "everything else" in the ordinary, everyday milieu.

Full disclosure: I first fell under Jackson's influence while an undergraduate architecture student in the late 1970s. His writings seemed radical and at odds with much of my coursework. Yet I remained drawn to the intellectual clarity of his core thesis. His writings continue to influence my teaching, writings, research, and community service work in Katrina's aftermath.[28] Perhaps Jackson's greatest contribution was to reintroduce Americans to their vernacular landscape, to teach them to see again—and in a new light—the common elements of roads, houses, yards, and towns. This ability to see anew will be essential in the rebuilding of New Orleans. His essays in *Landscape*, the magazine that he founded in 1951, sprang from a highly educated sensibility and careful literary craft. Moreover, they arose from a love of the baroque and a deep opposition to the International Style.[29]

Jackson often wrote under pseudonyms in the magazine's early years. In 1953, under the pen name of H. G. West, he wrote a harsh review of *Built in U.S.A.*, edited by Henry Russell Hitchcock and Arthur Drexler. He chastised the editors for championing only architects loyal to the teachings of Gropius, Mies van der Rohe, and Le Corbusier, and for their refusal to acknowledge the vital vernacular buildings of the postwar period, with their profusion of eclectic architectural forms and meanings: the tract house, the factory, and the drive-in as well as other businesses lining the highway. By contrast, the book focused on private houses, office buildings, and apartment houses, all large and expressive, and none of them needing to adapt to a neighborhood or commercial streetscape. They were, in fact, to be viewed and comprehended as "works of art." He argued that while they may be undeniably beautiful, they were not architecture. Here, West/Jackson defined architecture as "true expressions of domestic or communal life . . . these buildings of the International Style have been inspired less by a desire to accommodate existence as we know it today than by an almost fanatic rationalism."[30]

If Jackson sought to elevate the routine experience of going out for a drive, then the attractions and attractors of the roadside were logical, worthy subjects of inquiry by architects, urbanists, and others. To him, the lights and neon signs eased the workaday world and established their own sense of legitimacy, place, and identity. By the 1950s, attentive readers of *Landscape* had at hand a fundamental critique of the modern movement in architecture and planning and a set of new guiding principles, some of which anticipated, in important ways, postmodernism.[31] To him, everyday commercial vernacular buildings and artifacts were created by and for people who knew exactly what they wanted. While high architects were primarily advocates for the wealthy and powerful, he was a champion of the average citizen's desire for freedom of choice, convenience, and access.[32] His vision was antithetical to the utopian modernist vision.

He argued for that which was messy, indeterminate, naïve,

practical, unself-conscious, humble. He argued for an examination of new building types expressive of new rituals and routines. He embraced the delirious cacophony of franchises, gas stations, Airstream trailers, eye-catching signs, and parking lots. He sought to identify creative acts of newness in the built environment, but not from architects. Instead, from everyday people responding to the circumstances of their everyday lives.

The pre-automobile era in New Orleans would likely have been a source of fascination to him. But he was equally well versed in the visual and verbal languages of post–World War II America and how a new medium—television—was affecting attitudes toward technology, communication, and materiality. His dynamic, fluid perspectives on landscapes led him away from its traditional locus within painting. There, it had frequently been considered as little more than scenery, a static backdrop.[33] He celebrated relations between art, construction, commerce, consumption, beauty, satisfaction, freedom, transcendence, transgression, ethics, and meaning. The functions of racism, class inequalities, poverty, and politics in America rarely if ever were explicitly cited in Jackson's writings, however. Therefore, if alive today, would he have fused these issues with the case for rebuilding New Orleans, with its strong European roots and its Americanized suburban periphery? Probably so.

He recognized that a landscape need not always be only about harmony. Jackson's landscape was a process of sequences, perhaps an annual occurrence, such as a fragile flower unfolding. Fueled by unpredictable waves of economic opportunity, landscapes—including both medieval market crossroads and contemporary shopping centers—could blossom anywhere, anytime. He went so far in the 1950s as to hail the vehicular strip as the new American form of community and as part of an ongoing dialogue that knit together individuality and collectivity.[34]

It is one thing to argue to preserve a neon sign, but what about the larger issues lurking in the shadows? Jackson would have advocated for the preservation of the everyday vernacular expressed in such classic examples as the Crystal Preserves sign, the Stereo Lounge sign, and the Frostop Drive-In (see Part I). But what would Jackson have thought of New Orleans's post-Katrina roadside landscape (Fig. 5.31)? Would he have sought to reconcile, even celebrate, the indispensable role of the lowly, nondescript FEMA trailer as a vital force in the rebirth of New Orleans? I suspect the answer is yes. Jackson was wary of architectural or planning paradigms, or programs, emanating from a central bureaucracy. He would have championed the case for rebuilding New Orleans for everyone, not just for the New Urbanists.

5.31: *Deep South Motel, Airline Drive, Metairie, 2005 (post-Katrina).*

He would have found cause to celebrate the city's failings and shortcomings, because it is a place overflowing with complexity, uniqueness, intricacy, nuance, inexplicability, and the rhythms and cadences of life.[35] It is logical to conclude that Jackson would therefore have been highly skeptical of the extemporaneous imposition of ideology, whether the antiseptic pre-auto nostalgia of New Urbanism or that of egocentric, globe-trotting, avant-garde architects seeking to foist their latest signature building upon the city's landscape.[36]

Above all, Katrina magnified the importance of hanging onto that which is authentic in our lives. Authenticity is critical to the reconstitution of any city. An open gas station, convenience store, or roadside trailer dispensing po-boys becomes an emotive, transcendent experience when one has so little else to cling to. Reattachment to place can be fostered by the vernacular architecture of the everyday milieu. These are the places, as Jackson so adroitly argued, where we live out our lives. The everyday milieu is the central progenitor of place attachment: it is a catalyst. Such places, whether of recent or vintage origin, whether "permanent" or nomadic, whether modest in scale or otherwise, symbolize civic rebirth. Such places—as much as the art of place making—are lifesavers we can hold onto amid an ocean of uncertainty. I experienced this firsthand in Katrina's aftermath.

A real danger exists, however, that the intrinsic value of these everyday buildings and artifacts will be dismissed in the rebuilding process. If so, then a joyously indigenous, deeply authentic, delirious place will have been lost forever. Formalist "signature" architects and either-or planners tend to be dismissive of the everyday landscape. New Urbanists, for their part, disdain commercial strips in favor of neo-nineteenth-century "town squares." They view the funkiness of *both-and* landscapes as a contaminant, as having negligible value. By extension, they deem auto-centric strip environments unworthy of protection.[37] While pedestrian-scaled communities are praiseworthy in and of themselves, a homogenized, banal, anywhere-usa New Orleans can be avoided—whether pedestrian- or auto-centric—only if all who are concerned work together to ensure otherwise.

This book is ultimately a call to everyone—including community activists, architects, preservationists, investors, consumer advocates, private citizens, developers, and politicians—to authentically rebuild both-and funkiness, this endangered ingredient, into the extraordinary gumbo that makes New Orleans unique. Beyond, it is a call to action for Americans everywhere to rediscover and save these treasures before it is too late. Katrina taught us all a valuable lesson: do not take anything whatsoever for granted in the built environment—for it can be stripped away at any moment.

Architecture Under Siege

A Lesson from Katrina for Twenty-First-Century America

Right now, [the power elite's] whole thing is, "Let's take this opportunity to make a new city for the elite!" We have got to speak the truth as we know it and not be afraid.

—K. BRAD OTT, NEW ORLEANS GRASSROOTS NEIGHBORHOOD ORGANIZER

O N THE ONE-YEAR ANNIVERSARY OF KATRINA, August 29, 2006, the media descended upon disaster-stricken New Orleans. National and international media attention had been in sharp decline during the previous year. A horde of reporters and celebrities appeared. They scoured the city for any tangible signs of progress. Most reports would be about a tale of two cities. On the one hand there was the virtually untouched New Orleans that stretched along the high ground; it came to be known, as previously mentioned, in the days after the flooding as the *sliver by the river*. Here, the city was buzzing, reclaiming itself street by street and block by block. These returned families and individuals had a combination of money and the sheer will to return. Most also had a job, a house, or both. Generally, these were citizens of some means, and places of personal importance to them, along with their sense of place attachment, remained intact. The tale of the "other" city, which was reported globally on the one-year anniversary, was one of mile upon mile of still-ruined, mold-infested neighborhoods.

Even CNN, whose reporting from day one had been extensive, struggled to express the scope of this jarring urban paradox. That week, CNN would show a reporter (usually Anderson Cooper) stationed in the Lower Ninth Ward on a pitch-black street. In an instant, the producers would then cut to a reporter in the French Quarter, where a lively street scene played in the background. This stereotypical contrast proved highly irritating for returned residents and diaspora victims alike. *Which was the real New Orleans?* Those who were still suffering resented any "recovered city" storylines, whereas the relatively well-off segment of the returned population resented "city in ruins" storylines.

Meanwhile, the destruction of significant buildings, old and new, large and small, was being planned with worrisome frequency. Virtually nothing new was being built. There were a number of reasons for this. First, the federal levee system remained in tatters. Hastily concocted post-Katrina repairs had been made to the storm-weakened levee system during the first year of reconstruction. Because of this, the insurance industry had put the screws to New Orleans, redlining the city and much of the region south of Interstate 12. Where insurance policies were not cancelled outright, premiums skyrocketed. Insurance, beyond the reach of so many before Katrina, was now a near impossibility.

Second, with no federal funds flowing for rebuilding, private investors continued to sit on the sidelines. Developers in New Orleans were not availing themselves of the tax credits made available by Congress one year earlier through its Gulf Coast Opportunity Zone (GO ZONE) legislation. Given the precarious state of the levees, a climate of uncertainty permeated negotiations between lenders and builders. The cutoff date of December 2008 for projects to be completed in order for developers to receive the tax credits also became problematic. Construction costs by late 2006 had increased by 30 to 80 percent over pre-Katrina construction figures. Third, the city's expanding crime epidemic strongly deterred rebuilding efforts.

Finally, stillborn planning efforts and a continuing political-leadership vacuum continued to suppress public confidence in the city's elected officials. Promised federal rebuilding funds remained far on the horizon. The report by the Bring New Orleans Back (BNOB) Commission had been soundly rejected in early 2006 and nearly completely shelved (along with the volunteer efforts of many of its subcommittee members) as a result of the intense backlash against the commission's ill-fated proposal to reduce the geographic footprint of the city. In reaction, a quasi-feudal condition emerged in which ragtag neighborhood organizations sprang up across the city, each with its own self-interest, goals, and political constituencies. The Broadmoor Civic Improvement Association was one of the first such confederations to form, as if in direct defiance of the report's recommendation to create "dots" of green space at the center of their neighborhood's below-sea-level "bowl." Fired up, residents struggling to rebuild their homes and their upended lives banded together. At the time, the ire of these bands of roving neighborhood activists was largely directed at the Washington, D.C.–based Urban Land Institute, which had played a vital yet tormenting role in providing national and local financial support and "expert" guidance to the BNOB Commission.

The Broadmoor group (largely white), as well as the Association of Community Organizations for Reform Now (ACORN, largely African American), soon created an activist template for all other neighborhoods to follow. One by one, from the Lower Ninth to Gentilly to Lakeview to Mid City to flooded sections of Uptown, people united to share their frustrations with one another and with the snail-paced recovery. They clamored for effective officials at any and all levels of government and in particular in the U.S. Army Corps of Engineers (now widely referred to as the Army Corps of Amateurs). Still in a funk, trying to cope with a catastrophe of such magnitude, citizens collectively asked, "How could this have happened to us?"

This aggregation of quasi-feudal grassroots groups set out to make sure their voices were heard by someone. One such group, the Gentilly Civic Improvement Association, was organized by returned residents (most of whom were living in FEMA travel trailers) in the absence of any sort of citywide coordinated rebuilding plan. With no money and no government funding, such organizations were left to kiss the ring, so to speak, of any potential patron or suitor who may have come along with an offer of help. New Orleans was indeed now a quasi-feudal kingdom, in many respects, and a few seedlings were beginning to flower amid the ruins. As will be shown below, where this type of patronage flourished, New Orleans would come closer and closer to falling dangerously, even deliriously, into a post-Katrina dark age. Meanwhile, the New Orleans City Council, acting on its own, funded something known as the Lambert Plan, led by Paul Lambert of Miami, but this work was limited to the flooded neighborhoods. Lambert had had, pre-Katrina, a lucrative planning contract with the city.

Against this backdrop, when it became clear to outsiders that comprehensive planning efforts in the city were going nowhere fast, the Rockefeller Foundation, in New York City, stepped up with funding for a "unified recovery plan" for the city. With a grant of $3.5 million in hand, augmented by $1.5 million in matching funds, the Unified New Orleans Plan was auspiciously born in spring 2006 amid high hopes that finally a master plan for all neighborhoods—flooded and unflooded alike—would express the concerns of the ragtag assortment of neighborhood fiefdoms that had sprung up in the disaster's aftermath. The Rockefeller Foundation, naturally, was extremely wary of falling into the same morass that had swallowed up the BNOB Commission only a few months earlier. After sending out feelers and negotiating some backroom détente, the foundation finally delivered the funds, which were subsequently administered by the Greater New Orleans Foundation (GNOF), led by Ben Johnson.

The UNOP planning team presented its final report in January 2007. Like the bedeviled reports presented by the BNOB and Lambert, this one failed to completely satisfy anyone, but this time fewer people felt angry, hostile, or overtly disenfranchised. The plan presented detailed maps and scenarios for each of thirteen planning districts across the city.[1]

Meanwhile, national organizations continued to weigh in with their lofty, disconnected, utopian takes on the strange, unprecedented saga unfolding in New Orleans. The manifesto of the Katrina Task Force of the national organization Architects, Designers, and Planners for Social Responsibility stated in part:

> Disasters . . . tend to have a disproportionate effect on disenfranchised populations who are typically bypassed in rebuilding efforts. This invariably reinforces their pervious social isolation, lack of jobs and capital, and consequently sets them farther back in all the social capacities of life. The idea that poor people could be permanently displaced from their communities and not given a voice in its rebuilding, especially in New Orleans, in the name of "reconstruction" is unacceptable to responsible architects, designers, and planners. The current reconstruction effort is not a suitable response by our professions to the magnitude of these historic inequalities and new injustices. We must take this opportunity for a new Reconstruction by . . . [creating] new social and economic opportunities by empowering local communities.[2]

Such a screed, in the view of locals, amounted to little more than the rhetoric of well-wishing outsiders. The city's residents and their informal grassroots organizations were closing ranks by the fall of 2006. They had become increasingly suspicious of outsiders. During this period, and almost always behind closed doors, many architectural landmarks were being slated for demolition across the city, especially twentieth-century landmark buildings. These places included the 1950s-vintage Economical Supermarket and its prominent sign on the corner of Gentilly Boulevard and Elysian Fields, in Gentilly; the site was totally leveled in 2006, including the landmark sign (Figs. 6.1 and 6.2). Beyond this, modernism, and the International Style in particular, was now caught directly in the crosshairs. It was frightening enough that neighborhoods such as Holy Cross, which was filled with late-nineteenth-century Victorian shotguns and cottages that had flooded, were suddenly endangered by wholesale demolitions perpetrated by their owners and the city. In neighborhoods such as Holy Cross, a culture of expediency had emerged whereby demolition was seen as far more "efficient" than costly and time-consuming rehabilitation. The Preservation Resource Center and Squandered Heritage, the latter led by the indomitable, heroic Karen Gadbois, began to urgently sound the alarm about the ramifications of destroying so, so much of the city's irreplaceable cultural heritage.

6.1: *Economical Supermarket, Gentilly, 2005 (pre-Katrina).*

6.2: *Economical Supermarket, demolished, 2006.*

Numerous twentieth-century buildings were now being targeted for death, including brilliant art deco landmarks built in the 1930s. This list included the venerable yet obsolescent Charity Hospital (1938); a number of public housing projects, including St. Bernard, Iberville, St. Thomas, and Calliope (all built in the 1930s and early 1940s); the Blue Plate foods plant (1936); and Baumer's Foods factory and the landmark sign perched atop its roof (1942). International Style buildings of high quality were now also endangered. Their thoroughly senseless destruction was being justified on the grounds that they never "fit" into New Orleans in the first place; they were ugly, or so it was claimed; and no one ever really liked them in the first place. Suddenly, an "opportunity" existed for the opportunists—and presumably the prerequisite cultural climate of rebuild-at-any-cost-ASAP—to demolish these past "errors" of the twentieth century in a bold act of *architectural cleansing*. The pace of destruction was now quickening. By the summer of 2007, a total of nearly 6,000 structures from all periods had been bulldozed in Orleans Parish alone, although the twentieth-century sections of the city were now under the most intense attack.

Endangered modernist and moderne buildings now on architectural death row included the Pan American Life Building (1952) on Canal Boulevard in Mid City, by Skidmore, Owings and Merrill, which had sat empty since 1999; the city was desperate to unload it. The New Orleans Civic Center complex (1957) in the central business district was also on the hit list. This very handsome yet poorly maintained complex included the stately and well-appointed State of Louisiana Supreme Court Building, the New Orleans City Hall, and the State of Louisiana Office Building, all under the threat of demolition because of neglect and indifference. Another endangered building was the landmark Carver Theater (1950) on Orleans Avenue, built as a movie palace for African Americans. No films had been shown there since 1980, and before Katrina it had been used as a free health clinic. Another endangered building was the American Bank Building (1958, demolished 2008) by Moshe Goldstein. The estate of recently deceased millionaire oilman Patrick Taylor wanted to level this "eyesore," located on a prominent site on Lee Circle, and replace it with a pocket park. As for moderne commercial vernacular architecture, the 1950s-era Capri Motel (1955) on Tulane Avenue, which flooded, and other strip motels, along with their vintage neon signs, were suddenly endangered. However, none of these post–World War II buildings have, to date, elicited the unprovoked attacks and public fury that were directed at an exquisite International Style church that had been built in the lakefront section in 1963.

Crossing the Fine Line between Natural Catastrophe and War: The Battle for Cabrini Church

The built environment is at its greatest risk of violation in the aftermath of a catastrophe. When large numbers of residents are dead or scattered widely, as in the post-Katrina diaspora, a city's buildings and its neighborhoods cannot defend themselves from premeditated, hostile, or covert acts of aggression plotted against them. A building, of course, cannot advocate for itself. This is a key point in the following tale, a story of institutional arrogance and aggression. It is about *total* disregard for a city's collective memory. It is about local news media capitulating to historically powerful persons and institutions. It is about *myth* versus truth, about innuendo becoming propagandized and falsehoods coming to be seen as the truth. It is a case study of the condition of catastrophe becoming tantamount to the condition of war.

The St. Frances Cabrini Church was a masterpiece, designed by the celebrated New Orleans architectural firm of Curtis & Davis. It opened in 1963 in the Gentilly section of the city, only a few blocks south of the Lake Pontchartrain earthen levee. This section of New Orleans had been developed since World War II. Subdivisions had sprouted up on all sides of the twenty-acre parcel of land chosen in the early 1950s by the Archdiocese of New Orleans as the site for a much-needed church and school campus. It was a profitable plan for the Archdiocese, since many inner-city parishes in such neighborhoods as the Irish Channel and the Seventh Ward had begun to experience declines in their congregations and, as a consequence, in donations from these congregations. Most Gentilly residents were World War II vets who had started families. New Gentilly, as some called it, was to be, along with the nearby Lakeview section, which also straddled the lakefront landfill section, New Orleans's proud counterpart to Levittown and other prototype master-planned suburban communities across the nation.

According to an official account, the parish's namesake, St. Frances Xavier Cabrini, "was born Maria Francesca Cabrini on July 15, 1850, in Lombardy, Italy. She began her ministry as a teacher, but was soon drawn to religious life. In 1880, she founded the Missionaries of the Sacred Heart of Jesus (MSC), one of the first orders of women missionaries. In 1889, under the direction of Pope Leo XIII, Mother Cabrini traveled to America to help underserved Italian immigrants." She proceeded to found dozens of schools, orphanages, hospitals, and social services programs to serve the needs of immigrants in New Orleans, Chicago, and other American cities.[3]

Cabrini Church was striking in its originality, as indicated in a photo of the final presentation model in late 1959 (Fig. 6.3). Nathaniel (Buster) Curtis, the celebrated design prin-

6.3: *Architectural model of St. Frances Xavier Cabrini Church, 1959.*

cipal at the firm, set out to radically break with the conservative architecture of the stoic, neoclassical, pre–World War II churches that dominated the city's landscape at the time. Curtis and his design team, along with the parish pastor, Father Fyre, became fascinated with the progressive nature of the Vatican II proceedings in Rome, which had been initiated in 1959 by Pope John XXIII.

St. Frances Cabrini Parish had humble beginnings. The parish was founded in 1953 by a group of World War II vets, and at first operated from a metal Quonset hut chapel. The new church was absolutely stunning in its bold originality. It expressed the groundbreaking tenets of Vatican II, especially in the unfettered openness of the interior spaces, its structural dexterity and method of construction, the poetic use of natural light, a choir section and organ located behind the altar, and the decision to face its autonomous marble altar, carved from exquisite Italian Carrara marble, out toward a semicircular in-the-round seating configuration (Figs. 6.4 and 6.5, and Figs. 6.6 and 6.7).[4]

In Nathaniel Curtis's words:

We designed several Catholic schools and churches . . . our churches were first: Immaculate Conception Church, Our Lady Queen of Heaven Church, St. Frances Xavier Cabrini Church, and St. Angela Medici Church. Each one of these church buildings was given awards for design excellence. An architectural commission for a Catholic

6.4: *Interior, St. Frances Xavier Cabrini Church, 1963.*

Church presented an ideal situation for good design. There were no committees to satisfy—only the Pastor, who had sole authority. He controlled the budget, and could negotiate loans if need be. . . . Father Fyre—later to become an Archbishop—was the Pastor at St. Frances Xavier Cabrini, (it) owned a large tract of land . . . with a young and fast growing population. . . . there were several considerations that influenced the design . . . the strongest, of course, was the effect of the decisions taken as a result of Vatican II and its effect upon the plan.

The priest would no longer have his back to the congregation . . . there would be a sense of more participation . . . with the pews being placed in a semi-circle as close to the altar as possible. The spire, or steeple, utilized through the ages to draw attention to it as a place of supreme importance, was placed directly over the altar as the most important element. In fact, the altar was placed beneath the spire that grew up out of the roof as if pointing toward God. . . . the thin concrete shells . . . are reminiscent of the shape of the Quonset hut, in accordance with the wishes of Fr. Fyre since he had had a fond relationship with his first building.

All of the major components of the plan: altar, sanctuary, three-part nave and the baptistery, are enclosed within a fifteen-foot-high decorative brick wall, rectangular in plan. The only openings are at the entrances. The result is an honest expression of the activities that occur within, utilizing a forthright statement of the structural system and the materials employed. It was a church unlike any that had ever been built before.[5]

Its construction was a feat of originality in structural engineering. Curtis's initial design sketches depict a series of gravity-defying thin-shell barrel-vaulted lightweight concrete plates (Figs. 6.8 and 6.9) that rested gently upon a cast-in-place concrete baldachin (Fig. 6.10 and 6.11). Max Ingrand of Paris made the intricate stained-glass windows, which were arrayed in thin bands along the barrel-vaulted traceries and at the three vaults' outer termination points (Fig. 6.12). The ancestors of this same family had made the stained-glass windows for Chartres Cathedral in France more than six centuries earlier. The church cost $929,000 to construct in 1963, and its total replacement value was approximately $28 million in 2007. At its dedication ceremony on Sunday, April 21, 1963, Archbishop John P. Cody referred to Cabrini as "The Cathedral of the Lakefront." In blessing the church, Archbishop Cody said, "Many times as I knelt in St. Peter's in Rome during the Ecumenical Council my mind wandered across the sea and I wondered how the Cabrini Church would look when completed."[6]

6.5: *Demolition of St. Frances Xavier Cabrini Church, 2007.*

6.6: *Interior, St. Frances Xavier Cabrini Church, 1963.*

6.7: *Demolition of St. Frances Xavier Cabrini Church, 2007.*

It was these attributes that impressed me most when I first gazed upon the church's interior in the fall of 2002. My son's school (Isidore Newman School) was playing a basketball game at the nearby Redeemer-Seton High School, and I seized the moment. I had heard from my professional colleagues at Tulane of its minimalist beauty for years. From then on I attended mass at Cabrini on Sundays with my two initially reluctant teenagers in tow. They became immediately aware of its unique beauty, particularly when compared to the stoicism of the traditional design of our "home" parish church Uptown (Holy Name of Jesus). After nearly every mass they would ask questions about its architecture. Once, my son asked what the large freestanding circular objects were in the rear of the church, and I informed him they were the confessionals. They asked me questions about the delicate white barrel-vaulted roofs, which gently cantilevered outward high above the entrances, shading the large wooden doors and the stained-glass transoms above (Fig. 6.13). They commented on the slender spire-like steeple situated directly above the altar, perched high atop the baldachin.

Cabrini Church quickly became our adopted church. I was now donating to our "home" parish as well as to St. Frances Xavier Cabrini Church (henceforth referred to here as SFC or simply Cabrini Church). We attended mass there regularly for three years before the hurricane because we had become quite enamored with the church and its *genius loci*—sense of place—both in spiritual and physical terms.

In the blur of those first days after the levees broke, my wife, two children, and I arrived in Austin and became mindlessly transfixed by the wall-to-wall coverage on CNN of the horrific events taking place back home. We stared with open eyes at the unfolding chaos. On Wednesday of that first, highly surreal week, my son, Alexander, then seventeen, called out, "Look, Dad, there's the steeple of Cabrini Church!" Indeed, amid the floodwaters lapping at the eaves and rooflines of the hundreds of homes that surrounded the church, its long slender white steeple and large cross stood out proudly, majestically, as a beacon of hope—a symbol of the enduring spirit of New Orleans at its gravest moment (Figs. 6.8 and 6.9).

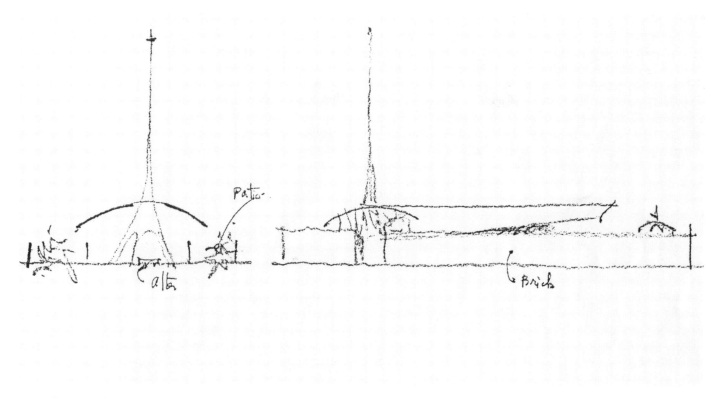

6.8: *Early concept sketches of St. Frances Xavier Cabrini Church, 1960.*

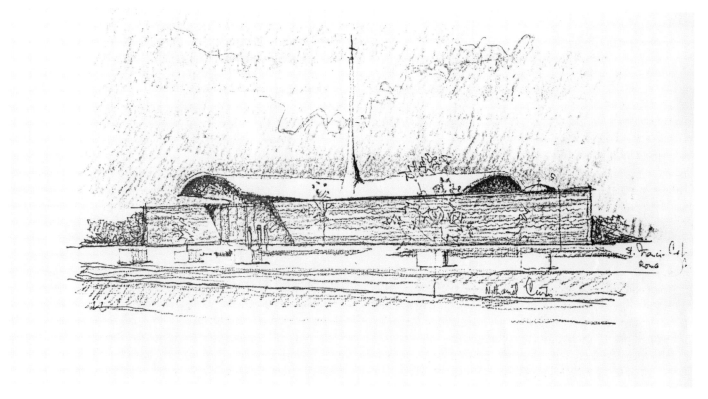

6.9: *Early rendering of St. Frances Xavier Cabrini Church, 1960.*

6.10: *St. Frances Xavier Cabrini Church, construction of baldachin, 1962.*

6.11: *Demolition of St. Frances Xavier Cabrini Church, 2007.*

6.12: *Construction of St. Frances Xavier Cabrini Church, 1962.*

From this point on, the status of the church became an object of intense curiosity to me and to its long-standing parishioners. Thanksgiving weekend 2005 was the first time my children would be able to return home to their place of birth. The church was among the first places they asked to be taken to, after seeing our flood-damaged home Uptown for the first time since the storm. As the three of us peered through the narrow panes of glass of the large wooden doors at the main entrance, we could see that nothing whatsoever had been touched in the interior, as if it had been frozen in Katrina time. As it turned out, shockingly, no restoration activity at all would occur at the church for an entire year.

No cleaning, no airing out, nothing.

Its immense wooden doors remained chained shut. Six feet of floodwater had stood in the church for many days after the storm, compared to the nine or more feet in the surrounding areas (since the church had been built upon a three-foot earthen foundation "platform"), and yet the church was in quite excellent condition structurally. In those

first days, soldiers had spray-painted the ubiquitous *X* marking on the skylight above the baptistery as part of the military's search-and-rescue mission across the city. Other than this, and the cross that was now leaning at a ninety-degree angle at the top of the slender steeple, there was no visible damage whatsoever to the exterior. My two children and I together suspected that, indeed, something was very wrong, something was amiss.

In early November 2006, the church was among the agenda items taken up at a meeting of New Orleans's official landmark oversight agency, the city-run Historic District Landmarks Commission (HDLC). Cabrini was the fifth or sixth item on the agenda. Glancing around the room, I noticed a number of concerned architects in attendance. Arthur Scully, a respected, astute local freelance historian, a week earlier had been the first to sound the alarm, in a letter strongly supporting the HDLC's granting of landmark status to the church as soon as possible. Scully's letter was entered into the official record that day, as were letters from

6.13: *Exterior, St. Frances Xavier Cabrini Church, 1963.*

the National Trust and the local chapter of the American Institute of Architects (AIA), all in strong support of saving this landmark.[7] A number of the church's supporters spoke, including me. The seven-member commission proceeded to vote, with little debate, to grant provisional landmark status to the church, despite the fact that it was only forty-three years old. In the vast majority of instances in the United States, landmark status is not accorded until a building is at least fifty years of age. The HDLC vote that day signified that the church was indeed worthy of being entered into the city's register of architecturally significant buildings. Yet this vote would touch off a major controversy. The stage was now set for the same honor to be bestowed at the national level, which, if it happened, would make Cabrini Church eligible for

candidacy and placement on the United States National Register of Historic Places (Figs. 6.13 and 6.14).

Immediately afterward, a group of energized and outraged friends, parishioners, and architects, including Frances Curtis, the eighty-eight-year-old widow of Nathaniel Curtis, and Arthur Q. Davis, the ninety-two-year-old surviving founding partner of Curtis & Davis, met informally in the public outer lobby of the city hall council chambers. It was then and there I first learned that demolition had surreptitiously begun at the church two weeks earlier and, worse, that many artifacts, including the exquisite stained-glass windows from France, were in the process of being carelessly removed. A thin white asbestos coating on the underside of part of the ceiling was being removed, and the church pews, built with a rare hard-

6.14: *Demolition of St. Frances Xavier Cabrini Church, 2007.*

wood, had been mindlessly, callously bulldozed into a pile of matchsticks in the middle of the church's central interior space, directly in front of the altar.

I immediately drove out to see this for myself. Once there, I learned that the situation was far worse than I had expected: the altar was gone, as was the brass communion rail; the wooden doors had been mutilated or removed completely, and were strewn across the lawn as if left for trash; sacred artifacts, including the vestments, were strewn about the lawn; and the marble baptismal font had been carelessly ripped out from its terrazzo pedestal by a Bobcat tractor and was nowhere in sight (Figs. 6.15 and 6.16). An asbestos-abatement crew was at work inside, removing the church's very small amount of asbestos on the ceiling beams.

By the end of the week, a group of about thirty people, built around the core group of fifteen supporters who had attended the HDLC meeting, met outside the church to express their outrage that apparently clandestine demolition was underway and that it had started at all. The morning after the HDLC meeting, I wrote a letter to the *Times-Picayune*. It was published the morning after that as the lead letter to the editor. In it I publicly decried the destruction of an architectural and civic landmark and called for the demolition process to cease at once so that a compromise could be reached with the archdiocese and with a local Catholic school, Holy Cross School, both of which were extremely eager to clear the entire twenty-acre site and demolish the church just as fast as possible so that the Holy Cross campus

6.15: *Baptismal, St. Frances Xavier Cabrini Church, 1963.*

could be relocated from the Lower Ninth Ward to Gentilly.[8] Opponents of the demolition, including me, questioned the possible motives and the need for expediency: Why demolish the church first when there are eight other buildings on the campus? Why the excessive urgency? Within days, the Friends of St. Frances Cabrini Church was formed expressly to save the church from, in the Friends' view, a brazen takeover end-run move, and its imminent senseless destruction.

Holy Cross School was an independent Catholic college-prep middle and high school with deep social and cultural roots in the city. It was founded by the Congregation of Holy Cross in 1879. Before Katrina, grades five through twelve were taught in its historic brick structures on a tree-shaded campus in the neighborhood that had become known as "Holy Cross." Its campus flooded in Katrina's aftermath, some of the buildings taking on as much as six feet of water. Since Katrina, the school was operating out of a mixture of FEMA trailers and some of its less-damaged structures. In the 2006–2007 school year, 887 male students were enrolled. Before Katrina, the median household income within its local zip code (70117) was reported as $19,567 a year (versus the Louisiana statewide average of $34,191), and the median value of the housing units was $57,140 (compared to the Louisiana statewide average of $94,303). The percentage of homeowners was only 46 percent (compared to statewide, 61 percent).[9]

By contrast, before Katrina the neighborhood where the Redeemer-Seton campus and the SFC school campus were located (70122 zip code) had a median household income of $31,104 a year, and the median value of the housing units was $83,400 (63 percent were owner-occupied). From these statistics the picture became crystal clear: Holy Cross was seeking to abandon its older, much poorer neighborhood in favor of far newer and "greener" pastures without having to leave Orleans Parish, its home for the past 128 years. Moreover, leaving Orleans Parish would have been politically incorrect. The school had been experiencing a gradual decline in enrollment before Katrina, presumably because of the unappealing aspects of its environs. The Gentilly site was significantly wealthier and had a far higher percentage of homeowners.

In short, Gentilly had been the more stable neighborhood and appeared to have a brighter future, according to the school's future enrollment projections, with or without the Katrina factor. Holy Cross had wanted out before Katrina, and now it had finally found the perfect reason to escape. But why move from one badly flooded neighborhood to another?

Just after the floodwaters had receded on its campus, Holy Cross began its search to relocate. Its board studied a number of sites during the fall of 2005, and two emerged as finalists:

6.16: *Skylight above baptismal, St. Frances Xavier Cabrini Church, 1963.*

one in west suburban Kenner, near the airport in Jefferson Parish, and the twenty-acre Gentilly site in Orleans Parish. The Kenner site did not have any buildings on it, whereas the Gentilly site contained Redeemer-Seton High School (a school with a predominately African American enrollment), St. Frances Xavier Cabrini Elementary School, the parish rectory, and a multipurpose activity center.[10] SFC Elementary had also been designed by Curtis & Davis, and the firm received national and local architectural awards upon its completion in 1955.[11] Combined, these two co-ed schools enrolled 592 students just before Katrina (compared to Holy Cross's enrollment of 887).

An article in the *Clarion Herald* (July 29, 2006) by Peter Finney, Jr. (an unabashed Holy Cross supporter and perhaps not coincidentally a lay member of the SFC Parish Council), announced that the Cabrini-Redeemer-Seton site had been selected as the location of a new Holy Cross School to be built from scratch.[12] All existing buildings on the twenty-acre

site were to be demolished. The school's architectural firm, Blitch/Knevel Architects, published a site plan accompanying the article. It showed a driveway and lawn on the 2.1-acre portion of the site where the landmark church presently stood. Meanwhile, the GCIA, the local press, and elected officials were being falsely told the new school would not fit on the site if the church remained. Worse, in a brilliant PR move seen by some simply as a bullying tactic, Holy Cross publicly threatened to move to the Kenner site if the church remained. Alice Kottmyer, a longtime parishioner, sent an e-mail to Bill Chauvin. It read:

As one of many Cabrini parishioners who are appalled by the plans to demolish our church, please be advised that the "open town hall meeting" at which the "Cabrini parishioners" supposedly "voted" on the sale to Holy Cross was poorly advertised. I saw the "notice" for it. There was no mention that a vote would be taken at that meeting on the future of the Parish (church), and so many parishioners—who at that time still lived at great distance—didn't feel it urgent that they attend.

They (including me, my mother, and my entire family, and many, many others) were certainly quite surprised and shocked to hear that "The Parish" had voted at that meeting to sell Cabrini's land. So do not cite the "town hall meeting" as any legal authority for your actions. That "vote" was a sham and, until a proper vote is taken, no one can assume that a majority . . . supported the sale, and certainly not the demolition of their church. What has happened up until now in this whole matter has been shockingly irregular, even by post-Katrina standards.[13]

In October 2006, Broadmoor Construction Company, acting on behalf of Holy Cross and the archdiocese, quietly applied for and received a demolition permit from the City of New Orleans. The demolition cost for the church was listed as $688,000. When what was happening came to light, the Friends immediately sought to halt demolition. As it turned out, and as clearly written in the parish charter, Cabrini Church and all its physical assets were owned in full by its parishioners—not the archdiocese. Furthermore, it was the parishioners themselves who had faithfully paid the premium on the church's flood-insurance policy all these years. This same policy had reportedly yielded a $4.2 million payout directly to the archdiocese following Katrina. Many parishioners who were aware of the details of the situation were incensed at having been cut entirely out of the decision-making "process." Worse, the archdiocese appeared to be well along in the process of formally suppressing the SFC Parish in order to seize its bank accounts together with the alleged $4.2 million flood payment. No mention whatsoever was made of any of this to the general public.

Cultural Cleansing

Milan Kundera asserts in *The Book of Laughter and Forgetting*, "The first step in liquidating a people is to erase its memory. Destroy its books, its culture, and its history. Then you have somebody write new books, manufacture a new culture, invent a new history. Before long the nation will begin to forget what it is and what it was."[14] Robert Bevan reasoned in his book *The Destruction of Memory: Architecture at War* (2006) that the machine-like destruction of symbolic buildings and the physical fabric of cities and civilizations is not merely collateral damage, but a deliberate campaign by attackers to "dominate, divide, terrorize, and eliminate" the memory, history, and identity of the opposing side. Cultural cleansing in times of intense uncertainty and conflict is inextricably linked

to ethnic cleansing, genocide, and holocausts.[15] The Geneva Conventions forbid churches to be destroyed in times of war, so how was it allowable for a landmark church to be destroyed in the aftermath of a natural disaster? In the rebuilding of cities after a war, Bevan argued, "the pitfalls of reconstruction in circumstances where there has been an attempt at forced forgetting by the destruction of material culture are particularly treacherous." The Hague and the Geneva Conventions consider the destruction of cultural heritage a war crime unless there is "imperative military necessity." Bevan argued for international principles to call attention to the importance of safeguarding the world's architectural record. His is a plea for heterogeneous, pluralist values, for integration and human justice, and for *cultural genocide* to be made a punishable "crime against humanity." This scenario certainly made sense in the case of the forcible seizure of Cabrini Church and its assets by an invading force.[16]

In war, religious buildings become key targets, as do libraries and museums. In the wars in the former Yugoslavia, Catholic Croatian and Serbian Orthodox structures did not escape targeting, although the Bosnian Muslims suffered the most severe losses. In his book, Bevan included before-and-after photographs showing first mosques and then the ruins or the parking lots that succeeded them. Such acts are far more than mere acts of aggression. The mayor of the town of Zvornik, once 60 percent Muslim with a dozen mosques, declared, "There never were any mosques in Zvornik."[17]

It appeared at this point that the destruction of collective memory was being used as a controlling device in New Orleans. Post-Katrina, cultural conditions in the city were disintegrating. In the past, the communists destroyed churches in Russia, Hitler burned synagogues, and China desecrated and destroyed temples in Tibet. In 1950 there were 6,000 Buddhist monasteries in Tibet. After thirty years of Chinese-government control, only ten monasteries remained. The Taliban in Afghanistan destroyed a pair of colossal 1,500-year-old Buddhas in 2001 after having forced local people at gunpoint to plant the explosives. In the Ukraine in the 1930s, architectural monuments of the Ukrainian baroque were destroyed in the cities, and unique wooden churches were razed in outlying villages. Today, Ukrainians are ashamed to recall this destruction, yet during this period almost every single wooden church was destroyed. Usually, such examples are about one religion or political order conquering another, as in Hitler's Third Reich and Stalinist Russia.[18] Paradoxically, the battle for Cabrini's survival had *intentionally* pitted Catholics against Catholics, and elected officials against rank-and-file preservationists and Cabrini loyalists. As for the local politicians, was *any* sign of "progress" tantamount to civic progressiveness? If so, the political urgency to build *anything*, *fast*, had deteriorated to a new low.

Initially, the so-called "town meeting" was supposedly called merely to discuss the future of "the Parish," although the meeting was not advertised as an occasion for voting on the future of the church building. Of course, nearly all the SFC parishioners remained in exile.[19] When the Holy Cross campus plan was presented at the meeting, no mention was made of any attempt to find a reasonable compromise, i.e., *to save the church by building the school around it*. The plan was presented as an all-or-nothing proposition. In retrospect, six months later, it appeared that, sadly, the parishioners had for all practical purposes unwittingly voted themselves out of existence that night. All their assets were later seized by the archdiocese, including the flood-insurance payout. Why would the parishioners vote to demolish their own church, using funds from their own flood-insurance proceeds?

Aside from the architectural significance of the church, the premeditated manner in which the situation evolved raised an entirely new set of questions. The Friends included many baby boomers who had been baptized and married at Cabrini Church and who had attended the parish school. Many were outraged to see their cultural heritage so brazenly dismissed. They tried to awaken and alert the Cabrini Parish Council, and then sought counsel from at least one canon law expert, although the Friends were, without question, most grateful for their talented, stalwart attorney, Jim Logan. Logan could see from the start what was going on, and he did what he could from a legal perspective to aid and guide the work of the Friends.

The archdiocese and Blitch/Knevel, their New Orleans–based architects, repeatedly exaggerated the true costs of repairing the church and its contents: estimates at first (before the rise of organized opposition) were as low as $1.1 million, but after staunch opposition emerged, they suddenly ran as high as *$6.1 million*! It was now a matter of gamesmanship. The Friends argued the church could be fully restored for no more than $2.1 million to $2.5 million (including the tragic post-Katrina human-inflicted destruction caused by the archdiocese itself), leaving the remaining funds for the creation of an operational endowment.

In response to the outcome of the town-hall meeting and the *Clarion Herald* article, the Friends produced an alternative site plan for the entire twenty-acre parcel, showing how the Holy Cross campus could fit comfortably next to the church, which would remain intact and fully restored. Holy Cross would hear nothing of it.[20] A tragedy was in the making. The church at this point fell prey to intense public verbal attacks.

Similarly, public housing in New Orleans was under attack at this time. By late 2006, public outrage was growing over the proposed demolition of thousands of Housing and Urban Development–sponsored housing units in the city. Angry former residents charged HUD and the Housing Authority of New Orleans (HANO) with racial cleansing and stealing land in order to resell it to private developers.[21] Before Katrina, more than 5,000 families had lived in public housing; two years after Katrina, only 1,000 had been able to return, although during this period rents had increased from 70 to 300 percent in the city. Similar to the by-now-standard Holy Cross party line, the HUD-HANO redevelopment plans were supposedly for the "betterment" of the residents. Both the Cabrini Church and HUD-HANO battles were being fueled by premeditated attacks on a slice of the city's collective memory.

Meanwhile, it became publicly known that Holy Cross would receive a massive payout from FEMA in disaster-mitigation funds. The school had managed to get FEMA to declare its historic Lower Ninth Ward campus as more than 51 percent damaged, based on what by that time in New Orleans had become widely referred to as the "Fifty-one Percent Rule." Here was a school abandoning its historic campus, with the option of selling it later to a developer at a profit, and electing to build a new campus in a newer yet worse flooded section of the city, and collecting as much as $24 million in federal taxpayer funds to do so. As this scenario played out, the church's comparatively small but determined band of supporters functioned as what the Holy Cross administration and the archdiocese would now label as "obstructionists." The enemy had been sighted.

The Upended Press Conference

By the week of Thanksgiving 2006, each side had firmly established its position. The anti-Cabrini camp had dug in its heels for a fight. It was now time for a direct confrontation. The first attack was launched by the Gentilly Civic Improvement Association, in this case functioning as no more than a mouthpiece for the invaders. The GCIA was one of the aforementioned quasi-feudal neighborhood confederations. Its PR person was the outspoken Angelle Givens, a short forty-something woman with a powerful set of vocal cords. On the Tuesday before Thanksgiving, the GCIA staged a press conference on the neutral ground (Paris Avenue median) across from the church. The sole purpose was to denounce us obstructionists and to extol the virtues of Holy Cross coming to Gentilly. Along the way, the group corralled the support of the district's beleaguered councilperson, Cynthia Hedge Morrell. Also in attendance was Oliver Thomas, president of the seven-member city council (and currently serving a three-year federal prison term for taking a bribe while in office).

These were indeed rough times for any elected official in New Orleans, but especially for Thomas and Morrell. Thomas had grown up in the Lower Ninth Ward and had witnessed firsthand the destruction of his old stomping grounds. Morrell, for her part, had lost two-thirds of the constituents in her heavily flooded council district. Thomas, one of two councilpersons-at-large, represented the entire city. To their credit, however, the two had been working tirelessly in crisis-management mode day and night to govern a city that was fiscally destitute, having laid off more than 3,000 city employees in the aftermath of the storm. There was no money to rebuild anything (except, it seemed, the resurrected Superdome for the city's pro football franchise, the New Orleans Saints). Together, along with the other five members of the council, they latched onto the Holy Cross relocation to Gentilly as a way to show that they were doing something, *anything*. That morning, they stood proudly side by side on the neutral ground, surrounded by GCIA members and a phalanx of TV cameras, as Givens led the charge. I had prepared large boards showing the Friends' proposed alternate site plan, with the church and the school on the same site. A handful of Tulane architecture students stood on the sidelines as I began to repeatedly shout "compromise, compromise" while Givens and the politicians took turns at the microphone. They had orchestrated the event for the cameras. I continued, "Why does it have to be either-or? Why can't Holy Cross *and* Cabrini coexist side by side in Gentilly?" They were clearly agitated. Members of the Friends stood nearby in a sort of defensive battle-line formation.

This action was necessary in order to demonstrate that a reasonable and logical alternative existed. Not surprisingly, no Holy Cross or archdiocese officials attended this event. A mêlée ensued, including some physical scuffles. The reporters rushed immediately to interview us, not the politicians. That same morning, an op-ed piece by David Villarrubia was published in the local newspaper. In it, he stated that while the Gentilly neighborhood embraced plans for the new school, many naturally assumed that the church would stay. He questioned the logic of revitalizing the community while tearing down its landmark church, its spiritual heart:

Why do I speak now? Because there were no public hearings—no chance to speak before. I grew up in this church. At the rate of demolition in New Orleans, we'll soon have nothing of quality left, no memories of pre-Katrina New Orleans. There is no reason why Cabrini Church, with minimal damage from Katrina, cannot coexist with the

new Holy Cross. This magnificent structure could easily be utilized for a chapel or performing arts center . . . or National Catholic Memorial Shrine named in honor of Mother Cabrini and dedicated to the victims of Katrina . . . as an adaptive use or mixed use with the church . . . [Its] demolition is a violent and immoral decision that goes against the emotional and societal fabric that makes us a civilized society. Throughout time, where wars are fought, churches are known as places of refuge, not unlike what is needed in these desperate times in New Orleans. How much loss is enough? The destruction of this church will rank among the worst and most painful post-Katrina decisions forever. How ironic it is that our church was spared by an act of God only to be destroyed by an act of man?[22]

The *Times-Picayune*, the local daily, immediately and repeatedly railed against us "obstructionists" for having waited, in its opinion, too long to protest, and for standing in the way of the city's rebuilding progress. Immediately, the archdiocese's PR machine entered the fray, launching its own intense attack campaign to discredit the supporters of SFC.[23]

The Questionable Section 106 Review

The following week, the city council squarely lined up in opposition to the SFC "obstructionists" when it unanimously passed an endorsement of the church's destruction, proclaiming the council's full support of Holy Cross's plans. Besides Morrell and Thomas, the five others who blindly fell into line were Arnie Fielkow, Shelly Madura, Stacy Head, James Carter, and Cynthia Willard-Lewis. To no one's surprise, Mayor Nagin was nowhere in sight on the issue. Meanwhile, the Friends and our attorney, Jim Logan, had contacted FEMA to inquire if FEMA realized that the church was architecturally worthy of local, even national, landmark status. FEMA, at first flustered, responded by instructing the archdiocese to halt further demolition at the site, and immediately launched what is called a *Section 106 Review*. This law was enacted in 1966 to provide a reasonable way to determine if buildings less than fifty years old are eligible for placement on the National Register of Historic Places. Additionally, the National Trust for Historic Preservation weighs in on this process, as does the State Historic Preservation Office (SHPO) in each of the fifty states. I had never heard of this federal law. Since Cabrini Church was only forty-three years old, FEMA's decision to now act fueled further loud controversy and yet another round of brutal verbal and written attacks on FEMA, the church, and the "obstructionists," this time centered even more squarely on the alleged physical ugliness of the church and how it had continued to be an albatross for the SFC Parish to fiscally operate.

Additional falsehoods about the church were hurled from the Holy Cross camp, not unlike an artillery barrage. Despite all the local hostility, the Friends quietly had garnered the support of the Cabrini Foundation in New York, and donations were beginning to accrue locally and nationally in support of the legal defense of the church.

This same week we learned that the famed structural engineer John Skilling had worked alongside Curtis & Davis on the design of Cabrini Church. Significantly, it was also learned that Skilling later worked with Minoru Yamasaki on the structural design of the ill-fated World Trade Center in New York City. In other words, Skilling was the structural engineer for the Twin Towers. The unprovoked attack on Cabrini Church was now attracting some national attention on the Internet via numerous preservation blog sites.[24]

Quickly, FEMA (under intense political pressure from Holy Cross and Louisiana lieutenant governor Mitch Landrieu) commissioned NISTAC, of Gaithersburg, Maryland, in a joint venture with URS Group, Inc., and Dewberry & Davis, to assess the significance of the SFC. This group in turn commissioned one of the most preeminent American architectural historians of mid-twentieth-century modernism in the United States, Dr. Richard Longstreth, to conduct the field and scholarly research for the report to FEMA. The deadline given to Longstreth was extremely short—little more than four weeks to complete his work. Longstreth, a professor of American studies and the director of the Graduate Program in Historic Preservation at George Washington University, in Washington, D.C., was eminently qualified for the task. He immediately set to work.

Longstreth's finished report was stunning in both its depth and scope, especially given the extremely short deadline.[25] Longstreth traveled to New Orleans twice and consulted with many experts, including Dr. Karen Kingsley, a well-respected professor emerita of architectural history who had taught in the School of Architecture at Tulane University for twenty-five years.[26] The Friends chose to lay low, since there was no point in attempting to turn around the tsunami of anti-Cabrini public opinion until the FEMA report was completed. However, just before Christmas 2006, Bill Chauvin and a fellow Holy Cross board member agreed to meet quietly with David Villarrubia, Jim Logan, me, and Walter Gallas, who represented the National Trust's New Orleans field office. We met one evening in an upstairs room at the Musicians Union Hall on Esplanade Avenue.

The Friends of Cabrini had been requesting a private meeting ever since the HDLC meeting six weeks earlier. The meeting was cordial, although hard as we tried, no real progress was made. We did all we could to justify our alternate site plan in detail and to show how we wanted both Holy Cross and SFC to coexist on the same twenty-acre site in Gentilly. They asked, "How are you going to pay for its repair and upkeep?" because "We [Holy Cross] do not have the money." We were told that the church was too big and ugly and would not fit into the neo-postmodern design of the new Holy Cross campus. From the start, we insisted that the church could be fully restored with a portion of the $4.2 million flood-insurance payout, that an endowment would be set up, and that the outer baptistery area would be an ideal setting for a Mother Cabrini National Shrine in memory of the 1,800 people who perished in Katrina. In fact, the poetic lighting and minimalist surroundings of the baptistery were perfectly suited to a memorial of this type—contemplative, restorative, understated.

The opposition would hear nothing of any memorial or of saving any part of the church. Holy Cross was intent on replicating to the extent possible its 128-year-old campus—in 2007. This seemed absurd to us that they repeatedly rejected our assertion that these two period styles could in fact coexist, just as a mixture of periods and styles exist side by side on college and university campuses across the country. Aside from our concerns, the rendering of the Paris Avenue elevation in the *Clarion Herald* article and on the Holy Cross Web site confirmed the worst suspicions of many leading local architects about the questionable architectural quality of the proposed design for the new Holy Cross.

The report commissioned by FEMA was delivered at the end of January 2007. The report was sent to the Louisiana SHPO office in Baton Rouge, to FEMA's headquarters in Washington, and to its New Orleans field office to assist in FEMA's determination of National Register eligibility for the church. The report's executive summary stated:

St. Frances Cabrini Church is exceptionally important as an example of Modern Architecture in New Orleans, with a plan, structural systems, and allusions to the local historical context that are unmatched in both their originality and sophistication . . . [It] is an exceptionally important example of its building type for being among, probably *the* most, singular design for a house of worship in New Orleans erected during the post-WWII period. It was on the front line of designs locally, and probably nationally, for a Roman Catholic parish church or cathedral in having its entire configuration developed in response to the drive for liturgical reform that subsequently culminated in Vatican II. Furthermore, the particulars of that configuration are unique locally and extremely unusual within a larger context. . . . [The church] is exceptionally important locally, and extremely unusual, for its innovative, complex structural design, interweaving several systems. The most prominent of these is a fan of three shallow barrel vaults of thin-shell reinforced concrete, pivoting on four structural columns, sheltering the worship space. The inspiration for this system was likely derived from the work of world-renowned Spanish structural engineer Eduardo Torroja. The church's structure is unique locally in having most if its remaining structure comprised of a baldachin of concrete parabolic arches that both forms the base of its tall spire and the structural anchor for a coffered concrete slab that radiates behind it.[27]

The report continued:

St. Frances Xavier Cabrini Church is unique locally and distinctive among houses of worship nationally in having its bold structure *not* be the generator of exterior form, instead having an exterior treatment that was intentionally differential to its residential context. The character of the exterior is further exceptional in the richness, sophistication, and subtlety with which it abstractly alludes to a variety of nineteenth-century iconic domestic and religious properties in New Orleans. . . . [It] is an exceptional example of the work of its architects, Curtis & Davis, who, in their own time and in retrospect were widely acknowledged as the preeminent architectural firm in New Orleans during the post-WWII era and a firm that enjoyed national and international distinction for much of that period. For most of its thirty-two-year existence, Curtis & Davis had a major impact on shaping the city during an important period of growth and change.[28]

Curtis & Davis also designed the Louisiana Superdome (1976), the Rivergate Convention Center (1966, demolished 1996), many private residences, office structures, medical facilities, and schools. Longstreth discussed this body of work and Cabrini's place within the impressive Curtis & Davis oeuvre:

The church ranks in the uppermost tier in the degree to which it integrates the three most distinguishing and significant attributes of the firm's approach to design: innovative planning in response to programmatic needs, innovative use of structure likewise tied to those needs, and innovative development of oblique historic references to nineteenth-century New Orleans architecture.

. . . [Cabrini Church] is exceptionally important as a local example of the work of John Skilling, a nationally renowned structural engineer. It was likely the first instance where Skilling and Curtis & Davis collaborated. The only other major work produced by this team locally was the Rivergate exhibition center, now demolished. Indeed, while the vast majority of distinguished twentieth-century architecture in New Orleans derives significance as examples of broader, national tendencies, St. Frances Xavier Cabrini Church stands in a league of its own—at once a striking emblem of modernity in appearance, structure, and program and a vibrant tribute to a rich, multi-faceted past.[29]

The report concluded:

St. Frances Cabrini Church meets the standard National Register eligibility requirements, and is significant under National Register Criterion C (Design/Construction) within a local historic context/level. It has a period of significance, which spans from 1961 to 1963, the years in which the building was designed and erected. Its boundaries extend to the curb of Paris Avenue to the east, extend eight feet from the west and south facades, and to the border of the parking lot north of the building . . . [It] meets the special eligibility requirements specified under Criterion Considerations A (Religious Properties) . . . [It also], while less than fifty years of age, meets the special eligibility requirements specified under Criteria Consideration G (Properties That Have Achieved Significance Within the Past 50 Years) . . . [and] maintains the seven aspects of integrity (location, design, setting, materials, workmanship, feeling, and association) required for National Register listing.[30]

The main body of the 125-plus-page report contained a lengthy justification for the conclusions stated above, a discussion of the history and development of modernism in the United States, the influence of modernism in liturgical architecture in the post–World War II period, and a detailed discussion of the significance of the buildings and accomplishments of Curtis & Davis in relation to the modernist canon. To supporters of Cabrini Church, this was absolutely the best news we could have hoped for.

Public Indifference to a Modernist Landmark

FEMA's public comment period of the Section 106 Review process occurred in February.[31] This protocol turned out to be a total circus. Nearly thirteen hundred comments were posted on FEMA's Cabrini Web site during a twenty-day period. The vast majority were hostile, taunting, and insulting, squarely aimed at the church and its "obstructionist" supporters near and far. Out-of-state supporters of SFC were seen as imposters, and singled out for intensely personal taunts, bullying, and ridicule. Holy Cross supporters attacked the church for being ugly, for never belonging in New Orleans in the first place, for being too expensive to maintain, and for having a leaky roof. Many posters (plus many imposters—ill-informed, self-anointed, overnight "experts" on the topic of architecture) chattered on about how Holy Cross School was of infinitely more value than any church could ever be, whether of landmark quality or otherwise. SFC supporters shot back: weren't two schools (Redeemer-Seton and SFC Elementary) already being sacrificed for Holy Cross? Why was Holy Cross somehow superior to the two schools that were already functioning as sacrificial lambs? Little though anyone knew, the church's roof had been completely repaired before Katrina, using a state-of-the-art polyurethane membrane roofing technology (see below). The roof did not leak a single drop of water during Katrina or after. Regardless, lies, innuendo, myth masquerading as fact, and ridiculous statements hijacked this supposedly "serious" facet of the federal Section 106 Review.

While this was occurring, a series of fruitless weekly consultation meetings were held, usually on Monday mornings, at which the aggrieved parties would gather at the FEMA offices on the west bank of the river with the aim of reaching a compromise. These sessions, often lasting four or more hours at a stretch, were governed by FEMA's out-of-state consultant-facilitators. Govern they did, simultaneously constricting any reasonably full airing of the pro-Cabrini camp's position in the ongoing controversy. The Friends were being firmly held in check. In more than ten hours of meetings, we were only given three minutes to formally defend the church. Adding insult to injury, we were disallowed from voting on the fate of the church. Meanwhile, every time we mentioned that the flood-insurance money was all that was needed to restore the church, Holy Cross cleverly replied, "Well, that is an issue you will have to bring up with the archdiocese, not us." When the archdiocese was approached on the issue, it stonewalled.

These private (no media) "consultative meetings" culminated in an event that unfortunately turned out to be a far bigger fiasco than the online comments during the Section 106 Review or the so-called consultative meetings. On Monday night, February 26, 2007, the requisite Section 106 public meeting took place in an auditorium at the University of New Orleans. Over two hundred people showed up, 95 percent of them Holy Cross students, parents, and sundry supporters. The church was subjected to nothing short of a total public bashing that night. Holy Cross students and parents taunted every supporter of Cabrini Church brave enough to approach the microphone. A lynch-mob mentality prevailed from start to finish. In fact, at the end, so many anti-Cabrini persons heckled and taunted church supporters that a police detail was required to escort us to the parking lot afterward.[32]

Not a single direct reference was made to the Longstreth report that night or thereafter by the FEMA machine. Nancy Niedernhofer, the FEMA administrative coordinator for the Section 106 Review of Cabrini, told the rambunctious audience at the start of the meeting, "FEMA has determined that the church is eligible for listing on the National Register of Historic Places." Hearing this news, a loud chorus of boos and sighs erupted. The newspaper account of the fiasco that night read in part:

> The room then exploded with applause when a mix of men, women and school-age children listened patiently as Bill Chauvin, chairman of the school's governing board, explained that parents of Holy Cross students cannot afford the tuition increases that would be needed to repair the church, which at 25,000 square feet [it was actually only 18,000 square feet—author's note] is too large to be incorporated into the school campus design. Robin Brou-Hatheway, a Gentilly resident and a parishioner, argued that the church should be preserved, noting Cabrini operated in the black before Katrina. The observation was greeted by many in the room with laughter. She characterized the earlier vote by parishioners to sanction the Holy Cross plan as "Infamous . . . only 92 people were there" for the vote.[33]

In November, Chauvin had arrogantly stated that keeping a modernist church would clash with Holy Cross's pseudo-1800s-styled campus, paradoxically designed to be in keeping with the architecture of the neighborhood it was *just about to abandon* in the Lower Ninth Ward:

> "That [modernism] is not what Holy Cross is, not what our history is." Chauvin said the church has been described as a "money pit" by the Archdiocese, the result of long-deferred maintenance, inadequate heating and air conditioning systems and a roof that has leaked since the church opened . . . "How can we go to parents and say your tuition has to be this high because we had to add a component to pay for maintenance on this facility?"[34]

Local investigative journalism was virtually nonexistent concerning the battle to save the church. Any public statements from the local Catholic political machine were taken as gospel. Nobody in the media ever checked the facts, in particular those regarding the behind-the-scenes money grab of insurance and taxpayer funds. Back in November, a front-page headline had read "Architect Says Church Should Be Preserved." Arthur Davis, the aged, surviving partner of Curtis & Davis, implored Holy Cross to find a compromise to keep the church and build the new school campus alongside it. Also in this piece, it was mentioned that Cynthia Hedge Morrell had written a few days earlier to Donald Powell, President Bush's Gulf Coast recovery czar, imploring him to immediately reverse FEMA's ruling that the church was deemed historically significant.[35]

In the end, FEMA would totally ignore Dr. Longstreth and its own consultants' recommendations. Longstreth's erudite, carefully constructed thesis for granting National Register status to the church was dismissed outright. In shelving the expensive report, the FEMA machine seemed to be searching for an easy victory amid the almost endless daily beatings it took in the local and national media for its dismal response to Hurricane Katrina and its aftermath. Perhaps FEMA saw succumbing—capitulating—to Holy Cross's and the archdiocese's demands as a local quick-fix public-relations coup. After all, buildings don't vote.[36]

By March 2007 it was clear the local media were not at all interested in airing the full dimensions of the controversy. Not a single investigative piece was published anywhere, and the "facts" publicly disseminated by the conquistadors went unchecked. The local paper published heavily slanted pieces. It portrayed the so-called agreement between the parties (which the Friends were never allowed to vote on) as having been orchestrated from behind the scenes by Mitch Landrieu (Landrieu, the head of the State Historic Preservation Office [SHIPO], had lost the nationally publicized 2006 mayoral runoff against incumbent Nagin, and he too was in search of *any* slam-dunk PR victory). This so-called agreement was between Holy Cross, the archdiocese, FEMA, and SHIPO—a classic case of the foxes guarding the henhouse. A photo accompanying the "agreement" article showed the Holy Cross board chairman, Bill Chauvin, speaking at a press conference with a beaming Landrieu and a sheepishly smiling Archbishop Alfred C. Hughes in the background. This "agreement" itself was in reality worthless because the National Trust for Historic Preservation and the Friends had *vociferously* protested its terms and conditions throughout the Section 106 Review.[37] No portion of the church was to be saved, except for perhaps the cross atop the steeple; a small

garden perhaps would be placed where the majestic altar once stood. FEMA was mandated to archive historical photos and drawings only.[38]

Jim Logan, attorney for the Friends, shot a letter (not published) to Jim Amoss, editor in chief of the *Times-Picayune*:

This morning's paper quotes [Hurricane Katrina] recovery czar Ed Blakely as saying that nothing is more important than preserving New Orleans' unique qualities, that "Maintaining the city's distinctiveness is the first order of business," and that in rebuilding any city, "It's very important to take care of its heart." Yet barely two pages earlier, the paper reported that the historic and architecturally significant Cabrini Church was considered an "obstacle" to rebuilding and that people "felt great" about its slated demolition . . . [however] the Gentilly neighborhood grew up around it with Cabrini at its heart.

Cabrini Church has recently garnered international support as people, watching the city's rebuilding effort, recognize it as special and unique, just as New Orleans is special and unique. But apparently this doesn't matter—we're supposed to feel good that perhaps a few trinkets are saved before this landmark is needlessly torn down. It's a sorry day, indeed, for preservation in New Orleans. This matter was poorly handled from the start. The Archdiocese acted too hastily to close a viable parish and structurally sound church. Holy Cross School stubbornly refused to adapt its plan to build at a location where both a church and a school have existed already for many decades. FEMA says its hands were tied—that it had *no influence* over this multi-million dollar, publicly funded project, since all it does is write the checks. And the State's Preservation Office, the supposed guardian of our historic legacy—well, it just whipped the historic review process into overdrive and inadvertently ended up as a key champion for the church's demise. There's a dangerous, false dichotomy afoot: it's being argued that for the city to rebuild, it has to demolish, that we can't have one without the other. *Wrong.* The reality is this: when buildings like Cabrini Church are torn down, we lose a bit of our historic core, and we lose a bit of the very soul of the city. Or, to paraphrase Mr. Blakely, the city will have just suffered a heart attack, only we won't know it until it's too late.[39]

However, a few days later the newspaper did publish a letter of rebuttal to its one-sided coverage, albeit a strategically edited one (see the italicized portion at the end of the original letter as added by this author). The writer was Nathaniel "Buster" Curtis's widow, Frances Curtis:

The "Agreement" between Holy Cross/Archdiocese of New Orleans/FEMA regarding St. Frances Cabrini Church apparently is whatever conforms to the desires of the powers that be, including the press, the broadcasting industry, the political establishment, and any others who are unwilling to hear the truth. To heck with a church, any church, the neighborhood only needs a school for boys ages 10–17, who will be bused in daily from the entire metropolitan area and the North shore to spark a building boom, they say. These shortsighted people are willing to demolish beauty for a tasteless pseudo nineteenth century architectural campus when they could have had both for the asking.

As far as the "devastated" church is concerned, the *only* damage from Katrina was to the mechanical equipment. In their haste to "remove" the building (did someone instruct Leslie Williams [in a recent article in the *Times-Picayune* on the church battle] to avoid the word "demolish" so much for semantics?) the contractors hired by Holy Cross, in order to avoid a possible Section 106 Review, carelessly damaged the eight-ton marble altar, the beautifully designed baptistery, the invaluable stained glass and, of course, the irreplaceable solid Honduras mahogany pews so callously bulldozed [Fig. 6.17]. Honduras mahogany is no longer available in any quantity, the slow growing trees having been decimated by the lumber interests. This wood was used in PT boats during WWII and is no stranger to water. It is found today only in fine antiques. Had FEMA not been forced to step in at the eleventh hour in compliance with the law, the church would have become a pile of rubble with nothing left to review (exactly what they intended) and suddenly those who wanted to save the church became "obstructionists." Did the SFC parishioners have anything to say about all of this? Of course not! They were locked out of their church with heavy chains from the beginning.

The so-called leaking roof was repaired eighteen months *before* Katrina with the finest roofing materials

6.17: *Interior, St. Frances Xavier Cabrini Church, 1963.*

available. The thin-shelled concrete was covered with elastomeric, a roof coating of exceptional durability used by the aerospace industry and on many government and industrial buildings. And what happened to the $4.2 million dollar insurance policy owned and maintained by the congregation all those years? Is it sitting in a bank somewhere earning interest? Has the Archdiocese confiscated it? Is it being used to repair the many other churches that were grossly underinsured? No one will answer these questions.

And what will the congregation have to show for the funds they worked so hard to raise to erect the church? An empty patch of real estate, that's what, where Holy Cross has egregiously and pretentiously offered to display "memorabilia." [Author's note—The following concluding passage was cut from Ms. Curtis's letter.] *What gall. How despicable, outrageous and insulting. The school even wants to take over the cross from the top of the steeple. By what right? If it does so, surely it should become known as the "Unholy Cross." The controversy has been from the beginning a done deal. Is the "mitigating" factor on which FEMA doomed the church its size, really? Or was it political pressure exerted at the highest levels of government?*[40]

Interest in the battle by this time had reached far beyond war-torn New Orleans, fueled by a piece appearing in December 2006 in the *New York Times*, titled "In Tale of Church vs. School: A New Orleans Dilemma."[41] Many were now starting to weigh in. In an unpublished letter sent to Jim Amoss from Paris by Lois Frederick Schneider, a strong case was made for the church's international importance as a work of modernist liturgical architecture:

Just recently I learned that Mr. Frederic Migayrou, Chief Conservator for Architecture of the Centre Georges Pompidou, had written a letter to FEMA during the period (February 6–26) when it was receiving comments, recommending that this remarkable architectural accomplishment be preserved. There has been a tragic deficit of communication between FEMA and the citizens of New Orleans. FEMA, intent on pursuing its action concerning the church, with Holy Cross School and the Archdiocese, did not appear to realize that the church could concern other New Orleans and Louisiana citizens attentive to the conservation of their patrimony. The church has been described by experts as a monument of extraordinary historical significance internationally, primarily because of its extraordinary structure of three cantilevered roofs designed by the structural engineer John Skilling, creator

of the ill-fated Twin Towers destroyed in New York on 9/11. After Al Qaida, do New Orleans citizens *really* want to be next to destroy a John Skilling masterpiece?

I know that your primary concern is your subscribers, and that is natural, but you must realize that other Americans, and in particular New Yorkers, have a right to be sensitive about a building structurally designed by the same engineer as the Twin Towers. Mr. Barry Bergdoll, Chief Conservator for Architecture and Design at New York's Museum of Modern Art, wrote to Mr. Paulson, Director of FEMA in Washington, to urge his office to ensure this church is preserved, as it is a unique aesthetic and structural accomplishment. Too few in New Orleans seem to have been aware of this.

Other experts beyond the Centre Pompidou in France have expressed concern because of the special ties felt toward New Orleans. In fact, a delegation of the French Ministry of Culture was created for Aid to Reconstruction for New Orleans. Its Director, M. Pierre-Antoine Gatier, President of the International Commission for Monuments and Historical Sites (ICOMOS France), the Chief Architect for Historical Monuments in France, has stated that this remarkable church must be saved. Lastly, Professor Richard Longstreth, in his report, commissioned by FEMA, cited numerous reasons why Cabrini Church was exceptionally important.

Please bring these facts to the attention of your readers so that later they can not say that all this was concealed.[42]

In a letter sent to the Vatican that same month, Georgi Anne Brochstein, a member of the Friends of SFC Church and the widow of Hamilton Frederick, one of the talented designers of Cabrini Church while at Curtis & Davis in the early 1960s, pleaded for last-minute intervention to remove Cabrini from the equivalent of architectural death row. The letter was addressed to "Most Reverend Mauro Piacenza":

Many of the Friends of Cabrini are second and third generation parishioners. This matter is both personal and intimate and extremely painful. It is because they continue to ask questions and request documentation that things come to light. Friends of Cabrini received copies of documents that indicate the reason given for the destruction of St. Frances Xavier Cabrini Church is based upon the "catastrophic damage to the church reported by Archbishop Hughes." This could not be further from the truth.

Rome has been either misled or lied to. Rome needs to take another good look at this before the destruction is allowed to take place. When the truth is exposed no one in this is going to be able to say that they were unaware that there was a discrepancy or that what looks like a conspiracy was some sort of misunderstanding. The Archdiocese's own experts put the damage to the church in the range of one million dollars, with no damage to the roof or structure whatsoever. It was during attempts to circumvent the (FEMA) Section 106 Review that work-men in haste caused at least another one million dollars in damage. Are you aware that these workmen bulldozed the irreplaceable Honduran Mahogany pews? Only when knowledgeable architects began questioning the Archdiocese's actions did the Archdiocese begin to recompute the damage estimates with constantly inflated figures.

Now the Parish finds itself in the incredible position of being made the "guilty" party in that the Archdiocese says *it isn't* tearing down the church. Holy Cross won't accept the property with the church still on it and now the Archdiocese is going to bankrupt the Parish by billing the Parish for its demolition. This is unbelievable. The Arch-diocese padlocked the doors and wouldn't let the parish-ioners in to clean, then the Archbishop deconsecrates the church, then the Archdiocese bills *the Parish* for the demo-lition. This is an outrage. Someone needs to step in and put a stop to this because the truth is coming to light. Any logical person has no choice but to conclude that no priest and no money and no church equal no Parish. When the truth comes out New Orleans will be horrified as will the rest of the Nation.[43]

At the same time, Archbishop Hughes was to be seen on local television gleefully talking about the importance of reopening flood-damaged churches other than Cabrini, including the nearby, far more damaged Resurrection of Our Lord Church.[44] Dr. Earthea Nance, of the mayor's Office of Recovery Management, remained silent. Dr. Nance was the city's rebuilding representative at the table during the FEMA Section 106 consultative meetings, and she represented Dr. Ed Blakely, the recently hired, jet-setting, highly compen-sated director of the city's Office of Recovery Management.[45] Blakely was widely referred to in the local press as Nagin's erstwhile recovery czar. Dr. Blakely, too, had apparently been muzzled by the city's Catholic machine establishment. By late April it was too late to save Cabrini. Intensely adverse public and political pressure stirred up a campaign designed solely to destroy a landmark church as a means to save a school. The conquering forces had been recalcitrant and had acted surreptitiously from the start. Ditto a punch-drunk, unquestioning local media. Jarvis DeBerry continued to slam the "obstructionists," dismissing them as maybe well inten-

tioned but very wrong to have slowed down the recovery of *his* neighborhood (before Katrina, he lived in a house directly across the street from where Holy Cross plans to build a football and baseball stadium, and his various pieces on the Cabrini issue will definitely not win him any national awards for unbiased investigative journalism).[46]

Tragically, the battle to save the church had been spun to the public and the local media from the start as a didactic either-or proposition rather than a *both-and* possibility. For FEMA's part in this saga, its unfortunate decision to cave in to misguided local political pressure became part of a larger and more dangerous pattern in post-Katrina New Orleans.[47] As for Blakely's silence, the demise of Cabrini Church flew directly in the face of the recovery czar's oft-stated goal of restoring valuable community and civic assets (such as churches) and to use them as key rebuilding elements in the city's most damaged neighborhoods. The church's senseless destruction would henceforth severely undermine Blakely's credibility among preservationists, and soon he himself would be lampooned by columnist James Gill in the local daily paper for his repeated disparaging remarks (always made in far-flung locales at conferences and to news media) toward the city and its citizens. However, no one dared to publicly castigate Blakely for his or his staff's callous indif-ference to the obvious value of keeping Cabrini Church.[48]

On April 27, the Friends of Cabrini filed two lawsuits. The first was filed in civil district court against the Archdiocese of New Orleans and the City of New Orleans. The second was filed in federal court against FEMA. On that same day, our attorney, Jim Logan, appeared before Judge Yada Magee and requested a temporary restraining order (TRO) to imme-diately halt the demolition until a trial date could be set. Although the judge seemed to be sympathetic to our cause, Holy Cross and archdiocese attorneys appeared at the hear-ing along with several political figures who objected, and the judge backed down from granting the TRO. The premise of the lawsuits maintained that the demolition paperwork was issued without proper authority of ownership. This was because the Congregation of St. Frances Cabrini Church, the church's legal owners, had not officially voted to sell their property and church to Holy Cross or the Archdiocese. Since a corporate resolution had not yet taken place to sell either the church or its land, and because the demolition permit was issued in the name of the Archdiocese of New Orleans and not the rightful ownership entity, the demolition permit had therefore been issued to a fraudulent third party.

Second, the lawsuit cited two additional technical points in the city's building codes and permitting laws that had not been met by the fraudulent third party seeking to demolish

Cabrini: no rodent-inspection permit was on file, and, additionally, the parcels of land being in effect stolen by this third party on behalf of Holy Cross School were in fact three separate tracts. These consisted of the St. Frances Xavier Cabrini Elementary School, the Parish Life Center and Rectory, and the parcel occupied by the church. Each was a separate tract according to city records dating from the early 1950s. In their reply to our TRO request, archdiocesan attorneys insisted that the proper corporate resolution had already taken place and that all necessary paperwork was in order. Denial of the TRO was based on a mere (untrue) verbal assertion at the hearing that all paperwork was already in order.

Meanwhile, the archdiocese and Holy Cross were engrossed behind closed doors in a furious game of catch-up. They knew they were being broadsided yet again by the enemy, but they had prevailed thus far on purely emotional public arguments, i.e., "It was best for the city." On May 10, before Judge Ernest Jones, a court hearing was held for a preliminary injunction in civil district court. At this hearing, archdiocesan attorneys were singing a new tune, stating that the corporate resolution had taken place *two days* before this court date, invalidating what had been falsely stated before Judge Magee only thirteen days earlier. In spite of the judge's regret and his good wishes that we should move on to appeals court, our request for a TRO was denied yet again.

On Tuesday, May 22, we returned once again, this time seeking a trial and again requesting that the demolition permit be pulled, which would allow us to have landmark designation confirmed through the local governing board, the Historic District Landmarks Commission. The HDLC unfortunately by this time also appeared to have been silenced on the matter of Cabrini Church by certain local political interests. Its pat reply to our plea for support was that it would have to wait in the very long queue of buildings the HDLC was researching for landmark eligibility, and that a vote by the HDLC might not occur for six months or more. Meanwhile, the National Trust had been approached by the Friends to enter the lawsuits as a coplaintiff with us, but it declined, despite the strong recommendation of its lead attorney assigned to the case. The issue of joining the lawsuits reached the desk of the head of the National Trust in Washington, but he appeared to have been dissuaded (muzzled?) by a certain Louisiana-based politician. The Southern Region office of the trust, based in Charleston, South Carolina, was similarly powerless to assist, as was its local representative in New Orleans, Walter Gallas.

The granting of the TRO would, we believed, have given the federal court time to rule on our request for a second (and hopefully balanced, this time) Section 106 Review for

landmark status, and would have allowed the church to survive or at the very least to get off architectural death row. Unfortunately, in spite of his best intentions, Judge Jones was overinfluenced by the unwaveringly staunch opposition, and he allowed the fraudulently obtained demolition permit from nearly eight months earlier to remain in force. On Tuesday, June 5, at 4:15 PM, the full-scale demolition of the church commenced. On the following morning, Jim Logan rushed back to federal court—the U.S. District Court for the Eastern District of Louisiana—to once again obtain a TRO. Again he was denied. That same morning yet another one-sided article ran in the *Times-Picayune* on the demolition, followed a month later by yet another distorted article on Holy Cross's exit from the Ninth Ward and its relocation to Gentilly as the be-all and end-all panacea for Gentilly's resuscitation.[49] The next morning we taped two TV segments in front of the demolition site, which aired that evening locally, calling for a halt to the demolition. I shot a photograph of the church with the baldachin still standing, and Jim Logan hurriedly e-mailed it to FEMA, Holy Cross, the National Trust, and anyone else who might have a say in its last-second reprieve.

The courts, sadly, allowed the demolition permit to remain in place, despite both legally sound arguments and facts that showed the opposition was clearly operating recklessly, even at times outside the bounds of Roman Catholic canon law. This had occurred from at least October 2006. We continued to maintain publicly that at the very least an orchestrated pattern of misinformation had begun while Katrina's floodwaters were still inside the church.

At this time the Cabrini Church Parish Council learned that the parish's financial coffers had been totally drained by the archdiocese. In an ultimate irony, these funds were being applied to the now $780,000 cost of demolishing the church. Could it be that the parishioners were now paying for the demolition of their own church? Incredibly, this appeared to be the case. Meanwhile, we had been trying to contact the Vatican to intervene to save the church. On April 11, we finally received (through the local archdiocesan office) a letter from Rome dated March 17, 2007, which was based on a letter of November 2006, pertaining to our request for the Congregation for Clergy to begin a full investigation into the "sale" of Cabrini and its land and the intended demolition of the church. Meanwhile, in order to make his case to the Vatican against Cabrini Church, Archbishop Hughes elected to travel to Rome for a personal meeting with the Pontifical Commission, which took place in Rome on March 14. The outcome of this meeting was recounted in a letter dated May 15 to Georgi Anne Brochstein, from the commission's president, Monsignor Mauro Piacenza, who is based in Rome.

On April 24, we had appealed to the Apostolic Signatura for intervention, through something called a Partition of Administrative Recourse, a request we fully expected would be approved, based on recent precedents in similar canon-law cases involving historic Roman Catholic churches around the world. This request for an investigation remained open at this writing, since we hoped the Vatican would render an opinion on the unnecessary demise of Cabrini Church because incomplete and misleading information was provided to the Vatican.[50] The Friends had been requesting a meeting with Archbishop Hughes since November to discuss the church. Exasperated, the Friends sent the archbishop a three-page letter dated May 3, 2007. This was still five days before the full-scale demolition work would begin on the church itself (before the Friends' court actions). In it, we refuted each and every claim he had apparently made to Msgr. Piacenza when he was in Rome. We presented the facts about the church's structural integrity, its historic status as a work of architecture on an international scale, the closing of the parish accounts, the demonstrated feasibility of building Holy Cross School alongside the church, the archdiocese's poaching of the $4.2 million flood policy held by the parishioners on their beloved church, and how human hands have damaged this "Cathedral of the Lakefront" far more seriously than Katrina did.[51]

Some weeks after the church was gone, the archbishop had the gall to request a meeting with members of the Friends group, including me. We declined, for obvious reasons. On June 28, 2007, nearly a month after the church was reduced to dust and rubble, the archbishop sent a bland, curt response letter in which he repeated his standard position on the matter.[52]

We were from the start always playing catch-up. Always working to string the dots together to make sense of the facts. If not for us, the Section 106 Review would not have occurred. Perhaps most troubling, we learned too late that the congregation had the right itself to initiate the appeals process with Rome, with or without the blessing of its Parish Council. In retrospect, it appeared we had been misled by a local deacon into believing that such action could be initiated only by Cabrini Church's Parish Council. Worse, an outspoken supporter of the archdiocese–Holy Cross compact sat on the Cabrini Council (it is naïve to assume that no subtle or overt intimidation of the other council members took place).

Thus, a piece of property the archdiocese did not technically own was sold to Holy Cross School, which insisted that the church must be eradicated in an act of cultural cleansing. This occurred before formal completion of the Vatican's internal appeals process in such matters under canon law.

As for the U.S. courts, at this writing the Friends' federal suit against FEMA remained open and may or may not be heard sometime in the future.

Architectural Landmarks, Place Attachment, and Cultural Cleansing

Voltaire once said that it was dangerous to be right in matters on which the established authorities are wrong. Unbridled power is an intoxicant. The Roman Catholic Church in New Orleans behaved egregiously in the case of Cabrini Church and in fact engaged in a conspiracy to eradicate Cabrini Parish and all of its assets, save for a few salvaged artifacts that are now somewhere in storage. The parishioners were told that these artifacts would be incorporated into a new Cabrini Church. But no one is holding his or her breath for that to occur in our lifetimes. Shockingly, all this took place at the parishioners' expense. Characteristically, the archdiocese and Holy Cross PR machines would later claim they merely had struggled to "do the right thing" in a difficult situation (this rationalization, "do the right thing," was by this point being invoked ad nauseam in post-Katrina New Orleans). Expediency, however, is an equally dangerous intoxicant, a poor justification upon which to make a claim to rebuild any city, let alone a ruined city as extraordinary as New Orleans. Why rebuild a city by first unbuilding its key landmarks? This, coupled with the denial of tradition, memory, and place, amounted to cultural cleansing. Rumor and myth had raged uncontrollably. For its part, Holy Cross saw this as a once-in-a-lifetime opportunity. Sadly, its abandonment of its old neighborhood was responded to entirely too late by the Holy Cross Neighborhood Association. What was to happen to them? Weren't they being left by the side of the road? In June 2007, Holy Cross struck a deal to open a state-run recovery district school in its abandoned buildings. This was yet another clever tactic for Holy Cross to get taxpayers to pay for the cleanup of its flooded seventeen-acre campus. Moreover, at the same time it issued a request for proposals to private developers for schemes to profitably redevelop the old campus.

Cabrini's senseless destruction was also a win-win for FEMA, as seen from within its ranks. The agency clearly abused its oversight powers in looking for a quick-and-easy PR fix that would turn aside the tidal wave of hostile local sentiment. As for FEMA's payout to the school, the $24 million question remained, "Why did the unbuilding of a landmark place of worship have to occur?" This debacle proved if nothing else that the art of compromise had been entirely cast aside in Katrina's aftermath. Watching this, would others now be emboldened to try the same tactics?

When I returned full time to New Orleans after Katrina, in December 2005, it was not in my plans to become a preservation warrior. Yet a diverse band of knowledgeable and equally determined colleagues and I found ourselves thrust into the front lines. None of us had experience in preservationism per se, but we knew that if we didn't help, who would? We were the foot soldiers, by default. Social scientists might refer to our field method as participant observation, although to us the alternative was unconscionable. To passively sit on the sidelines would have been spineless in such dire circumstances. Fortunately, Katrina created a small but determined cadre of new street fighters battling for the life of their city. Sadly, these battles require well-trained foot soldiers and new waves of reinforcements periodically because the rate of "Katrina burnout" is high. My fear is that there are too few souls willing to take on the myriad inevitable skirmishes and full-scale confrontations that lie ahead. It is difficult to challenge a political machine as entrenched as an archdiocese, a venerable Catholic boys school, the major local daily newspaper, the federal government, and the lieutenant governor, let alone all five at once.

The Future

This sad tale need not repeat itself in future post-disaster rebuilding efforts in twenty-first-century America. Six cautionary provisos briefly outlined below may help guide interested parties toward a simultaneously passionate and compassionate approach to reconstructing ruined cities:

BE ENGAGED

It is useless to stand on the sidelines in a time of great urban turmoil and upheaval, especially whenever cultural cleansing rears its ugly head. Get personally involved, if possible, in saving your city, your neighborhood, and places of importance to you. This can be difficult, because in the eyes of many, you are damned if you leave the setting of the disaster (by those who return and stay), and nearly equally damned if you stay (by those who left and never returned). It is an act of civic disingenuousness to expect others to stick their necks out while you stand silently by and watch.

DO NOT TRUST POLITICIANS TO SAFEGUARD THE BUILDINGS AND PLACES THAT YOU VALUE

It is senseless and foolhardy to look to your local elected political leaders for rational leadership. This is especially true when it comes to architectural preservation. In post-disaster contexts, nothing is considered sacrosanct, whether the "cleansing" target is a modernist masterpiece or a funky vintage neon sign atop an old brewery. It is probably prudent

to expect the worst and hope for the best. It is naïve to expect that otherwise rational people will think and act rationally in uncontrollable, irrational situations.

BE WARY OF OUTSIDE EXPERTS

It can be naïve to over-rely on prestigious "experts" from afar, since, first, they do not have knowledge of the inner profundities of the challenges at hand, and, second, they will probably be dismissed by the locals as out-of-touch outsiders (witness Blakely and a parade of others before him, and even Longstreth). In the case of post-Katrina New Orleans (as with the torpedoed BNOB excursion), the term *carpetbagger* was frequently whispered by locals behind the backs of "just trust me because I am here to help you" northern "experts." Worse, such experts may unknowingly advocate "cleansing" without realizing it.

STRIVE TO OVERCOME BARRIERS OF RACE AND CLASS

Everything in New Orleans in one way or another seems to eventually come down to deep-rooted racial and class inequities. Post-disaster planning can degenerate into a tug-of-war between the haves and the have-nots, and the "flooded" versus the "unflooded." In New Orleans's case, as was broadcast to the entire world, life and death was determined by geography—those who lived on low ground suffered far worse than those who lived on high ground. The "cleansing" of low-lying neighborhoods, whether intentionally through a premeditated process of land reclamation and redevelopment, or otherwise, became a subject of intense debate as the city's raw scabs continued to be revealed to the nation and the world.

AVOID COUNTERPRODUCTIVE GRIDLOCK AND PARALYSIS THROUGH OVERANALYSIS

Conflicting constituencies with conflicting political agendas for rebuilding can and will cancel one another out if allowed the opportunity to do so. This will result in reconstruction gridlock. This pattern dominated the first three years of life post-Katrina and was most often the direct result of the aforementioned acute political-leadership vacuum, particularly at the city and state levels of government.

BE AWARE THAT RECOVERING FROM A SEVERE DISASTER IS THE SAME AS RECOVERING FROM A WAR

It is prudent to equate the post-disaster rebuilding of a city with rebuilding after a war. Everything is a struggle, and nothing is built or saved except through the sheer will and determination of someone or some group. In an age of skyrocketing federal deficits, Middle East tensions, and increasing competition from rising superpowers such as China, do not look to the federal government for any type of windfall of post-disaster funds for reconstruction. To some critics, New Orleans was a postindustrial welfare state long before Katrina. However, there is some reason for optimism: since 1990, many Armenian churches in Iran and the Republic of Georgia have been restored using state funds. The Georgian restorations occurred after independence from the Soviet Union, long after Stalin had destroyed eighty churches in the region in a premeditated act of "cleansing."[53]

History's record of violent acts against architecture and against the survival of historically significant cities has been well documented and remains a catalogue of repeatedly broken sociocultural contracts in which individual liberties are sacrificed to a domineering new order.[54] Doctors, lawyers, engineers, pop musicians, writers, historians, and many others have all played a role in helping alleviate the chronic human and physical suffering wrought by the alarming acceleration of wars and natural disasters in recent years. And the recent (July 2007) Live Earth global concert extended this movement into the realm of global warming. *But where have the architects been in all this?* A focus on aesthetics per se, rather than on ethics and engagement, and on the making of form per se, rather than on any genuine interest in its societal or environmental ramifications, only ensnares us in a self-perpetuating, vacuous architectural discourse that remains dangerously confined to the ranks of a small professional elite class.

Esther Charlesworth argues that architects miserably failed to provide effective reconstruction strategies for cities polarized by ethnic and economic conflict after World War II.[55] She proposes that architects should work as part of interdisciplinary teams (as in the case of the battle to save Cabrini). Second, she urges that any planning processes should be incremental and not governed by abstract, top-down bureaucratic machines. In the case of Cabrini, the core group of activists included an accountant, an attorney, architects, business owners, close relatives of the building's designers, the surviving founding partner of the firm that designed the building, a journalist, neighbors, parishioners of all ages, a nurse, parish rights activists, and a freelance historian. We were drowned out by a large chorus of ill-informed naysayers uninterested in hearing anything about compromise, uninterested in hearing any both-and possibilities. As for Charlesworth's second point, the hyperaccelerated pace of the scheme from the start, the reckless FEMA Section 106 Review, the Catholic PR machine, and local and state politicians' desperation to demolish "yesterday" made

meaningful discourse next to impossible. Of course, that had been their intent from the outset.

What was achieved by working so hard to save Cabrini Church? The church was granted a stay of execution of eight months. Big deal. Yet beyond this, maybe local awareness of the importance of saving the city's twentieth-century architectural landmarks will be slightly greater from here on out. But it will be a long struggle. The public's very low level of education on architecture in general was a major impediment in the battle to save Cabrini Church. Neighbors bizarrely thought the church's value to be less than that of their own ruined homes across the street: "Gee, my house is older than forty-three years old, so why can't my house also be listed on the National Register?" "It doesn't look the way a church is supposed to look." "Jobs and neighborhoods are more important than saving a church." "People are more important than bricks and mortar." "Tear down the church and build the school because at least it is more than the government is doing to help us." And so on.

Around midnight on the evening of June 6, while standing in front of the church in its then partially demolished state, a group of the Friends formed a new organization, the Council on the Protection of Parishes, or COPP. We vowed to do what we could to make sure this would not happen to other churches in post-Katrina New Orleans or in other post-disaster communities across the United States.

The both-and possibilities of preservation—versus a knee-jerk tear-down-to-rebuild-fast mentality—need to be positioned front and center in post-disaster architectural discourse. This and other hard lessons learned in Katrina's aftermath need to be told for the benefit of people elsewhere engaged in the battle to preserve collective memory and to hold onto the meaning of important places. This applies to a landmark modernist church as much as to a vintage roadside diner. The victims of disaster in other places need to know what can happen if no one stands up to fight. Yet how does one decide what to stand up for? In the battle over Cabrini Church, the term *silent majority* was turned on its head as an army of heretofore "nonexpert" passive observers (pre-Katrina) were manipulated, post-Katrina, into becoming a lynch mob of misinformed screechers for whom any sort of compromise was wholly unthinkable. Shame on all of you who worked to bring about the senseless loss of Cabrini Church and its parishioners' cultural and spiritual legacy.

Conclusion

This tale has been about how the first three years of life after Katrina were similar to the aftermath of a war. Excessive private and public turf struggles, animosity, mistrust, institutional greed, and the denial of cultural legacies defined the first three years of reconstruction. They were about the eradication of collective memory and the triumph of placelessness over place making. This period was too often about personal and civic loss, institutional arrogance, and blind institutional opportunism.[56] As Mat Schwarzman put it: "In an increasingly homogenized, corporatized, simulated world, the extent to which this rebuilding process can save what's authentic and positive about New Orleans, while improving the circumstances of our residents, will say a lot not only about this city, but the general direction of our society. I hope the world pays full attention."[57]

Buildings are about emotion, memory, and spirit as much as about bricks and mortar. The preservation of collective memory requires a willingness to reflect, recollect, and think rationally. Cultural cleansing denies this. It was no accident that in 2006 the entire city of New Orleans was added to the World Monument Fund's list of most endangered places on the planet.[58]

Even the Internet search engine Google was guilty of attempting to expunge New Orleans's collective consciousness. In April 2007 the search engine once again was showing the city in ruins in the aerial maps posted on its Web portal. A few days earlier, Google had come under heavy fire for replacing post-Katrina images on its popular site with views of the city and the Mississippi coast as they existed before Katrina. After an Associated Press article highlighted the changes, a U.S. House of Representatives subcommittee accused Google of "airbrushing history" and thereby insulting the memory of storm victims.[59]

Katrina is perhaps the only national disaster in United States history whose effects may have been profoundly and repeatedly understated, despite virtually wall-to-wall media coverage of its immediate aftermath. The extent of the wreckage—mile after mile of darkened windows and trash-strewn landscapes—was simply too far-reaching to be captured on video, in photos, or in words. The amount of uninsured damage alone topped $55 billion (as of December 2007), greater than that from Hurricane Andrew, the World Trade Center attacks, and the Northridge earthquake combined. More than 124,000 homes were destroyed or severely damaged.[60] This statistic itself would prove to be an underestimate. By July 2007, more than 150,000 applications were on file with Louisiana's tedious, much-maligned, federally funded Road Home program.

Three-plus years out, uncertainty reigned. The flood-protection system remained nowhere near being guaranteed to hold up in a category 4 or category 5 hurricane. Many experts, both near and far, were convinced that the city's lack of political leadership and its many false starts in the planning process were the main reasons for the city's lethargic pace of recovery. The city had truly become delirious, but in the negative sense. In just a single week in May 2007, three examples of this syndrome dominated local conversation. First, NBC aired a national piece on the hazards to human health posed by the ubiquitous FEMA travel trailer, while FEMA itself on the same day publicly offered to sell a used trailer to anyone for as little as $650. That same week, the New Orleans Redevelopment Authority was granted unprecedented local power to accumulate and redevelop abandoned homes, but no funds whatsoever were provided by the city or any other governmental source for staffing or property acquisition. Third, recovery czar Ed Blakely was finally lampooned by the local newspaper as being out of touch, arrogant, ineffective, and overcommitted; yet on the day the column appeared, he was out of town (once again) to receive praise at a national planning conference for his heroic "brilliance."

To favor the basest of economic priorities in the rebuilding of a city as important as New Orleans is to deny New Orleanians their rich and unique cultural legacy. No public relations campaign alone could rebuild New Orleans's shattered image in the eyes of the nation and world. However, this was precisely what was being attempted.[61] By contrast, rebuilding needed to occur transparently and democratically. As in a war, individual freedoms had been serially lost, and wholesale acts of aggression had been perpetrated against a victimless built environment, a built environment that could not stand up to defend itself.[62] Three years after Katrina, invading forces—whether they took the form of the Roman Catholic Church, a big-box developer, an arrogant private school, FEMA, HUD, an overzealous and ill-informed neighborhood organization, or even Google—appeared more than willing to impose a new order. As for the continued assault on modernism, death row included the Pan American Life Building, the State of Louisiana Supreme Court Building, and the State of Louisiana Office Building. Memorable buildings, places, and artifacts of a suddenly discardable past were now subject to degradation and destruction—and with each loss a part of New Orleans's extraordinary heart and soul was gone forever (Fig. 6.18).

6.18: *Demolition of St. Frances Xavier Cabrini Church, 2007.*

Notes

Part 2

1. Malcolm Heard, *French Quarter Manual* (Jackson: Univ. Press of Mississippi, 1997). Many excellent guidebooks have been written on the city's mainstream architectural treasures. See Eve Zibart, *The Unofficial Guide to New Orleans*, 4th ed. (New York: Wiley, 2003). Samantha Cook's *Rough Guide to New Orleans*, 2nd ed. (New York: Rough Guides, 2001), focuses on the city's indigenous cultural amenities and mentions many architectural landmarks. I fondly recall an informal conversation from more than twenty years ago. It occurred only a few weeks after I had moved to New Orleans, although it remains as vivid as if it had taken place yesterday. It was with Eugene Cizek, a colleague I admire greatly for his vast knowledge of the city. I listened to him describe at some length a New Orleans neighborhood and its patterns of growth in the late '20s and early '30s. It was not until near the end of his detailed narrative that I realized he was referring to the 1820s and 1830s, not the 1920s and 1930s. Having been born and raised in a city incorporated at the time he was referring to (Chicago, 1833), I was taken aback. I was an ingénue, an uninitiated *archi-cidental* tourist about to embark on a strange voyage, becoming immersed in a place with ancient roots by American standards. Without question, there was much to learn. Fortunately, this journey was greatly aided by the many insightful books on New Orleans architecture written by the late Samuel Wilson and others. It remains among the most written-about places in the United States. Also without question, the majority of written work on the architecture of the city has centered on the Vieux Carré.

2. Pierce Lewis, *New Orleans: The Making of an Urban Landscape* (Charlottesville: Univ. Press of Virginia, 2003). Also see Craig Colten, *An Unnatural Metropolis: Wrestling New Orleans from Nature* (Baton Rouge: Louisiana State Univ. Press, 2004); Richard Campanella and Marina Campanella, *New Orleans Then and Now* (New Orleans: Pelican Press, 1999); and Michael Brown, *Streetwise New Orleans* (Sarasota, Fla.: Streetwise Maps, 1997).

3. Lewis Mumford, *The City in History: Its Origins, Its Transformations, and Its Prospects* (New York: Harvest Books, 1968).

4. Richard O. Baumbach, *The Second Battle of New Orleans: A History of the Vieux Carré Riverfront Expressway Controversy* (Tuscaloosa: Univ. of Alabama Press, 1980).

5. Professor Cizek has become well known for his forays into the field with his architecture and preservation students at Tulane University. In 1998 he initiated a master of science degree program in historic preservation. He has received many national awards for his work, often in collaboration with Lloyd Sensat.

6. Samuel Wilson, Patricia Brady, and Lynn D. Adams, *Queen of the South: New Orleans in the Age of Thomas K. Wharton, 1853–1862* (New Orleans: Historic New Orleans Collection and the New York Public Library, 1999). The book contains Wharton's firsthand account of New Orleans's golden era, a time when fortunes were made and multiplied, the population doubled and redoubled, mansions and grand hotels were built, yellow fever raged, and armed men took to the streets during elections. The era ended abruptly with the outbreak of the Civil War and the capture of the city by the Union Army.

7. *Webster's Universal College Dictionary* (New York: Goldmercy Books, 2001), 726.

8. Chester H. Liebs, *Main Street to Miracle Mile: American Roadside Architecture* (Boston: Little, Brown, 1985). Interest in this quirky, idiosyncratic mode of architectural expression dates from a century earlier. See "Colossal Elephant of Coney Island," *Scientific American*, July 11, 1885, 21–27; and "World's Queerest Eating Places," *Science and Invention*, April 1931, 12–16.

9. Toon Michiels, *American Neon Signs by Day and Night* (New York: Idea Books, 1982). Also see Robert Swinnich, *Contemporary Beer Neon Signs* (Gas City, Ind.: L-W Books, 1994); John A. Jakle and Keith A. Sculle, *Fast Food: Roadside Restaurants in the Automobile Age* (Baltimore: Johns Hopkins Univ. Press, 1999); Len Davidson, *Vintage Neon* (Atglen, Penn.: Schiffer, 1998); and Colin Davies, "Lessons at the Roadside," *Architectural Research Quarterly* 8, no. 1 (2004): 27–37.

On motels, see John A. Jakle, Keith A. Sculle, and Jefferson Rogers, *The Motel in America* (Baltimore: Johns Hopkins Univ. Press, 1996).

On gas stations, see John A. Jakle and Keith A. Sculle, *The Gas Station in America* (Baltimore: Johns Hopkins Univ. Press, 1994). Also see Jakle, "The American Gasoline Station, 1920 to 1970," *Journal of American Culture* 1, no. 3 (1978): 520–542; John Margolies, *Pump and Circumstance* (Boston: Bullfinch, 1993); and Margolies's book of postcards, *Signs of the Times* (New York: Abbeville Press, 1993).

On travel lodges and resorts, see John Baeder, *Gas, Food, and Lodging* (New York: Abbeville Press, 1982). Also see Keith A. Sculle, "Oral History: A Key to Writing the History of American Roadside Architecture," *Journal of American Culture* 13, no. 3 (1990): 79–88; and Stephen Sears, *The Automobile in America* (New York: American Heritage, 1977).

On bizarre signs, see Jack Barth, Doug Kirby, Ken Smith, and Mike Wilkins, *Roadside America* (New York: Simon & Shuster, 1986). Also see Philip Langdon, *Red Roofs, Golden Arches: The Architecture of American Chain Restaurants* (New York: Knopf, 1986); and John Margolies, *Fun Along the Road* (Boston: Bullfinch, 1998).

On diners, see Richard J. S. Gutman, *American Diner: Then and Now* (Baltimore: Johns Hopkins Univ. Press, 2000). Also see Robert O. Williams, *Hometown Diners* (New York: Abrams, 1999); Michael K. Witzel, *The American Diner* (St. Paul, Minn.: Motorbooks International, 1999); and Randy Garbin, *Diners of New England* (New York: Stockpile Books, 2005).

On drive-ins and movie palaces, see Michael Putnam, *Silent Screens: The Decline and Transformation of the American Movie Theater* (Baltimore: Johns Hopkins Univ. Press, 2000). Also see Jenna Jones, *The Southern Movie Palace* (Gainesville: Univ. Press of Florida, 2003); Michael D. Kinerk and Dennis Wilhelm, *Popcorn Palaces: The Art Deco Movie Theatre Paintings of Davis Cone* (New York: Abrams, 2001); Ross Melnick and Andrea Fuchs, *Cinema Treasures: A New Look at Classic Movie Theaters* (St. Paul, Minn.: Motorbooks International, 2004); Maggie Valentine, *The Show Starts on the Sidewalk: An Architectural History of the Movie Theatre, Starring S. Charles Lee* (New Haven, Conn.: Yale Univ. Press, 1996); and Don Sanders and Susan Sanders, *The American Drive-in Movie Theatre* (St. Paul, Minn.: Motorbooks International, 1997).

10. Debra Jane, *Roadside Architecture*, http://www.agilitynut.com (accessed December 14, 2005).

11. John A. Jakle and David Wilson, *Derelict Landscapes: The Wasting of America's Built Environment* (Savage, Md.: Rowman and Littlefield, 1992). Also see Jakle, *The Visual Elements of*

Landscape (Amherst: Univ. of Massachusetts Press, 1987).

12. Jim Heimann, *California Crazy and Beyond: Roadside Vernacular Architecture* (San Francisco: Chronicle Books, 2001). Also see Sally Wright Cobb and Mark Willems, *The Brown Derby Restaurant* (New York: Rizzoli, 1996); David Gebhard, *Robert Stacy-Judd* (Santa Barbara: Capra, 1993); David Gebhard and Harriette Von Bretton, *L.A. in the Thirties* (Salt Lake City: Peregrine Smith, 1975); Robert Oberhand, *The Chili Bowls of Los Angeles* (Los Angeles: Los Angeles Institute of Contemporary Art, 1977); Charles Jencks, *Bizarre Architecture* (New York: Rizzoli, 1979); Steve Harvey, "Eating Away at Oddball Architecture," *Los Angeles Times*, July 20, 1985; Stacy Enders and Robert Cushman, *Hollywood at Your Feet: The Story of the World Famous Chinese Theatre* (Los Angeles: Pomegranate, 1992); and Beth Dunlop, *Building a Dream: The Art of Disney Architecture* (New York: Abrams, 1996).

13. Paul Hirshhorn and Steven Izenour, *White Towers* (Cambridge, Mass.: MIT Press, 1979).

14. "About the SCA," http://www.sca-roadside.org (accessed December 7, 2005). Established in 1977, the SCA is the oldest national organization devoted to the buildings, artifacts, structures, signs, and symbols of the twentieth-century commercial landscape. The SCA offers publications, conferences, and tours to help preserve, document, and celebrate the structures and architecture of the twentieth century: diners, highways, gas stations, drive-in theatres, bus stations, tourist centers, neon signs, and related places and artifacts. Membership includes four annual newsletters, two issues of the journal published by the SCA, and tour information. Also see "Great American Roadside," *Fortune*, September 1934, 35–43; J. D. Reed, "Tacky Nostalgia? No, These Are Landmarks," *Time*, December 11, 1989, 41–43; Philip S. Gutis, "Roadside Relics of Early Auto Days Are Being Saved," *New York Times*, September 3, 1987; Daniel P. Gregory, "Billboard Buildings," *Sunset*, November 1992, 21–24; and David Blanke, "Signs in America's Auto Age: Signatures of Landscape and Place," *Journal of Popular Culture* 38, no. 5 (2005): 957–958. In Japan, roadside commercial vernacular architecture has also been examined. See Yoshinobu Ashihara's excellent bilingual book, *The Aesthetics of Tokyo: Chaos and Order* (Tokyo: Ichigaya, 1998).

15. "About the National Trust," http://www.nationaltrust.org (accessed December 7, 2005). Founded in 1949, the National Trust for Historic Preservation is a private nonprofit membership organization dedicated to saving historic places and revitalizing America's communities. Staff at the Washington, D.C., headquarters, six regional offices, and twenty-six historic sites work with the trust's 270,000 members and thousands of preservation organizations in all fifty states. The organization's mission is to provide leadership, education, advocacy, and financial resources.

16. In 2003 this structure was adapted to a Whole Foods grocery store, with a considerable amount of architectural panache, despite major opposition from neighbors.

17. Wilson, Brady, and Adams, *Queen of the South*, 114.

18. Joan E. Fisher, *Automobile and Culture* (New York: Abrams, 1984).

19. George Lipsitz, *Time Passages: Collective Memory and American Popular Culture* (Minneapolis: Univ. of Minnesota Press, 1988).

20. Richard Longstreth, *City Center to Regional Mall: Architecture, the Automobile, and Retailing in Los Angeles, 1920–1950* (Cambridge, Mass.: MIT Press, 1997). Also see Longstreth, *The Drive-in, the Supermarket, and the Transformation of Commercial Space in Los Angeles, 1914–1941* (Cambridge, Mass.: MIT Press, 1999); and Karal Ann Marling, *The Colossus of Roads: Myth and Symbol along the American Highway* (Minneapolis: Univ. of Minnesota Press, 1984).

21. Recently, the medical and public health communities have publicly adopted antisprawl positions on the grounds that long commutes and sedentary suburban lifestyles contribute to excessive rates of heart disease and obesity among Americans in nearly every age group. See special issues of the *American Journal of Public Health* (September 2003) and the *American Journal of Health Promotion* (September 2003).

22. Philip Collier, with J. Richard Gruber, Jim Rapier, and Mary Beth Romig, *Missing New Orleans* (New Orleans: Ogden Museum of Southern Art / University of New Orleans, 2006).

23. Baumbach, *Second Battle of New Orleans*, 87–104.

24. Robert Venturi, Denise Scott Brown, and Steven Izenour, *Learning from Las Vegas* (Cambridge, Mass.: MIT Press, 1972). Six years later, Charles Jencks published his seminal *The Language of Post Modern Architecture* (New York: Rizzoli, 1978). These author-architects were the first to feature examples of American roadside commercial vernacular in their books. Jencks included a photograph of the Tail o' the Pup hotdog stand in Los Angeles.

25. Ellen's Kitchen, "King Cake 2001," http://www.ellenskitchen.com (accessed June 21, 2006).

26. Eric Ulken, "World's Longest King Cake Takes a Lot of Baking," http://www.nola.com/mardigras/food/?longestkingcake.html (accessed January 6, 2008).

27. Collier et al., *Missing New Orleans*, 168.

28. Blake Pontchartrain, *Gambit Weekly*, "New Orleans Know-it-All," http://www.nola.com (accessed June 20, 2006). *Gambit Weekly* has now moved to bestofneworleans.com, and Pontchartrain's column can be found at http://www.bestofneworleans.com/dispatch/current/blake.php.

29. Andrew Hurley, *Diners, Bowling Alleys, and Trailer Parks: Chasing the American Dream in the Postwar Consumer Culture* (New York: Basic Books, 2001).

30. Michael Tisserand, "Mid City Lanes," *Bowler's Journal*, November 1992, 100–102.

31. "A History of Frostop," http://www.frostop.com (accessed December 10, 2005).

32. Alan Hess, *Googie Redux: Ultramodern Roadside Architecture* (San Francisco: Chronicle Books, 2004). Hess's earlier book, *Viva Las Vegas* (San Francisco: Chronicle Books, 1993), paid homage to the vintage architecture and signage of the casino strip.

33. Rally's, "Company History," http://www.fundinguniverse.com/company/histories (accessed June 20, 2006).

34. AFC Enterprises, Inc., "Popeye's: Our History," http://www.popeyesgulfcoast.com (accessed June 20, 2006).

35. Ground Pat'i Corp., "History of Ground Pat'i International, Inc.," http://www.ground-pati.com (accessed June 20, 2006).

36. Smoothie King, "The Smoothie King History," http://www.smoothieking.com (accessed June 18, 2006).

37. *Webster's Universal College Dictionary*, 494.

Part 3

1. Henry Glassie, *Pattern in the Material Folk Culture of the Eastern United States* (Philadelphia: Univ. of Pennsylvania Press, 1969). Also see Glassie, *The Spirit of Folk Art*, 2nd ed. (New York: Abrams, 1995); and Glassie, *Vernacular Architecture* (Bloomington: Indiana Univ. Press, 2000).

2. Terry G. Jordan and Matti Kaups, "Folk Architecture in Cultural and Economic Context." *Geographical Review* 77 (1987): 52–75.

3. Stacy C. Hollander, "A Place for US: Vernacular Architecture in American Folk Art," Traditional Fine Arts Organization, Inc., http://www.tfaoi.com/aa/5aa/5aa74.htm (accessed January 7, 2008).

4. William Ferris, ed., *Afro-American Folk Arts and Crafts* (Jackson: Univ. Press of Mississippi,

1983). The discussion centers on quilt making, instrument making, and folk architecture.

5. By this time, being situated along a rail line became as vital to a community's cultural development, including its folk-architecture traditions, as being situated along a major waterway had been only a few years before.

6. Dell Upton and John Vlach, eds., *Common Places: Readings in American Vernacular Architecture* (Athens: Univ. of Georgia Press, 1986).

7. Dr. Bob, "About Bob," http://www .drbobart.net (accessed January 7, 2008).

8. UCM Museum, http://www.ucm@ ucmmuseum.com (accessed January 7, 2008). The online tour of the museum is an excellent introduction to founder Preble's offbeat vision of a folk-architecture dystopia.

9. Terrance Osborne, http://www .galleryosborne.com/catalog/statements. php?menu=3 (accessed January 7, 2008).

10. Common Ground, "Mission and History of the Common Ground Collective," http:// www.commongroundrelief.org/mission_and _vision (assessed January 7, 2008).

11. Hansen's, on Tchoupitoulas Street near the riverfront, is among the most famous in the city, because in 1939, according to local folklore, Ernest and Mary Hansen invented an ice-shaving machine that replaced the old method. There is some dispute, however, whether the Hansens or George J. Ortolano was the actual inventor. This is where myth and fact become blurred, as often happens in New Orleans folklore.

12. Ortolano continued to modify his early wooden machines. Incorporating knowledge gained through his shipyard experience, he developed new models built of galvanized metal and, later, stainless steel, and marketed them to enterprising entrepreneurs throughout New Orleans and beyond.

13. SnoWizard, "History," http://www .snowizard.com/history (accessed January 7, 2008).

14. No Limit began its ascent to fame with Master P's *The Ghetto Is Trying to Kill Me!* (1994) and subsequent hits by Rappin-4-Tay (*Don't Fight the Feeling*, 1994), Silkk the Shocker (*Charge It 2 Da Game*, 1998), and C-Murder (*Life or Death*, 1998). Corey Miller, aka C-Murder, was arrested and charged with killing sixteen-year-old Steve Thomas with a single gunshot to the chest during a dispute at a club in Harvey, Louisiana. In 2003 he was found guilty of second-degree murder, which carried a mandatory life sentence. Despite incarceration, he managed to release an entire album (*The Truest Shit I Ever Said*, 2004) and a music video, without the knowledge of prison authorities.

15. This label was cofounded by brothers Ronald "Suga Slim" Williams and Brian "Baby" Williams in 1991. By the end of the 1990s, it was the preeminent label in southern rap. Its biggest stars were the members of the Hot Boys: Terius Gray (aka Juvenile), Lil' Wayne, The B.G., and Turk. Juvenile and many other fellow rappers were born and raised in the Magnolia housing project in Uptown.

16. "B.G. Explodes Back on the Hip Hop Scene," http://www.rapnews.net/ 0-202-260722-00.html (accessed January 7, 2008).

17. "Gangsta Rap," http://en.wikipedia.org/ wiki/Gangsta_rap (accessed January 7, 2008).

18. Nolan Strong, "Details in Soulja Slim Shooting," http://slumz.boxden.com/ showthread.php?t=652424 (accessed January 7, 2008).

19. "Seventh Ward Neighborhood Snapshot," Greater New Orleans Community Data Center, http://www.gnocdc.org/orleans/4/14/ snapshot.html (accessed January 7, 2008).

20. "Tremé/Lafitte Neighborhood Snapshot," Greater New Orleans Community Data Center, http://www.gnocdc.org/orleans/4/42/ snapshot.html (accessed January 7, 2008).

21. Ibid.

22. Katy Reckdahl, "Best Reason to Drive 'Downstairs,'" *Gambit Weekly*, August 31, 2004, http://www.bestofneworleans.com/dispatch/ 2004-08-31/cover_story6.html (accessed January 7, 2008).

23. Reid Mitchell, *All on a Mardi Gras Day: Episodes in the History of New Orleans Carnival* (Cambridge, Mass.: Harvard Univ. Press, 1995). Also see Michael P. Smith, *Mardi Gras Indians* (New Orleans: Pelican Press, 1984).

24. Mitchell, *All on a Mardi Gras Day*, 30.

25. Dena J. Epstein, *Sinful Tunes and Spirituals: Black Folk Music to the Civil War* (Urbana: Univ. of Illinois Press, 2003). For further discussion of the history of African American visual and musical culture in America, see Shane White and Graham White, *Stylin': African American Expressive Culture from its Beginnings to the Zoot Suit* (Ithaca, N.Y.: Cornell Univ. Press, 1998).

26. Mitchell, *All on a Mardi Gras Day*, 31.

27. Ibid., 127.

28. "Traditional Mardi Gras Returns to Claiborne Avenue," *Louisiana Music Archive and Artist Directory*, February 9, 2004, http://po88 .ezboard.com/flouisianamusicarchivemardi-grascentral.showMessage?topicID=1495.topic (accessed January 7, 2008).

29. He crossed over into the pop mainstream with "Ain't That a Shame" (1955), although, as was common at the time, it took

a white singer, Pat Boone, to have a number one hit with a cover of the song. Domino proceeded to release an unprecedented string of thirty-five Top 40 singles, including "Whole Lotta Loving," "Blue Monday," "Walking to New Orleans," "I'm Walkin' (Yes, Indeed, I'm Talkin')," and a funky version of the old ballad "Blueberry Hill."

30. His induction into the Rock and Roll Hall of Fame and an invitation to perform at the White House failed to cause Domino to make an exception to his no-travel policy. He does, however, make annual appearances at the New Orleans Jazz and Heritage Festival as well as at certain other special events in the city.

31. Roger Friedman, "Fats Domino Missing in New Orleans," September 1, 2005, http:// www.foxnews.com/story/0,2933,168122,00 .html (accessed January 7, 2008).

32. Kevin Krolicki and Nichola Groom, "Fats Domino Returns Home to New Orleans" (Reuters), October 15, 2005, available at http:// www.redorbit.com/news/general/272803/ fats_domino_returns_home_to_new _orleans/ (accessed January 7, 2008).

33. While the World's Fair was regarded as an artistic and aesthetic success, its financial failure seemed to have left a permanent stain. It took the external resources of a national hotel chain to rescue the piazza from becoming the world's first postmodern ruin (it was finally restored in 2004). The twenty-five-year period of architectural stagnation, commencing with the closure of the fair, is discussed in greater detail in the following section.

34. Marissa Bartolucci, "Power," *Metropolis*, December 1994. Also see Richard Moe and Carter Wilkie, *Changing Places: Rebuilding Community in the Age of Sprawl* (New York: Holt, 2002).

35. Mary Foster, "Ruined City Is Still Picturesque," *Times-Picayune*, October 10, 2005.

36. In theory, whites' avoidance of black neighborhoods was no different from what it was fifty years ago. Only then, avoidance was sanctioned and enforced by Jim Crow laws. Recently, the problem has worsened because of the deleterious effects of a subculture dominated by drugs and the associated turf-war rivalries between thugs. In post-Katrina New Orleans, fifty-six murders were committed between January 1 and June 1, 2006. This prompted Governor Blanco and Mayor Nagin to once again send in the National Guard to police the city. One hundred fifty heavily armed troops arrived on June 20. They were assigned to the least populated areas of the city, including Gentilly, New Orleans

East, Lakeview, and the Lower Ninth. These neighborhoods experienced the worst flooding and were now plagued by the looting of ruined houses and houses in the process of being repaired. Troops were still on patrol in these neighborhoods in mid-2008.

Part 4

This chapter's narrative foundation has been inspired by and has drawn from the writings of Carol Flake and James Gill, two observers who have together come closest to capturing the essence of this key portion of a complicated story. I am greatly indebted to them for their critical insights.

1. Chris Erskine, "Upbeat Notes from a City That's Down but Not Out," *Los Angeles Times*, http://www.latimes.com/travel (accessed September 23, 2005).

2. Carol Flake, *New Orleans: Behind the Masks of America's Most Exotic City* (New York: Grove, 1994). By 2000 the city had withered to 485,000 people from a peak of 627,000 in 1960. Louisiana had been shrinking as well; between 1995 and 2000 it was the only state in the nation to lose population. During a period of record high immigration in the rest of the country, New Orleans's total of Hispanic and Asian-born residents did not change at all in twenty years. By contrast, New Orleans has the nation's highest percentage, 77 percent, of native-born residents of any large metropolitan area in the nation (18).

3. Kate Moran, "Shrinking City," *Times-Picayune*, October 23, 2005, http://www.nola.com (accessed October 24, 2005).

4. John Logan, "Nurture Social Ties to Bring City Back," *Times-Picayune*, November 25, 2005. The situation in Louisiana was not much better. Louisiana fell to the bottom of the fifty states in 2002 in all three measures used by the Corporation for Economic Development (CED) in Washington, D.C., which studies and compares state economies and their prospects for growth. In the 2002 report, using a scale of A to F, Louisiana scored Fs in all three core CED categories: economic performance, including such measures as employment, earnings-job quality, equity of income, quality of life, and use of the state's resources; development capacity, a measure of the quality of workers through education, financial resources available for businesses, and other factors, such as the number of doctoral scientists and engineers, households with computers, university research grants, and patents issued to inventors in the state; and business vitality, measured by such factors as the competitiveness of existing businesses, the number of new and entrepreneurial firms, and the diversity of the state economy. At the other end of the study's spectrum were five states that earned As in all core categories: Colorado, Connecticut, Massachusetts, Minnesota, and Virginia (Alan Sayre, "State Economy Bottoms Out in Study," *Times-Picayune*, December 18, 2002).

5. Mel Leavitt, *A Short History of New Orleans* (San Francisco: Lexikos, 1982). For this reason, architects and students of architecture must conjure the motivation to learn all they can about the past lives of a site and its neighborhood context. Such methodologies can yield a tremendous amount of information about the inhabitants' social status, race, and perhaps even their political predilections.

6. Pierce F. Lewis, *New Orleans: The Making of an Urban Landscape*, 2nd ed. (Charlottesville: Univ. of Virginia Press, 2003). Often, more data on land transactions are available in Louisiana compared to most other parts of the United States. This is the result of the civil law system, a system based on the Napoleonic code. This code, historically, required more information than was required by civil legal codes in the other forty-nine states.

7. Ibid., 49.

8. Leavitt, *Short History of New Orleans*, 87.

9. Craig E. Colten, *Transforming New Orleans and Its Environs: Centuries of Change* (Pittsburgh: Univ. of Pittsburgh Press, 2001); also see Colten, *An Unnatural Metropolis: Wresting New Orleans from Nature* (Baton Rouge: Louisiana State Univ. Press, 2004). Also see Jeffrey Kluger, "Global Warming: The Culprit?" *Time*, October 3, 2005, 42–46; and Don Melvin, "Dutch Are Spending Billions in Their Defense against the Sea," *Milwaukee Journal Sentinel*, September 25, 2005.

10. LaNitra Walker, "More than Black and White," *American Prospect Online*, http://www.prospect.org (accessed September 10, 2005). She added:

Not all black people in New Orleans are poor. The city has a substantial population of middle-class blacks and Creoles, as well as people of mixed-race background. Because of its geographic proximity to the Caribbean islands and its history as an outpost in the French and Spanish empires, New Orleans has become as rich and culturally mixed as its famous gumbos and jambalayas. In the years following the Haitian revolution, which raged from 1791 to 1894, black slaves and French slave owners sought refuge in New Orleans, bringing new ideas about race and class to our budding nation. In addition to these refugees, thousands of free blacks, known as "free persons of color," lived in New Orleans in the nineteenth century. Many of these blacks were educated and owned property, and some even owned slaves. The mixture of landowners of French, Spanish, Indian, Acadian, and African descent created a middle class of Creoles who have helped to define New Orleans' culture.

11. John M. Barry, *Rising Tide: The Great Mississippi Flood of 1927 and How It Changed America* (New York: Simon & Shuster, 1997).

12. Lolly Bowean, "In New Orleans, Land Elevation Was a Matter of Race, Experts Say," *Kansas City Star*, http://www.kansascity.com (accessed September 26, 2005). Dozens of homes went underwater in The East that could have contained valuable letters, portraits, and other artifacts from generations ago, as well as invaluable documents on the period of slavery and Reconstruction.

13. Richard Sexton, *New Orleans: Elegance and Decadence* (San Francisco: Chronicle Books, 2000). Also see Frederick S. Starr, *Southern Comfort: The Garden District of New Orleans* (San Francisco: Chronicle Books, 2001).

14. Flake, *Behind the Masks*, 72.

15. Ibid., 22.

16. Ibid., 24.

17. Certain underlying assumptions have perpetuated this culture: the city would remain poor but picturesque; the supply of musical and artistic talent was replenishable; the Vieux Carré would remain both a national architectural treasure and a gaudy tourist trap; well-connected interests would be able to sway elected officials to build inappropriate buildings, e.g., Harrah's Casino on Canal Street at the river; outside investors would be able to purchase properties that locals could no longer afford; and the shrinking yet entrenched Uptown enclave of Mardi Gras bluebloods would always dominate New Orleans society.

18. Leonard V. Huber, *Mardi Gras: A Pictorial History of Carnival in New Orleans* (Gretna, La.: Pelican, 1977).

19. Mardi Gras actually began first in Mobile, Alabama, and is celebrated to some extent in a number of other cities, but in New Orleans the conditions proved ideal for incubating a permanent carnival culture.

20. Flake, *Behind the Masks*, 5.

21. Ibid., 7.

22. The bickering that ensued over the ordinance threatened to escalate into a divisive social and political conflict that opponents thought would forever disfigure, perhaps even destroy, the blithe, giddy façade of Carnival that had endured for a century and a half. This battle was also over the heart and soul of a city—the dwindling base of power centered in New Orleans—plagued with a rising crime rate, deteriorating housing stock, and an epidemic of white flight.

23. Flake, *Behind the Masks*, 8.

24. In the end, after eight hours of arguing and heated rhetoric, the ordinance passed unanimously, 7–0, with the three white members of the city council voting in favor.

25. This spirit is so captivating that one becomes drawn into it, unknowingly, even against one's will at times.

26. Flake, *Behind the Masks*, 171.

27. An indicator of how completely Carnival dominated the traditional social power structure: between 1920 and 1970, the total percentage of new blood brought into the Krewe of Comus was less than 1 percent. Some observers were writing newspaper columns about a conspiracy of social control held tightly over the entire population by the elite white krewes, even if this was just a self-fulfilling civic myth.

28. Until 2007 the city was subdivided into seven tax assessment districts, each with its own elected tax assessor. This has led to wildly uneven tax assessments within and between districts over the generations. Most large American cities have a single tax assessment office or commissioner, aided by external consultants. Remarkably, New Orleanians in 2007 voted to condense the tax assessor offices into a single citywide office. Soon after the vote, all properties in Orleans Parish were reassessed. More than 5,000 property owners protested their higher reassessments. It was a classic case of "Be careful—you just might get what you wish for."

29. Flake, *Behind the Masks*, 45.

30. Meanwhile, in the aftermath of the fair, critics charged that the self-absorbed social elites turned even further inward and left the majority of the population to fend for itself. Making matters worse, the white egocentric social elite of the uptown Mardi Gras subculture offered few new ideas for the city's future, since their immediate neighborhoods, while threatened by the crime epidemic that was overtaking the entire city, appeared to be under control for the time being. This attitude persisted up to the day Katrina struck. It was as if the course of events had inevitably reached a turning point, leading to an attitude of learned helplessness. A few within these cultural substrata privately acknowledged that

new partnerships were desperately needed across neighborhoods and across social, racial, and economic class boundaries. These persons were tied by blood or marriage to the city for economic and social reasons.

31. Flake, *Behind the Masks*, 60.

32. Carnival was canceled during the Civil War, and following a brief resumption during Reconstruction, it was again canceled in 1875, following the clash between the Crescent City White League, a paramilitary and political coalition, and the metropolitan police, a largely black force then under the control of Republican carpetbaggers. Although the White League won the "Battle of Liberty Place," federal troops arrived immediately thereafter to restore civil order. In 1891, an obelisk to commemorate the battle was dedicated on Canal Street. David Duke once marched around it, chanting, "White power!" He and other racists often referred to it as a rallying point. For blacks, on the other hand, the monument symbolized the legacy of Jim Crow. In 1989 it was removed to a nearby side street. See Samuel Kinser, *Carnival American Style: Mardi Gras at New Orleans and Mobile* (Chicago: Univ. of Chicago Press, 1990).

33. Flake, *Behind the Masks*, 160.

34. James Gill, *Lords of Misrule: Mardi Gras and the Politics of Race in New Orleans* (Jackson: Univ. Press of Mississippi, 1997), 57.

35. This club and others like it followed the precedent of the northern clubs until the outbreak of the Civil War, when the issue of slavery divided clubs in the North as well as the South. By the 1880s, this club had become synonymous with the city's small, elite ruling class, highly restrictive in its membership. It was as if a form of social Darwinism was in operation—only the fittest would survive (Flake, *Behind the Masks*, 233).

36. Monisha Sujan, "A Sad Aftermath of Katrina: Perpetuating Poverty," http://www .blogforamerica.com (accessed September 23, 2005). This neighborhood was leveled by the storm surge of Katrina.

37. "Blake Pontchartrain: New Orleans Know-It-All," *Gambit Weekly*, August 13, 2002, http://www.bestofneworleans.com (accessed June 12, 2006).

38. Ibid.

39. AIA New Orleans Chapter, "Bywater," *A Guide to New Orleans Architecture* (2005), http://www.neworleansonline.com (accessed December 15, 2005).

40. Gill, *Lords of Misrule*, 143:

New Orleans was probably the filthiest and least salubrious city in the Union, while

government starved the public schools of money, ensuring that the populace would remain largely ignorant and illiterate. Recovery from the economic depression of 1873–1877, which had ruined many a rich man and sent Garden District values into precipitous decline, was slow. The vigorous entrepreneurial spirit of the pre–Civil War era seemed to have been dissipated, and the Anglo-Americans now joined the Creoles in posing as the refined products of a vanished civilization that put them above vulgar commercialism . . . in race relations, the city continued to move steadily backward. Gangs of underfed black convicts, leased to construction and levee companies, labored under such brutal conditions that they died in appalling numbers . . . the few remaining pockets of interracial association disappeared from New Orleans in the 1880s.

41. Leonard V. Huber, *New Orleans: A Pictorial History from the Earliest Times to the Present Day* (New Orleans: Pelican, 1971).

42. The city seemed to bask in a state of relative delirium, as if it were intrinsically better to not be like any other American city. The question loomed: Could uniqueness alone continue to function as a sufficient prerequisite for this self-imposed autonomy from mainstream America?

43. Gill, *Lords of Misrule*, 241:

Carnival sympathizers' fondest wish—that Comus, Proteus, and Momus might one day return to the streets—now seemed unlikely. The main problem occurred when krewes continued to delude themselves that their parades were meritorious in their own right. However, the supposed beneficiaries no longer saw it that way. They were feeling patronized. Carnival was seen as a smokescreen, obscuring deep fissures in the civic life of the city. Some members even complained of a backlash of blacks against whites, and to some extent this was true. This makes some sense when viewed against the broader social context of the descendants of slaves' seeking reparations from the federal government. The old-line view was dying: the masses in the streets were no longer grateful to the krewes as their great benefactors. The old-line organizations have played a major role in perpetuating the delirious view that the South sustained a great civilization until it was destroyed by the evil, aggressive North.

44. Many of these people attended Tulane as undergraduates and later earned a graduate degree from an Ivy League school. These fortunate sons (very few daughters) would return to New Orleans with the intellectual "endorsement" credential of a prestigious East Coast university, combined with the best undergraduate education New Orleans could provide.

45. Because the architecture schools at Tulane and LSU were segregated until the 1960s, the only source of trained black architects in the state was Southern University, in Baton Rouge. Southern, a historically black school, graduated a small number of highly talented architects, who then would return to the city to embark on careers, but remained locked out of the city's real power circles.

46. Flake, *Behind the Masks*, 205.

47. Jason DeParle, "What Happens to a Race Deferred?" *New York Times*, September 4, 2005, http://www.truthout.org/docs (accessed September 19, 2005). Anyone who knew New Orleans knew that danger lurked behind the festive façade. Let the good times roll, the tourists on Bourbon Street were told. Unusually poor, with 27.4 percent living under the poverty line in 2000, the Big Easy was also disproportionately murderous, with a rate that was for years among the nation's highest. Thirty-five percent of black households did not own a car, compared to just 15 percent for white households.

48. Dru Oja Jay, "The Battle of New Orleans: Race, Class Disparity Set Stage for New Orleans Disaster," *Dominion*, September 3, 2005, http://www.dominionpaper.ca (accessed September 19, 2005). Also see John Lewis, "This Is a National Disgrace," *Newsweek*, September 12, 2005, 52.

49. Susan Cutter, "The Geography of Social Vulnerability: Race, Class, and Catastrophe," *Understanding Katrina: Perspectives from the Social Sciences*, September 29, 2005, http://www.understandingkatrina.ssrc.org (accessed September 30, 2005).

50. Moran, "Shrinking City," October 23, 2005.

51. Susan L. Cutter, Bryan J. Boruff, and W. Lynn Shirley, "Social Vulnerability to Environmental Hazards," *Social Science Quarterly* 84, no. 1 (2002): 242–261.

52. Gordon Russell, "New Orleans, 77054," *Times-Picayune*, October 10, 2005, http://www.nola.com (accessed October 10, 2005). Also see Audrey Singer, *The World in a Zip Code* (Washington, D.C.: Brookings, 2005); James Dao, "No Fixed Address," *New York Times*,

September 11, 2005; and Gwen Filosa, "I Came to See What God Had Done," *Times-Picayune*, October 28, 2005, http://www.nola.com (accessed October 28, 2005). Critics asserted that physical vulnerability must be reduced through the construction of disaster-resistant buildings, changes in land use, the restoration of wetlands and floodways, and a marked reduction in social vulnerability. These steps were seen as prerequisite, even if they resulted in a more compact urban footprint, fewer profits for developers, and a smaller tax base.

53. Editorial, "New Orleans Revisited," *USA Today*, December 1, 2005, http://www.usatoday.com (accessed December 4, 2005). Also see Nicole Gelinas, "Who's Killing New Orleans?" *City Journal*, Autumn 2005, http://www.city-journal.org (accessed October 31, 2005).

54. Lynne Jensen, "Trailer Confusion Abounds in City," *Times-Picayune*, December 12, 2005, http://www. nola.com (accessed December 12, 2005). An editorial on the corrosive effects of racism and classism in New Orleans's resurrection clearly stated their potential threats to the city's future ("The New Xenophobia," *Times-Picayune*, December 3, 2005, http://www.nola.com [accessed December 3, 2005]).

55. Logan, "Nurture Social Ties to Bring City Back."

56. Cutter, Boruff, and Shirley, "Social Vulnerability to Environmental Hazards," 257.

57. Jonathan Alter, "How to Save the Big Easy," *Newsweek*, September 12, 2005, 53.

58. Michael Sorkin, "After the Flood: Rebuilding the Physical and Social Fabric," *Architectural Record*, October 2005, http://www.archrecord.construction.com (accessed October 14, 2005).

59. Manuel Roig-Franzia, "If New Orleans Is a Blank Canvas, Many Are Poised to Repaint," *Washington Post*, September 14, 2005, http://www.washingtonpost.com (accessed September 18, 2005). Also see Julia Reed, "Hope in the Ruins," *Newsweek*, September 12, 2005, 58.

Part 5

1. Inga Saffron, "A Planner's Historic Opportunity, Impossible Task," *Philadelphia Inquirer*, February 19, 2006, http://www.philly.com/inquirer (accessed June 1, 2006). A well-respected planning firm from Philadelphia, WRT, developed a detailed report, which in part recommended that the lowest-lying, most flood-prone neighborhoods of the city should be abandoned and converted to green space. This ignited a firestorm of controversy,

and the ramifications of the commission's recommendations were reported widely in the national and international media. The local newspaper, the *Times-Picayune*, and its editorial writers agreed, and urged the city to adopt WRT's ideas. The city, they wrote, can't wave a magic wand and return New Orleans to its pre-Katrina state; what it can do is embrace a responsible plan for redeveloping a great city.

2. This consistent inconsistency, or flip-flopping, extended to his views on the army of FEMA trailers descending upon the city. Sometimes he would give one opinion on the "footprint" debate over the trailer villages when speaking to a predominately white audience in the morning, and then give a contrary opinion on the same issue to a predominately black audience later that same day. The absence of visionary or even decisive leadership on these critical issues during this early period of stabilization was, to laypersons and to planning and design professionals alike, seen as worrisome, quixotic, and exasperating. As of 2008, the situation had improved little in this regard.

3. Before Katrina, Mayor Nagin was not known as being particularly versed or even interested in urban planning, architecture, or historic preservation. He portrayed himself as a business executive—nothing more, nothing less. Many critics saw this as a profound irony: a mayor of one of the most historic cities in America appeared to be blind, or the equivalent of tone-deaf, to the built environment. The catastrophe would do little to alter his predisposition on these matters, unfortunately. While this apparent indifference will undoubtedly be the subject of books and symposia for years to come, space is insufficient here to go into great detail on the inner profundities of the strange period of paralysis that descended upon the city as a result of the political indecisiveness and sheer ineptitude exhibited by the city's elected politicians, particularly in the aftermath of the debacle involving the Bring New Orleans Back urban planning committee.

4. These events were sponsored by private donations solicited under the auspices of the newly created Louisiana Recovery Authority (LRA). The LRA, created in the immediate aftermath of Hurricanes Katrina and Rita in 2005, is a quasi-public state agency mandated to distribute the $10.2 billion in federal Community Development Block Grant (CDBG) funds distributed through the U.S. Department of Housing and Urban Development, as approved by Congress in 2006 and 2007. These funds were intended for the rebuilding of the region's devastated housing and urban infrastructure. The first charrette was conducted in the Lake Charles region, in areas affected by Rita; a second charrette occurred soon thereafter in Vermillion Parish, an area hit hard by both Rita and Katrina; a third was conducted in St. Bernard Parish, and a fourth in the Gentilly neighborhood in New Orleans. St. Bernard and Gentilly were devastated by twelve feet and more of floodwater from Katrina. See the Web site http://www.lra.gov for additional information on the LRA.

5. Andres Duany, Elizabeth Plater-Zyberk, and Jeff Speck, *Suburban Nation: The Rise of Sprawl and the Decline of the American Dream* (New York: North Point, 2000). The scope of devastation was something that Duany had never encountered in his years of planning communities across the United States. This fact he openly admitted to his audiences and to the charrette participants. The tenets of the charter of the Congress for the New Urbanism advocate walkable, compact neighborhoods, corner stores versus convenience stores, main street versus shopping malls, traditional land-use zoning versus current zoning laws, traditional town planning versus suburban sprawl, and by extension, they reject the suburban roadside strip, since it is the main conduit through which sprawl propagates. To many architects, design and planning professionals, and laypersons, this polemic seems like common sense, and this is why the New Urbanism became the poster child in the United States for "smart growth" over the past decade. However, when set against the sheer scale of ruin in post-Katrina New Orleans, this polemic appeared to be overwhelmed and unconvincing, even naïve. To be sure, the surreal atmosphere created by the charrettes was largely due to the intense urgency of the region's immediate housing crisis, the depopulation and snail-paced repopulation of the city and its hardest-hit suburbs, continuing uncertainties surrounding the ineffective and tattered federal levee system, and the profound lack of political leadership on planning issues. Duany's design for a "Katrina Cottage," an affordable mass-produced house prototype, of which one was built in the Wal-Mart parking lot in Chalmette in early 2006, was the closest he came to acknowledging the harsh reality of the ubiquitous yet barely inhabitable, faceless FEMA trailer. It was hard to take seriously his images of bucolic streetscapes rendered in pastels, grand fountains, and canals with promenades and light-rail systems when most people in the audience remained tragically homeless and at wit's end.

6. In the neighborhoods where the charrettes were held, the streets were nearly impassable, filled with the stench of litter and mountains of post-flood debris; any convenience store was a welcome sight, no matter what it looked like aesthetically; drinkable water was welcomed over a vision of a grand fountain in the center of a new town square; and the return of natural gas and electricity service was viewed especially as an act of grand civic munificence.

7. Most units are manufactured by the following thirteen domestic suppliers: Keystone, Forest River, Jayco, Adventurer, Fleetwood, Zinger, Gulf Stream, Thor Industries, Cross Roads, Sun-Ray, Sunline Coach, R-Vision, and Coachman. The various manufacturers were contracted to build the two basic prototype models: the Deluxe FEMA Trailer, for installation on multiple-unit sites, and the Standard Travel Trailer, for installation on private residential sites. The former type contains a full kitchen and a full-size washer and dryer. The latter type consists of two rooms, is straight tongue (not pop out or fifth wheel), and is 29–35 feet long. The subcontractor transported its trailer units from the manufacturer's plant to the distribution yard in Texarkana, Texas, or to other staging yards, including those in Jasper, Texas, and Purvis, Mississippi. An assigned installation contractor then transported the unit to its final destination. The installation of the vast majority of units in New Orleans was completed by Bechtel, CH2M, Flour Enterprise, or the Shaw Group and its subcontractors.

8. Assigned prime contractors are also responsible for providing adequate underground sewage lines, a municipal sewer tap, the telecommunications power pole with meter, a 50-amp travel-trailer electric-power pole and meter loop, water-line winterization, and direct wiring to the well-pump switch. In addition, the prime contractor is responsible for any aboveground electrical excess capacity and for state and local permits, as well as for providing an additional 25-foot potable-water hose and a 5-kilowatt generator, directly burying the 50-amp service, and refilling the propane tanks as needed.

9. Based on data posted online by FEMA's PFO Logistics Unit at FEMA.gov. Meanwhile, thousands of the bland, colorless trailers sat idle in staging lots in Arkansas and Mississippi.

10. Keystone Corporation, *Cover America II: A New Direction*, http://www.keystonecorporation.com/ (accessed May 12, 2006).

11. Ibid., 12.

12. Jenny Hurwitz, "Little Matchboxes,"

Times-Picayune, November 13, 2005, http://www.nola.com/features (accessed May 28, 2006).

13. Laura Maggi, "It's No Place Like Home," *Times-Picayune*, April 12, 2006.

14. Jenny Hurwitz, "FEMA Trailers First Arrived as Hope on Wheels for Those Rebuilding, but Now They Seem to Bring More Frustration than Hope," *Times-Picayune*, April 23, 2006. By 2007, the trailers were being blamed for a host of physical ailments—including nausea, vomiting, eyestrain, muscle contractions, and sleep disorders—among occupants. After many stories appeared in the national media, FEMA finally launched a study of its own in late 2007.

15. Ibid. By June 2006, additional fires and propane-gas explosions had occurred, causing deaths; for example, a Slidell man died from an explosion caused by a propane leak inside his trailer.

16. Frustration often won out when people attempted to negotiate the phone-booth-sized bathrooms, head-skimming ceilings, and "efficiently" proportioned bunk beds. Other problems frequently cited included too-small hot-water tanks, flimsy particleboard cabinetry, and mattresses that quickly lost their firmness. Worse, as mentioned, the trailers were blamed for causing illnesses: many residents' eyes teared up after they sat in their trailers for too long. FEMA officials attributed this to toxic molding glue used in constructing the interior. As a result, many occupants had to keep the windows open for ventilation as often as possible. Claustrophobic quarters, combined with indoor-air-quality problems, including the omnipresent odor of sewage, forced many to limit their time indoors.

17. Keith Darcé, "Powerless, Residents Waiting for Trailers," *Times-Picayune*, January 14, 2006.

18. Karen Turni Bazile, "St. Bernard Getting 6,000 Trailers," *Times-Picayune*, January 24, 2006.

19. Michelle Krupa, "Trailer Sites," *Times-Picayune*, December 22, 2005.

20. Michelle Krupa, "Algiers Neighbors Fight FEMA Trailer Park," *Times-Picayune*, April 12, 2006.

21. Rob Nelson, "Nagin Halts Trailer Site Work," *Times-Picayune*, April 4, 2006.

22. Frank Donze, "Trailers Get the OK after Dust-up," *Times-Picayune*, April 27, 2006.

23. Jarvis DeBerry, "Afraid of Trailers—or What's Inside?" *Times-Picayune*, December 4, 2005.

24. Amy Liu, Matt Fellows, and Mia Mabanta, "Katrina Index: Tracking Variables of Post-Katrina Recovery" (Washington, D.C.: Brookings Institution, June 1, 2006), http://www.brookings.edu/ (accessed June 10, 2006).

25. Mike Von Fremd, "Finding the Christmas Spirit in New Orleans," *ABC News*, December 23, 2005, http://www.abcnews.go.com/ (accessed June 10, 2006).

26. Venturi, Scott Brown, and Izenour, *Learning from Las Vegas*.

27. J. B. Jackson, "Other Directed Houses," *Landscape* 6, no. 2 (1956): 29–35.

28. During my twenty-two years in New Orleans, I lived a few blocks from a small neighborhood shopping district. It included a convenience store, pizza parlor, health-food restaurant, card shop, drive-in, video rental store, gas station, parking lot, and a branch bank. It lacked a cohesive visual identity or theme, but this is just as Jackson would have preferred. It was a visual jumble of what at first appeared to be competing commercial interests, and yet lurking beneath the surface there was a remarkable degree of harmony and unanimity among the various storeowners. While far from cohesive from a purely aesthetic perspective, it possessed considerable meaning and virtue. This district took on six feet of floodwater in Katrina, and from all accounts will return as a viable shopping district. And in the process of overcoming extreme hardship, it will, one hopes, be stronger than before.

Throughout 2006, I was an active member of the Claiborne University Neighborhood Association (CUNA). This was one of the dozens of activist planning entities created by citizens on their own in the weeks after the disaster. We sponsored a successful urban-redevelopment design competition that was funded by a group of storeowners in the neighborhood. The area is now known as University Village. Many thanks to Jay Dufour and others for their hard work and continued leadership in 2008.

29. Helen L. Horowitz, "J.B. Jackson as a Critic of Modern Architecture," *Geographical Review* 88, no. 4 (1998): 465–473.

30. J. B. Jackson (as H. G. West, pseudonym), "Review of *Built in U.S.A.*, edited by H. R. Hitchcock and A. Drexler," *Landscape* 3, no. 1: 29–30.

31. Horowitz, "Jackson as Critic," 470.

32. Neil Campbell, "Much Unseen Is Also Here: John Brinckerhoff Jackson's New Western Roadscapes," *European Journal of American Culture* 23, no. 3 (2004): 217–231.

33. Horowitz, "Jackson as Critic," 468.

34. Mitchell Schwarzer, "J. B. Jackson's Writings," *Harvard Design Magazine* 6 (Fall 1998), http://www.gsd.harvard.edu/hdm (accessed June 10, 2006).

35. The scope of the devastation in New Orleans was vast. Heartbreaking scenes could be found, replete with bitter irony, all over the city. These were the vivid reminders of severe cultural and physical dislocation. How does a large American city start to rebuild itself? Four places to begin: construct a first-class levee system and work to restore Louisiana's vanishing wetlands; provide affordable housing in sustainable neighborhoods for the victims of the Katrina diaspora; create incentives for reinvestment and new investment in New Orleans; and, reinvent a public school system that was failing even before Katrina.

36. The scenario unfolds daily with respect to the uncertain road ahead regarding planning for the recovery and reconstruction of New Orleans. Calls for grassroots neighborhood planning initiatives are considered politically correct, but hidden even within these populist, so-called participatory agendas are the agendas of those who seek personal gain over the public good.

37. Blair Kamin, "Architecture Augments Don't Help Housing," *Metropolis*, April 2006, 43–45. Ideological catfights over housing and other facets of the rebuilding of New Orleans threaten to marginalize and undermine the work of all architects involved. Kamin writes, "Can we close the great divide between fetishistic formalism and social responsibility? Or are we doomed to a world in which architecture's leading practitioners use their work merely to comment on social tumult rather than actually trying to do something about it? Forget the rampant aestheticism and architectural blunders of the twentieth century. We live in a pluralistic age, and it demands a new pragmatism. We are beyond either/or—we live in a world of both/and . . . the issue is real urbanism, not some polite, politically palatable 'lite' version thereof. I'll take good urbanism, just like I'll take good modernism." Competing ideologies will cancel each other out. An excellent source to learn more of the background of the pros and cons of the ongoing bitter debate over New Orleans's future is "My Urbanism Is Better than Yours," by Alan A. Loomis. It is a review of a symposium held at the Harvard Graduate School of Design in 1999; see http://www.deliriousla.net/essays/1999-debates.htm (accessed April 21, 2006).

Part 6

The epigraph for this part was taken from K. Brad Ott, "A Healthcare Activist in New Orleans Tells the Story of Charity Hospital," *Breaking Ground* 3 (Winter 2007): 22–24.

1. City of New Orleans, Bring New Orleans Back Commission, *Final Report*, January 2006. Also see the Greater New Orleans Foundation, *Unified New Orleans Plan Final Report*, January 2006. The latter report yielded for the first time a set of somewhat clearer goals and priorities for infrastructural improvements, such as the city's decrepit sewage and water system, subterranean gas-line system, roads, and the restoration of essential city services, including schools, fire stations, community libraries, parks, police stations, and the like. The price tag was nearly $13 billion. No concrete method for financing the plan's recommendations was put forth, but the good news was that at least a citywide wish list had been articulated for the first time based on a (although appearances were deceiving in some instances) genuinely bottom-up, grassroots participation and the "buy in" of hundreds, even thousands, of New Orleanians, rather than the top-down methods that had permeated the earlier Bring New Orleans Back (BNOB) planning process. The Greater New Orleans Foundation was the clearinghouse for this second planning process. Along the way, a report called the Lambert Plan, started under the direction of the city council as a reaction to the BNOB report, was also worked on, but this in-between effort left out many "dry" neighborhoods, and so it too was denounced. The Unified New Orleans Plan's teams began their work in September 2006. More than a dozen teams of planners and architects were hired to carry out the planning process. The teams themselves were a loose confederation of local firms paired with national architectural and planning firms.

2. Architects, Designers, and Planners for Social Responsibility, "ADPSR Katrina Task Force Statement of Principles," http://www.adpsr.org/ (accessed January 17, 2008). In its Katrina manifesto, this organization argued for five planning and rebuilding principles: "establish community participation and control in the reconstruction processes; preserve communities; reconstruct a more equitable economy and grow social capital; design for long-term ecological stability; and act as public advocates and responsible professionals."

3. "Mother Cabrini," Cabrini Mission Foundation, New York, http://www.cabrinifoundation.org/About/cabrini.html (accessed January 17, 2008). According to the Web site: "Despite poor health and frailty, Mother Cabrini crossed the ocean 25 times during 29 years of missionary work, and with her sisters founded 67 institutions in nine countries on three continents—one for each year of her life. . . .

Her message [was] 'all things are possible with God.' . . . She was a progressive, strategic visionary, willing to take risks . . . In recognition of her extraordinary service to immigrants, Mother Cabrini was canonized in 1946 as the 'first American saint,' and was officially declared the Universal Patroness of Immigrants by the Vatican in 1950."

4. Gary Hymel, "St. Frances Cabrini Church Plans Dedication Sunday," *New Orleans States-Item*, April 19, 1963. See also "New St. Frances Cabrini Church to Be Dedicated," *Times-Picayune*, April 20, 1963; and "Cabrini Church Dedication Set April 21," *Clarion Herald*, April 18, 1963.

5. Notes from the personal diary and sketchbook of Nathaniel Curtis, 1964.

6. "New Cabrini Church Gets Cody's Praise," *New Orleans States-Item*, April 22, 1963. The photographer who took the interior photos, Frank Lotz Miller, remarked, "The lines of Cabrini Church are such that a whole book of pictures could be done on the church." Also see Bodil W. Neilsen, "Curtis & Davis," special issue of *Interiors*, February 1967, 101–134. Dozens of articles appeared in national professional publications on the work of Curtis & Davis in the 1960s and 1970s. The firm also won dozens of major design awards during this period and operated offices in New York and Berlin in addition to the base office in New Orleans.

7. In 2006, the HDLC received letters from, among others, Walter W. Gallas (National Trust for Historic Preservation, dated November 7), Stephen Braquet (AIA New Orleans Chapter, dated November 8), and Arthur Scully (freelance New Orleans historian; two, dated November 3 and November 17).

8. Stephen Verderber, "Landmark Gentilly Church Deserves to Be Saved," *Times-Picayune*, November 10, 2006.

9. "Holy Cross School," http://www .privateschoolreview.com/school_ov/school _id/11605 (accessed January 17, 2008).

10. Leslie Williams, "Study Sought for Church Being Razed for Holy Cross," *Times-Picayune*, November 10, 2006. The next day an editorial appeared, headlined "Too Late to Interfere." The day after that, a reporter whose ruined house was across the street from Cabrini and Redeemer-Seton High School again weighed in with a negative piece: Jarvis DeBerry, "Now You Tell Us? Controversy Over Razing 1963 Church Comes Out of Nowhere," *Times-Picayune*, November 12, 2006. A few weeks later, James Gill weighed in with an antipreservation piece on Cabrini, including a thinly veiled attack on me: "FEMA Swift to

Gum Up the Works," *Times-Picayune*, November 26, 2006. In the previous two weeks, a barrage of anti-Cabrini letters, but only a smattering of pro-preservation ones, had been published (only a small number of the "pro" letters sent to the editorial page were ever published).

11. "The No-Corridor School," *Architectural Forum* 98 (April 1955).

12. Peter Finney, Jr., "Cabrini Parishioners OK Holy Cross Talks," *Clarion Herald*, July 29, 2006. This propaganda article stated that parishioners of Cabrini Church voted "overwhelmingly" for a proposal that would allow Holy Cross to purchase the land occupied by the church. It was also publicly announced in this article that Holy Cross would demolish all buildings on the site. Also see "New Orleans Modern," *Fortune* 52 (April 1955); "New Orleans Architects Given Citation," *Times-Picayune*, October 10, 1956; "Schools Lead List of Design Awards," *New York Times*, June 17, 1954.

13. Alice Kottmyer to Bill Chauvin, November 13, 2006.

14. Milan Kundera, *The Book of Laughter and Forgetting* (New York: Knopf, 1980).

15. Robert Bevan, *The Destruction of Memory: Architecture at War* (Chicago: Univ. of Chicago Press / Reaktion Books, 2006).

16. Ibid., 43.

17. Ibid., 51.

18. Ibid., 64. Also see Reinhold Martin, "Architecture at War," *Angelaki: Journal of Theoretical Humanities* 9 (August 2004): 217–225.

19. No announcement of a vote on the fate of the church was publicized before this meeting. However, and to the surprise of many in attendance, a vote was announced—with a yes vote apparently indicating archdiocese approval to demolish the church, and a no vote indicating opposition to demolition. The suddenness of this ad hoc straw vote stunned many in attendance. Eyewitness accounts corroborated the Friends of SFC's position that the vote was a "done deal" long before that day, and the intent of the meeting was to surreptitiously obtain rubber-stamp approval in order to proceed with demolition posthaste. However, many who were not there disputed these facts or opted to ignore them. See Carolyn Lousteau's letter to the editor, headlined "Parishioners Were Consulted in Church's Closing," *Times-Picayune*, November 17, 2006.

20. Mark Schleifstein, "Church Is Designated as Historic by FEMA," *Times-Picayune*, November 21, 2006. The headmaster, Charles DiGange, and the head of the board, Bill Chauvin, led the charge by falsely claiming there

was absolutely no practical way to incorporate the church into the Holy Cross campus plan. Reasons given were that it would be too expensive to repair and too expensive to maintain; it was ugly; Holy Cross had no daily programmatic use for it; and their campus plan simply could not be reworked at this "late date."

21. Matt Olson, "Resistant as Brick: Months of Covering Public Housing," *Breaking Ground* 3 (Winter 2007): 25–31. Also see Brendan McCarthy, "Bloodshed Greeted with Outrage, Apathy," http://www.nola .com/news/t-p/frontpage/index.ssf?/base/ news-8/1176271533107970.xml&coll=1 (accessed January 17, 2008). As in a time of war, the citizens of the city had become desensitized to bloodshed. A culture of complacency had become culturally ingrained regarding the horrific post-Katrina crime epidemic. People did not describe it openly as war, but we all were aware. If violence "don't hit your block, nobody cares," said one attendee at a recent funeral.

22. David Villarrubia, "In Katrina's Wake, How Much More Loss?" *Times-Picayune*, November 21, 2006. The reaction to the upended press conference was swift: about twenty-five hostile letters were sent from GCIA members— a campaign entirely orchestrated by Angelle Givens—to Dr. Scott Cowen, president of Tulane University. The university did not deserve nor wish to be attacked on this issue. Regardless, our action was a success, even if we had to employ quasi-guerrilla media tactics. It was the only way to delay the church's razing. Otherwise, it would have been completely destroyed by early December 2006. That night, members of the Friends of SFC, including me, were on every evening newscast, and numerous blog sites discussed the controversy. The following days included our appearances on local radio talk shows, including an on-air verbal battle on WWL-AM that I fought with diehard Holy Cross banner carrier Clancy Dubos, an alumnus, former board chair, and key disseminator of the Holy Cross propaganda line (and also editor of the local free weekly paper *Gambit*), and Bill Chauvin, the current board chair.

23. Stephen Maloney, "Sacred Ground: FEMA Blocks Holy Cross Plans," *New Orleans CityBusiness*, http://www.neworleanscity-business.com/viewStory.cfm?recID=18451 (accessed January 17, 2008). Father William Maestri, the acting superintendent of schools for the archdiocese, had little choice but to go on the attack, because the Holy Cross initiative in Gentilly was largely his brainchild. His style was intense, caustic, and confrontational. His public encounters with the Friends frequently disintegrated into personal attacks on us. For instance, he told me on a 10:30 evening news program on WGNO, in a voice that was only a shade this side of a yell, that "I was not a [Cabrini] parishioner, and therefore I had no business getting involved!" Each time I politely countered that I had attended mass faithfully at SFC church for three years with my children before Katrina. Regardless, his attacks continued unabated. He was a controversial figure in his own right, having only recently stirred up the hostilities of neighbors and parents alike in the case of Archbishop Hannan High's planned expansion of its football stadium. He stepped down from his post in early 2007. See "Maestri to Resign as School Leader," *Times-Picayune*, January 31, 2007; and Bruce Nolan, "Maestri Holds Many Jobs at Archdiocese," *Times-Picayune*, February 1, 2007.

24. Blog sites advocated sparing the church from attack. These Web sites included the New Orleans–based *Squandered Heritage* (http://squandredheritage.com) and the Washington, D.C.–based *Rebuilding Place in the Urban Space* (http://urbanplacesandspaces.blogspot.com).

25. Richard Longstreth, *St. Frances Xavier Cabrini Church, New Orleans, Louisiana: Assessment of National Register of Historic Places Eligibility Report* (Gaithersburg, Md.: NISTAC—A Joint Venture of URS Group, Inc., and Dewberry & Davis, January 2007). Also see *Protecting Historic Properties: A Citizen's Guide to Section 106 Review* (Washington, D.C.: Advisory Council on Historic Preservation, 2002). At the time, we feared vandalism might occur at the church site, so I met with the local commander of the Louisiana National Guard to ensure that nightly patrols were stepped up in the vicinity of the church.

26. Karen Kingsley, *Buildings of Louisiana* (New York: Oxford Univ. Press, 2003). Kingsley herself was in the midst of writing the first career-spanning book on the work of Curtis & Davis. Kingsley provided Longstreth with many scholarly sources about Cabrini and other Curtis & Davis buildings.

27. Longstreth, *St. Frances Xavier Cabrini Church*, 1–2.

28. Ibid., 2–3.

29. Ibid.

30. Ibid., 3.

31. Bruce Eggler, "Hundreds Weigh In on Demolition of Church," *Times-Picayune*, February 9, 2007. On February 1, James Stark, director of the FEMA Louisiana Transitional Recovery Office, sent out a letter regarding the public comment period (February 5–26) and the public meeting on the evening of February 26. Contact information for Nancy Niedernhofer, FEMA deputy environmental liaison officer for historic preservation in New Orleans, was provided in the letter.

32. Leslie Williams, "Cabrini Hearing Draws Big Crowd," *Times-Picayune*, February 27, 2007. Worse, later that night my wife received a series of threatening phone calls at home from what sounded like high-school-age boys. The propaganda machine that was instigated, perpetuated, and creatively spun by the conquering Holy Cross together with the quasi-feudal Gentilly-area neighborhood group clearly had triumphed.

33. Ibid.

34. Schleifstein, "Church Is Designated as Historic."

35. Susan Finch, "Architect Says Church Should Be Preserved," *Times-Picayune*, November 22, 2006.

36. "Lt. Governor Mitch Landrieu Announces Resolution in Holy Cross–Cabrini Issue," press release, Baton Rouge, March 21, 2007. Landrieu made certain there was no opportunity in the Section 106 Review to debate the issues rationally or to discuss the $4.2 million in flood-insurance money and the many millions in FEMA federal-taxpayer mitigation funds. Hedge Morrell, a Cabrini parishioner herself for many years, had mixed emotions about the issue, yet she capitulated.

37. Frances Curtis, the widow of Buster Curtis, was in the second row with two of her daughters that night at UNO, and we all became concerned for her health because she was visibly shaking throughout the unruly spectacle that somehow passed for a "meeting" that night. Control was barely maintained over the boisterous crowd. A week later, the actual "agreement" was titled *Memorandum of Agreement Among the Federal Emergency Management Agency, The Louisiana State Historic Preservation Officer, The Advisory Council on Historic Preservation, The Louisiana Governor's Office of Homeland Security and Emergency Preparedness, Holy Cross College, Inc, and the Roman Catholic Church of the Archdiocese of New Orleans regarding the Construction of Holy Cross School in New Orleans, Louisiana*.

38. Leslie Williams, "Cabrini to Make Way for Holy Cross," *Times-Picayune*, March 22, 2007.

39. Jim Logan, unpublished letter to the editor of the *Times-Picayune*, March 23, 2007.

40. Frances Curtis, "The *Former* Cabrini Church," *Times-Picayune*, March 31, 2007.

41. Adam Nossiter, "In Tale of Church vs. School: A New Orleans Dilemma," *New York Times*, December 18, 2006, http://www.nytimes.com/2006/12/19/us/19orleans.html (accessed January 17, 2008).

42. Lois Frederick Schneider, unpublished letter to James Amoss, editor, *Times-Picayune*, April 11, 2007.

43. Georgi Anne Brochstein to the Reverend Mauro Piacenza, April 13, 2007.

44. E-mail correspondence received from Robin Brou-Hatheway, April 22, 2007. In point of fact, that church sustained far less flood damage and only about thirty percent of the people in that neighborhood were back in their homes or in their FEMA trailers. Meanwhile, SFC parishioners were being told they would from now on be worshiping at neighboring churches (Pius the X, or St. Leo the Great).

45. Tom Murphy, "New Orleans: Where Are the Leaders?" *Urban Land*, February 2007, 47.

46. Jarvis DeBerry, "It's Slow, It's Imperfect—It's Democracy," *Times-Picayune*, April 1, 2007. In the next sentence in this article, he actually compared the Cabrini battle with a then-ongoing trashcan-maintenance-contract controversy in the French Quarter.

47. Bruce Alpert, "FEMA Jumps the Gun, Landrieu Says," *Times-Picayune*, April 7, 2006. More than 101,000 FEMA trailers were deployed after Hurricanes Katrina and Rita in 2005. Also see Alpert, "Memo: FEMA Ignored Its Own Advice," *Times-Picayune*, April 25, 2007. Mississippi got 72.5 percent of the $400 million that Congress appropriated to help FEMA develop alternatives to trailers and mobile homes. Louisiana received only twenty percent, although Louisiana sustained much more damage to its housing stock. Under the FEMA consultant's recommendation, Louisiana would have received 39.3 percent, and only 36.7 percent would have gone to Mississippi.

48. Frank Donze, "City's Redevelopment Plan Unveiled," *Times-Picayune*, http://www.nola.com/newslogs/tpupdates/index.ssf?/mtlogs/nola_tpupdates/archives/2007_03_29.html (accessed January 17, 2008). It was most puzzling that no mention of neighborhood churches was made in Blakely's presentation. The sole emphasis appeared to be commercial hubs at major intersections. The sole exceptions were the Lower Ninth Ward and New Orleans East. Also see James Gill, "Jet-Lagged Savior: Ed Blakely Flies In, Out and Flies Off the Handle," *Times-Picayune*, May 20, 2007.

49. Daniel Monteverde, "Gentilly Church Demolition Proves Bittersweet for Many: Parishioners Keep Bricks as Mementos," *Times-Picayune*, June 6, 2007. Also see Monteverde, "Faith in Gentilly: Holy Cross School Is

Breathing Life into its New Neighborhood, but Its Longtime Home in the Lower 9th Ward Is Feeling the Loss," *Times-Picayune*, July 8, 2007. On May 14, 2007, Pamela Dashiell, president of the Holy Cross Neighborhood Association, wrote to James Stark, director of the FEMA Louisiana Transitional Recovery Office in New Orleans. She decried the harmful loss of Holy Cross School to her neighborhood and called for a reopening of the FEMA Section 106 Review process. Her intent was to see to it that her neighborhood was included in any mitigation actions that involved allowing Holy Cross to relocate to Gentilly. Curiously, her organization declined to join the Friends' two lawsuits aimed at saving Cabrini Church.

50. The appeal procedure in canon law was described in correspondence dated June 6, 2007, from Sister Kate Kuenstler and Chris Schenk, national advocates for the rights of Roman Catholic parishes (http://www .futurechurch.org), to Georgi Anne Brochstein: "The suspension of administrative acts pending appeal is as follows: An appeal to the Archbishop shall be understood as also petitioning for the suspension of administrative action which has occasioned the dispute (Canon Law 1734.1), and automatically suspends the execution of the administrative decree (Canon Law 1736.1) until a definitive decision is passed by the Vatican. Appeal to the Congregation for Clergy may give a negative reply but the Parish is then permitted to file an appeal to that decision to the Signatura. Nothing is to be done in the diocese until all steps of the administrative recourse process have been attempted and the final appeal to the Signatura is given." Also see Christine M. Roussel, "1911 Vatican Directive to Bishops of the United States Concerning Church Property" (2003), an unpublished translation by Roussel and others from the Latin original published in *Ecclesiastical Review* 45 (1911): 596–598.

51. Friends of St. Frances Xavier Cabrini Church to Archbishop Alfred C. Hughes, May 30, 2007. Our letter was copied to nearly three dozen individuals and organizations internationally, including the national office of the American Institute of Architects, the Voice of the Faithful, DOCOMOMO, Mario Botta, Michel Ragon, Richard Longstreth, Barry Bergdoll, Louisiana governor Kathleen Blanco, FEMA, *Architectural Record*, the Associated Press, *60 Minutes* (CBS), and CNN.

52. Archbishop Alfred C. Hughes to David Villarrubia, June 28, 2007.

53. Bevan, *Destruction of Memory*, 57–59.

54. Jon Calame and Esther Charlesworth, *Divided Cities* (Charlottesville: Univ. of Virginia Press, 2006).

55. Esther Charlesworth, *Architects without Frontiers: War, Reconstruction, and Design Responsibility* (Oxford: Architectural Press / Elsevier, 2006). Also see Keith Mallory, *The Architecture of War* (New York: Pantheon, 1973).

56. Jaime Guillet, "Stafford Act behind Slow Moving Recovery Funds," *New Orleans CityBusiness*, April 1, 2007, http://www.neworleanscitybusiness.com/uptotheminute.cfm?recid=9731&userID=0&referer=dailyUpdate (accessed January 17, 2008). Cary Grant, New Orleans's assistant chief administrative officer, was quoted as saying, "This is at least my seventh or eighth major (disaster) event and this is the first one that has had more bureaucratic nightmares than any (other disasters) have had. I know everybody's got their stake in this . . . But it's almost to the level it grinds to a halt because you have to elaborate on everything over and over. It bogs everything down."

57. Mat Schwarzman, "New Orleans, as It Is," Community Arts Network Reading Room, http://www.communityarts.net/readingroom/archivefiles/2006/04/new_orleans_as.php (accessed January 17, 2008).

58. Mac Margolis, "Travel: The World's Most Endangered Destinations," *Newsweek International*, April 10, 2006, available at http:// www.globalheritagefund.org/news/conservation_news/newsweek_vanishing_acts_7 _endangered_wonders.asp (accessed January 17, 2008).

59. Associated Press, "Under Fire, Google Goes Back to Maps Showing Katrina Damage," *New Orleans CityBusiness*, April 2, 2007, http://www.neworleanscitybusiness.com/ UpToTheMinute.cfm?recID=9739 (accessed January 17, 2008). The subcommittee's chairman, Representative Brad Miller, asked Google's CEO, Eric Schmidt, to explain what happened and to disclose whether federal or local officials asked the company to use the old imagery, perhaps in an effort to portray the stalled recovery more favorably. Miller wrote to Schmidt in a letter, "Google's use of old imagery appears to be doing the victims of Hurricane Katrina a great injustice by airbrushing history."

60. Peter Whoriskey, "Gulf Coast's Post-Katrina Rebuilding Efforts Stall; Many Who Fled Storm Wary of Coming Back," Washington Post News Service, August 28, 2006, http://www.neorunner.com/archive/2006/ 08/28/62_2104196.php (accessed January 17, 2008).

61. Deon Roberts, "Mixed Messages: Ambassadors Launch Campaign to Put Positive Spin on New Orleans' Recovery," *New Orleans CityBusiness*, April 2, 2007, http://www .neworleanscitybusiness.com/viewStory .cfm?recID=18653 (accessed January 17, 2008). The Fleur-de-lis Ambassadors Program was launched in March 2007 to help counter the barrage of negative national media coverage of post-Katrina New Orleans. Ironically, at least three of the group's twenty members were against saving Cabrini Church. In 2006 around 3.7 million visitors spent $2.9 billion in New Orleans, down from 2004, when over 10 million visitors came to the city and spent $4.9 billion. The city was even poised to spend $100,000 to have a public relations firm attempt to rebuild the city's gravely shattered image (Frank Donze, "N.O. Plans to Hire PR Firm," *Times-Picayune*, May 29, 2007).

62. Jay Winter and Emmanuel Sivan, *War and Remembrance in the Twentieth Century* (Cambridge: Cambridge Univ. Press, 1999).

Index